Frommer's®

Barcelona
day BY day

1st Edition

by Neil Edward Schlecht

1807
WILEY
2007

Wiley Publishing, Inc.

Contents

15 Favorite Moments   1

1 The Best Full-Day Tours   7
The Best in One Day   8
The Best in Two Days   14
The Best in Three Days   18

2 The Best Special-Interest Tours   23
Modernista Barcelona   24
Ciutat Vella: Ancient Barcelona   30
Barcelona for Art-Lovers   36
Barcelona for Design & Architecture
   Fans   40
Gourmet Barcelona   46
Barcelona for Kids   50

3 The Best Neighborhood Walks   55
La Rambla   56
Barri Gòtic   60
La Ribera   64
L'Eixample   68

4 The Best Shopping   71
Shopping Best Bets   72
Barcelona Shopping A to Z   76

5 The Best of the Outdoors   83
Montjuïc   84
Parc de la Ciutadella   86
The Waterfront   88
Barcelona by Bike   90

6 The Best Dining   93
Dining Best Bets   94
Barcelona Dining A to Z   98

7 The Best Nightlife 107
Nightlife Best Bets 108
Barcelona Nightlife A to Z 112

8 The Best Arts & Entertainment 119
Arts & Entertainment Best Bets 120
Arts & Entertainment A to Z 124

9 The Best Lodging 131
Lodging Best Bets 132
Barcelona Lodging A to Z 136

10 The Best Day Trips & Excursions 145
Montserrat 146
Sitges 148
Girona 150
L'Empordà & Costa Brava 154

The Savvy Traveler 159
Before You Go 160
Getting There 162
Getting Around 163
Fast Facts 164
Barcelona: A Brief History 167
Barcelona's Architecture 169
Useful Phrases 171
Recommended Spanish Wines 173
Recommended Vintages for Rioja &
    Ribera del Duero Wines 174
Toll-Free Numbers & Websites 174

Index 176

Published by:

Wiley Publishing, Inc.

111 River St.
Hoboken, NJ 07030-5774

ISBN: 978-0-470-16540-9

Editor: Cate Latting
Production Editor: Jana M. Stefanciosa
Photo Editor: Richard Fox
Anniversary Logo Design: Richard Pacifico
Cartographer: Andrew Murphy
Production by Wiley Indianapolis Composition Services

For information on our other products and services or to obtain technical support, please contact our Customer Care Department within the U.S. at 800/762-2974, outside the U.S. at 317/572-3993 or fax 317/572-4002.

Wiley also publishes its books in a variety of electronic formats. Some content that appears in print may not be available in electronic formats.

Manufactured in China

5   4   3   2

A Note from the Publisher

Organizing your time. That's what this guide is all about.

Other guides give you long lists of things to see and do and then expect you to fit the pieces together. The Day by Day guides are different. These guides tell you the best of everything, and then they show you how to see it *in the smartest, most time-efficient way*. Our authors have designed detailed itineraries organized by time, neighborhood, or special interest. And each tour comes with a bulleted map that takes you from stop to stop.

Hoping to tour the best in *modernista* architecture, stroll down La Rambla, or taste your way through gourmet Barcelona? Planning a walk through La Ribera, or plotting a day of fun-filled activities with the kids? Whatever your interest or schedule, the Day by Days give you the smartest routes to follow. Not only do we take you to the top attractions, hotels, and restaurants, but we also help you access those special moments that locals get to experience—those "finds" that turn tourists into travelers.

The Day by Days are also your top choice if you're looking for one complete guide for all your travel needs. The best hotels and restaurants for every budget, the greatest shopping values, the wildest nightlife—it's all here.

Why should you trust our judgment? Because our authors personally visit each place they write about. They're an independent lot who say what they think and would never include places they wouldn't recommend to their best friends. They're also open to suggestions from readers. If you'd like to contact them, please send your comments my way at mspring@wiley.com, and I'll pass them on.

Enjoy your Day by Day guide—the most helpful travel companion you can buy. And have the trip of a lifetime.

Warm regards,

Michael Spring,
Publisher
Frommer's Travel Guides

About the Author

Neil Edward Schlecht is a freelance writer based in northwestern Connecticut. His first exposure to Spain was teaching English for a summer at a Col.legi Sant Ignasi in Barcelona. He returned to the Catalan capital just before the 1992 Olympics and spent most of the decade there, working on social and economic development projects for the European Union and later as a contributing writer for a Spanish art and antiques magazine. Neil is the author or co-author of a dozen travel guides, including *Frommer's Peru, Frommer's Cuba, Frommer's South America, Frommer's New York, Frommer's Texas,* and *Spain For Dummies*. But little motivates him like the chance to discover new restaurants and wines in Spain.

Acknowledgments

Thanks to my editor, Cate Latting, for her gentle prodding, tireless attention to the peculiarities of the Catalan language, and welcome doses of sarcasm.

An Additional Note

Please be advised that travel information is subject to change at any time—and this is especially true of prices. We therefore suggest that you write or call ahead for confirmation when making your travel plans. The authors, editors, and publisher cannot be held responsible for the experiences of readers while traveling. Your safety is important to us, however, so we encourage you to stay alert and be aware of your surroundings.

Star Ratings, Icons & Abbreviations

Every hotel, restaurant, and attraction listing in this guide has been ranked for quality, value, service, amenities, and special features using a **star-rating system.** Hotels, restaurants, attractions, shopping, and nightlife are rated on a scale of zero stars (recommended) to three stars (exceptional). In addition to the star-rating system, we also use a **kids icon** to point out the best bets for families. Within each tour, we recommend cafes, bars, or restaurants where you can take a break. Each of these stops appears in a shaded box marked with a coffee-cup-shaped bullet.

The following **abbreviations** are used for credit cards:

AE	American Express	DISC	Discover	V	Visa
DC	Diners Club	MC	MasterCard		

Frommers.com

Now that you have this guidebook to help you plan a great trip, visit our web-site at **www.frommers.com** for additional travel information on more than 3,600 destinations. We update features regularly to give you instant access to the most current trip-planning information available. At Frommers.com, you'll find scoops on the best airfares, lodging rates, and car rental bargains. You can even book your travel online through our reliable travel booking partners. Other popular features include:

- Online updates of our most popular guidebooks
- Vacation sweepstakes and contest giveaways
- Newsletters highlighting the hottest travel trends
- Online travel message boards with featured travel discussions

A Note on Prices

In the "Take a Break" and "Best Bets" sections of this book, we have used a system of dollar signs to show a range of costs for 1 night in a hotel (the price of a double-occupancy room) or the cost of an entree at a restaurant. Use the following table to decipher the dollar signs:

Cost	Hotels	Restaurants
$	under $100	under $10
$$	$100–$200	$10–$20
$$$	$200–$300	$20–$30
$$$$	$300–$400	$30–$40
$$$$$	over $400	over $40

An Invitation to the Reader

In researching this book, we discovered many wonderful places—hotels, restaurants, shops, and more. We're sure you'll find others. Please tell us about them, so we can share the information with your fellow travelers in upcoming editions. If you were disappointed with a recommendation, we'd love to know that, too. Please write to:

Frommer's Barcelona Day by Day, 1st Edition
Wiley Publishing, Inc. • 111 River St. • Hoboken, NJ 07030-5774

15 Favorite
Moments

15 Favorite **Moments**

1. La Rambla
2. La Pedrera
3. Barri Gòtic
4. Mercat de la Boqueria
5. Palau de la Música
6. Catalan cuisine*
7. La Sagrada Família
8. Old-school Barcelona*
9. Biking along the Beach
10. Cava crawl*
11. La Ribera fashion
12. Classic Catalan culture*
13. Santa María del Mar
14. Blue Tram to Tibidabo
15. Catalunya*

* categories not mapped

Previous page: The rooftop chimneys of La Pedrera.

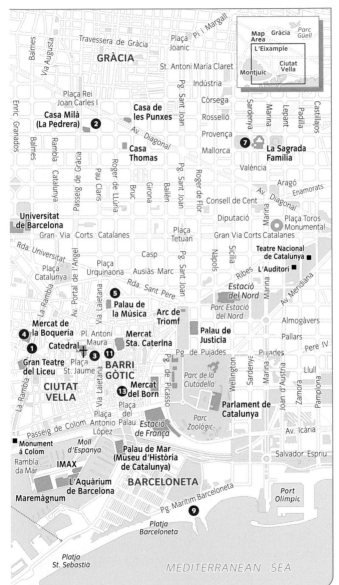

Travessera de Gràcia

Plaça
Joanic

GRÀCIA

St. Antoni Maria Claret

Balmes

Via Augusta

Enric Granados

Plaça Rei
Joan Carles I

Casa Milà
(La Pedrera) ❷

Balmes

Rambla

Passeig de Gràcia

Pau Claris

Roger de Llúria

Bruc

Girona

Bailèn

Casa de
les Punxes

Av. Diagonal

Casa
Thomas

Pg. Sant Joan

Roger de Flor

Pg. Sant Joan

Indústria

Còrsega

Rosselló

Provença

Mallorca

València

Catalunya

Universitat
de Barcelona

Gran Via Corts Catalanes

Rda. Universitat

Plaça
Catalunya

La Rambla

Plaça
Urquinaona

Av. Portal de l'Angel

Plaça
Antoni
Maura

Casp

Ausiàs Marc

Rda. Sant Pere

Plaça
Tetuan

Pg. Sant Joan

❼

Sardenya

Marina

Lepant

Padilla

Castillejos

La Sagrada
Família

Aragó

Enamorats

Av. Diagonal

Consell de Cent

Diputació

Gran Via Corts Catalanes

Nàpols

Sicília

Ribes

Marina

Plaça Toros
Monumental

Teatre Nacional
de Catalunya ■

L'Auditori ■

Estació
del Nord

Av. Meridiana

Mercat de
la Boqueria ❹

Catedral ❶

Gran Teatre
del Liceu

CIUTAT
VELLA

La Rambla

❺

Palau de
la Música

Pl. Antoni
Maura

Mercat
Sta. Caterina

Via Laietana

Plaça
St. Jaume

❸ ⓫

BARRI
GÒTIC

Mercat
⓭ del Born

Plaça
del
Antonio
López

Arc de
Triomf

Palau de
Justícia

Pg. de Pujades

Pg. de Picasso

Parc de la
Ciutadella

Parlament de
Catalunya

Wellington

Parc Estació
del Nord

Sardenya

Marina

Joan d'Àustria

Almogàvers

Pallars

Pujades

Pere IV

Zamora

Llull

Pamplona

Av. Icària

Estació
de França

Parc
Zoològic

Passeig de Colom

Monument
á Colom ■

Rambla
da Mar

Moll
d'Espanya

IMAX

Plaça
Palau

L'Aquàrium
de Barcelona

Palau de Mar
(Museu d'Història
de Catalunya)

BARCELONETA

Salvador Espriu

Maremàgnum

Pg. Marítim Barceloneta

❾

Port
Olímpic

Platja
Barceloneta

Platja
St. Sebastià

MEDITERRANEAN SEA

Map
Area

Gràcia

Parc
Güell

L'Eixample

Montjuïc

Ciutat
Vella

It's hardly a shock that Barcelona has become such a hot destination. What's surprising is how long it took the world to discover Barcelona's diverse charms, which draw architecture and design fanatics, foodies, culture hounds, history buffs, and those merely in search of a happening, all-night party. These are some of my favorite things to do in the thriving Catalan capital.

1 Joining the throngs on La Rambla. Barcelona's pedestrian-only boulevard is anything but commonplace; it's the epicenter of life in the capital, and joining the vibrant street parade is the best way to immerse yourself in the city. Pick up fresh flowers and come face-to-face with outrageous human statues. *See p 56.*

2 Grooving to jazz at La Pedrera. The dreamlike rooftop of Antoni Gaudí's finest building is topped by surreal-looking chimneys, but it really comes to life during a summer eve's music program of jazz, swing, flamenco, or tango. You can tap your toes, sip *cava,* and watch the elegant Passeig de Gràcia below turn to night. *See p 127.*

3 Wandering the Barri Gòtic. Barcelona's Gothic Quarter is a mesmerizing labyrinth of medieval buildings and narrow streets, and it's a joy to take a stroll and discover a quiet square or picturesque patio. Meander down Sant Sever and slip into Plaça Sant Felip Neri, or along Carrer Banys Nous, lined with antique shops. *See p 60.*

See some outrageous performers on La Rambla.

4 Breathing in La Boqueria. Barcelona's wonderfully redolent food market is a feast for the senses, with hundreds of colorful stalls overflowing with fresh seafood, wild mushrooms, meats, and vegetables. For a special treat,

Explore the antique stores in the Barri Gòtic.

La Boqueria is a food-lover's paradise.

pop into a kiosk such as Bar Pintxo or El Quim for breakfast or lunch at the counter. *See p 58.*

⑤ Tuning into El Palau de la Música. This spectacular 1908 *modernista* museum piece draws hordes for its architectural tours. But there's nothing quite like experiencing a concert here; the spine-tingling monument to art-nouveau excess takes a back seat to no musician, whether a chamber quartet or Lou Reed. *See p 124.*

⑥ Sampling cutting-edge Catalan cuisine. Led by the likes of Ferrán Adrià, Catalan cooking has exploded, making Barcelona the hottest dining scene in Europe. From chic tapas bars to minimalist haunts known for their celebrity chefs, Barcelona is a destination for gastronomic pilgrimages. *See p 93.*

⑦ Gazing up at La Sagrada Família. Gaudí's legendary, futuristic church remains a work in progress nearly a century after work on it began, but its soaring spires—like melting candles—never fail to amaze. Try to take in all its dense symbolism, realizing it's only half finished. *See p 25.*

⑧ Dipping into old-school Barcelona. Unfazed by today's fashions and fast pace are authentic, time-stopping treasures in the old city: a 1920s *modernista* chocolate shop; a *granja*, or "milk bar," serving thick chocolate drinks as it has for 125 years; and a gourmet food and wine shop in the same family for four generations. All are portals to an earlier era. *See p 46.*

⑨ Biking along the beach. Only 20 years ago Barcelona turned its back on the Mediterranean and its polluted port; today the revitalized waterfront is lined with leisurely bike paths and immaculate beaches. Take a pit stop at one of the city's most traditional seafood haunts in Barceloneta. *See p 90.*

Be sure to try the cava (Catalan sparkling wine) while you're visiting the region.

⑩ Traipsing along on a *cava* crawl. You can do a tapas crawl anywhere in Spain, but in Barcelona pre-meal snacks are washed down by glasses of *cava*, Catalan sparkling wine. *Xampanyerías* are friendly spots where good cheer bubbles over. *See p 117.*

⑪ Discovering cutting-edge fashion on medieval streets. Against a backdrop of Gothic palaces, churches, and centuries-old shops, the tangle of dark but suddenly chic alleyways of the La Ribera/Born district now are also home to dozens of edgy fashion and home design shops, a delight to discover. *See p 64.*

⑫ Experiencing classic Catalan culture. La Mercé, Barcelona's signature folklore festival, has something for everyone: *castellers* (human towers rising eight levels); *gigants* and *cab grosses* (massive costumed royal figures parading the streets); and devils running, chasing each other down with fireworks in *correfocs*. It's a blast and a quintessential expression of Catalan pride. *See p 161.*

⑬ Reveling in Santa Maria del Mar. This Gothic church, in the heart of bustling La Ribera, is architectural perfection, a model of graceful, soaring dimensions. A sublime sanctuary on a quiet afternoon, it's also thrilling if you catch a society wedding spilling out onto the steps—which you can watch from a wine bar across the plaza. *See p 65.*

⑭ Hopping the Blue Tram to Tibidabo. Appreciate how Barcelona gracefully stretches from the surrounding hills out to the sea on the old trolley (*Tramvía Blau*) up to Tibidabo, the small mountain overlooking the city. On a clear day, you can pick out the perfect grid system of the Eixample and maybe even see Mallorca. *See p 21.*

⑮ Getting a taste of Catalunya. Sample even more Catalan flavor just a couple of hours outside the capital: Ride an aerial cable car to Montserrat, a monastery cleaved into a mountain; discover the idiosyncratic spots where Salvador Dalí's mad genius erupted; or lose yourself in the pristine, ancient Jewish quarter of Girona. *See p 146.* ●

Explore Dalí's stomping grounds, including the Teatre Museu Dalí in Figueres.

1

The Best
Full-Day Tours

The Best **in One Day**

Diagonal 🅜
Provença ②
Mallorca
València
L'EIXAMPLE
Aragó ④
⑤ 🅜
Consell ⑥ **Passeig**
de Cent **de Gràcia**
Diputació ③
Universitat
de Barcelona

Rambla
Pg. de Gràcia
Pau Claris
Roger de Llúria
Bruc
Girona
Bailèn

Mercat de la
Concepció
Aragó
🅜
Girona
■ **Torre**
d'Aigües
Plaça
Tetuan

Plaça
Sagrada
Família ①
Mallorca 🅜
Sagrada Família
València
Av. Diagonal
Nàpols
Consell de Cent
Diputació
Sicília
Sardenya
Gran Via Corts Catalanes

Gran Via Corts Catalanes
Tetuan 🅜
Casp
Ausiàs Marc
Roger de Flor

Balmes
Ronda Universitat
Casp
Plaça
Catalunya ⓘ
Fontanella 🅜 **Urquinaona**
Catalunya 🅜
Pelai
Ronda Sant Pere
Tallers
La Rambla
Portaferrissa
Portal
de l'Angel
Av.
⑧
⑨
⑦
Sta. Maria
✝ **del Pi**
Generalitat
⑩ **Catedral**
Liceu
Ajuntament ⓘ
BARRI
GÒTIC
CIUTAT
⑫ ⑬
VELLA
Llotja
de Mar
La Mercè ✝ Mercè
Passeig de Colom
(Ronda Litoral)

Pau Claris
Roger de
Llúria
Bruc
Girona
Bailèn
Pg. Sant Joan
Roger de Flor

Palau de la
Música Catalana
LA RIBERA
Mercat
Sta. Caterina
Plaça
Allada
Vermell
Princesa
Museu
Zoologia
Museu
Geologia
Lluís Companys
Montcada
Comerç
Rec
Passeig de Picasso
Passeig de Pujades

Ribes
Alí Bei
Estació
del Nord
Arc de
Triomf 🅜
Arc de
Triomf
Palau de
Justícia
Buenaventura Muñoz
Almogàvers
Av. Meridiana
Parc Estació
del Nord

Jaume I 🅜
Ataülf
Ajuntament
Mercat
del Born
Plaça
del
Palau
La Mercè
Plaça
Antonio
López
Estació
de França
Barceloneta 🅜

Parc de la
Ciutadella
Parlament de
Catalunya
Zoo de
Barcelona
Wellington
Sardenya

ⓘ *Tourist Information*
🅜 *Metro Station*

Moll
d'Espanya
Rambla
da Mar
Port
Vell
IMAX
L'Aquàrium
de Barcelona
Maremàgnum

Palau de Mar
(Museu d'Història
de Catalunya)
Plaça
Poeta Boscà
BARCELONETA

Platja
Barceloneta
MEDITERRANEAN
SEA

St. Martí
L'Eixample
Parc de la
Ciutadella
Ciutat
Vella
Map
Area
Montjuïc

Scale:
0 — 1/2 mile
0 — 1/2 km

① La Sagrada Família
② La Pedrera
③ tapaç 24
④ Casa Batlló
⑤ Casa Amatller
⑥ Casa Lleó Morera
⑦ La Rambla
⑧ Mercat de la Boqueria
⑨ Café de la Ópera
⑩ Catedral de Barcelona
⑪ Museu Picasso
⑫ Santa María del Mar
⑬ La Vinya del Senyor

Previous page: An artist captures La Sagrada Família.

This **very full day, a "greatest hits" tour,** begins with the best of Barcelona's *modernista* architecture in the morning, is followed by a stroll down the epic Rambla, and ends with the highlights of the *Ciutat Vella,* or Old City. You'll need your walking shoes. START: **Metro to Sagrada Família.**

1 ★★★ kids La Sagrada Família. Antoni Gaudí's unfinished legacy, the soaring "Holy Family" church, is a testament to his singular vision: the art of the impossible. This mind-altering creation—the best-known, if not necessarily the best example, of *modernisme*—has become Barcelona's calling card. Begun in 1882, its eight bejeweled spires drip like melting candlesticks, and virtually every square inch of the surface explodes with intricate spiritual symbols. Gaudí was run over by a tram long before it could be finished, and at present it remains only an otherworldly facade. Though many believe it should be left unfinished, a private foundation works furiously to finish the church—now projected for 2026, the centennial of Gaudí's death. ⏱ *1 hr. Mallorca 401.* ☎ *93-207-30-31. www.sagradafamilia.org. Admission: 8€ adults. Daily Jan–Mar and Oct–Dec 9am–6pm; April–Sept 9am–8pm. Metro: Sagrada Família.*

2 ★★★ kids La Pedrera. Thought by many to be the crowning glory of

La Pedrera is considered one of Antoni Gaudí's masterpieces.

the *modernista* movement, Antoni Gaudí's avant-garde apartment building Casa Milà is better known as La Pedrera, or Stone Quarry, for its wavy mass of limestone. The exterior seems carved out of nature: It undulates like ocean waves along Passeig de Gràcia and around the corner onto Provença street. The fascinating roof, what most people come to see, is guarded by a set of warrior-like chimneys that look like the inspiration for Darth Vader. ⏱ *1 hr. Passeig de Gràcia 92 (at Provença).* ☎ *902-40-09-73 or 902-10-12-12 for advance tickets. www.fundaciocaixacatalunya.org. Admission 8€ adults, 4.50€ students; also part of ArticketBCN joint admission. Daily 10am–8pm. Closed: Dec 25–26 and Jan 1–6. Tours in English, Spanish, and Catalan. Metro: Diagonal or Provença.*

Detailed carving work on La Sagrada Família.

3 ★★ **tapaç 24.** The informal tapas bar of acclaimed chef Carles Abellán, who's in the kitchen at Comerç 24, is a good-looking pit stop just off Passeig de Gràcia. Grab a snack or lunch of tantalizing small bites with big flavors, and wine and cava by the glass. *Carrer Diputaciò, 269.* ☎ *93-488-09-77. $$.*

4 ★★★ **Casa Batlló.** The centerpiece of the so-called "Block of Discord," Casa Batlló owes its extraordinary facade to Antoni Gaudí, who completed a remodeling in 1906. Thought to represent the legend of Saint George (patron saint of Catalonia) and his dragon, the house glimmers with fragments of colorful ceramics, while the roof curves like the blue-green scales of a dragon's back, and balconies evoke Carnavalesque masks or menacing monster jaws. The sinuous interior, full of custom Gaudí-designed furniture, is similarly stunning (though tours are unexpectedly pricey). ⏱ *30 min. Passeig de Gràcia, 43.* ☎ *93-488-06-66. Admission 17€ adults, 14€ children and students, free for children under 5. Daily 9am–8pm. Metro: Passeig de Gràcia.*

The "dragon's back" atop Casa Batlló.

5 ★★ **Casa Amatller.** Puig i Cadafalch, a Gaudí contemporary, created this brilliant house—the first building on the Manzana de la Discòrdia block of Passeig de Gràcia—in 1900. It has a medieval-looking, ceramics-covered facade, topped by a distinctive Flemish-inspired roof and beautiful carved stone and ironwork of themes related to the chocolate business and hobbies of the original owners. ⏱ *10 min. Passeig de Gràcia 41.* ☎ *93-488-01-39. Ground floor open to public Mon–Sat 10am–7pm. Metro: Passeig de Gràcia.*

6 ★ **Casa Lleó Morera.** This gorgeously ornate corner house (1905), the final member of the Block of Discord triumvirate, is the work of Domènech i Montaner, who designed El Palau de la Música Catalana and Hospital Sant Pau. Especially appealing when illuminated at night, the building is now home to the upscale leather-goods purveyor Loewe, which lamentably destroyed a good part of the lower facade and sumptuous interior ground floor. *Passeig de Gràcia 35. Except for the Loewe store, the house cannot be visited. Metro: Passeig de Gràcia.*

Fresh flowers are for sale daily on La Rambla.

7 ★★★ kids **La Rambla.**
Barcelona's great strolling boulevard is the centerpiece of life in the Catalan capital. It throbs with activity, as crowds at all hours of the day file past vendors, food markets, cafes, and historic buildings (in the evening, the lower parts can get a little sketchy). Subdivided into five separate ramblas, each of different character and attractions, are a lively succession of newspaper kiosks, fresh flower stands, bird sellers, and crowd-friendly human statues (mimes) in elaborately conceived costumes and face paint. About halfway down the boulevard,

to the left as you face the port, is the Plaça Reial, a grand square with cafes, palm trees, arcades, and lampposts designed by *modernista* master Antoni Gaudí. ⏱ *30 min. Begin at Plaça de Catalunya. Metro: Plaça de Catalunya.*

8 ★★★ kids **Mercat de La Boquería.** Europe's largest and surely most dynamic food market, this Catalan classic is the foundation of Barcelona's fascination with food. Wander among the more than 300 stalls and several small bar/restaurants to see and smell an amazingly lively gastronomic scene: the slicing,

Top Attractions: Practical Matters

ArticketBCN Discounts: With a single ticket (www.articketbcn.org) you can visit seven top art museums in Barcelona, including the Museu Picasso, Museu Nacional d'Art de Catalunya (MNAC), Fundació Joan Miró, and the Museu d'Art Contemporani de Barcelona (MACBA). Purchase the ticket (20€; good for 6 months) at individual museum ticket offices, the Plaça de Catalunya Tourist Information Office, branches of Caixa Catalunya bank, or by phone or online with Tel.Entrada (☎ 902-101-212 or 34-93-326-29-46 from abroad; www.telentrada.com).

Mercat de La Boquería is a Barcelona institution.

9 ★ **Café de la Ópera.** A Barcelona institution, this 1929 Belle Epoque cafe facing the Rambla and opposite the Teatre Liceu opera house is a low-key, Old-World spot during the day and a bar that occasionally gets much more animated late in the evening, especially if groups of fun-loving gay and bohemian patrons stop by. Good pastries and desserts. *Rambla 74.* ☎ *93-317-75-85. $.*

dicing, and selling of fresh fish, meats, produce, and more. Keep an eye out for bolets and ceps (wild mushrooms), massive prawns, eels, and octopus. The colorful bounty is a testament to the fertile region and Catalans' desire for the freshest and tastiest foodstuffs available. 🕐 *30 min. La Rambla 91–101.* ☎ *93-318-25-84; Mon–Sat 8am–8pm; Metro: Liceu.*

10 ★★ **Catedral de Barcelona.** The cathedral, the focal point of the Old City and a splendid example of Catalan Gothic architecture, was begun in 1298 but largely completed in the 14th and 15th centuries. Don't miss the carved choir and surprisingly lush cloister—a welcome oasis in the midst of the Medieval Quarter with its pond, magnolias, orange and palm trees, and white geese. 🕐 *45 min. Plaça de la Seu s/n.* ☎ *93-315-15-54. Free*

Café de la Ópera is an old-school spot, perfect for a midday snack or a late-night drink.

The Museu Picasso holds 2,500 paintings and sculptures.

admission to cathedral; museum 1€. Elevator to roof: 10:30am–1:30pm and 5–6pm, 2€. Global ticket for 1–4:30pm guided visit to museum, choir, rooftop terraces, and towers, 4€. Cathedral daily 9am–1pm and 5–7pm; cloister museum daily 10am–1pm and 4–6:30pm. Metro: Jaume I.

⓫ ★★★ Museu Picasso. Pablo Picasso was born in southern Spain, but he spent much of his youth and early creative years in Barcelona on his way to becoming the most famous artist of the 20th century. The museum is the largest collection of his works in his native country: 2,500 paintings and sculptures, many of them early works, including several from his blue period. The highlight of the collection is *Las Meninas,* a series of 59 interpretations of Velázquez's masterpiece. The Picasso museum occupies several exquisite 15th-century palaces on a lovely pedestrian-only street lined with medieval mansions. 🕐 *1 hr. Montcada 15–23.* ☎ *93-319-63-10. www. museupicasso.bcn.es. Admission 6€ adults, 4€ students and those under 25, free for children under 16. Admission part of ArticketBCN. Free*

admission first Sun of every month. *Tues–Sat 10am–8pm; Sun 10am–3pm. Metro: Jaume I.*

⓬ ★★ Santa Maria del Mar. A stunning14th-century Catalan Gothic church that's neither opulent and jewel-encrusted nor home to a fabulous art collection. Instead, it's a simple and solemn, but wholly inspired, space—the kind of place about which architects understandably wax poetic, with perfect proportions in its three soaring naves, wide-spaced columns, and handsome stained-glass windows. 🕐 *15 min. Plaça de Santa Maria.* ☎ *93-215-74-11. Free admission. Mon–Sat 9am–1:30pm and 4:30–8pm, Sun 9am–2pm and 5–8:30pm. Metro: Jaume I.*

⓭ ★★ La Vinya del Senyor. A hip little wine bar with much-coveted tables on a terrace at the lovely square across from Santa María del Mar, it features an excellent selection of a 100 or so wines from across Spain, including two dozen by the glass, as well as Spanish ham, salami, and cheeses. *Plaça de Santa María, 5.* ☎ *93-310-33-79. $$.*

The Best **in Two Days**

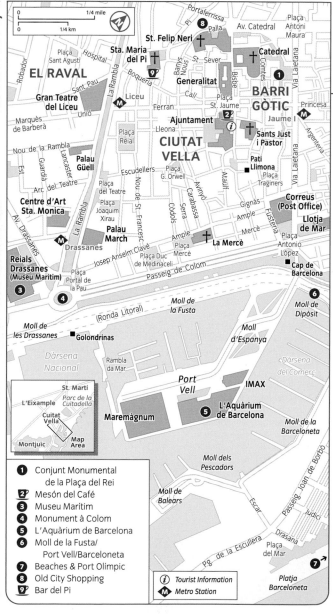

❶	Conjunt Monumental de la Plaça del Rei
2️⃣	Mesón del Café
❸	Museu Marítim
❹	Monument à Colom
❺	L'Aquàrium de Barcelona
❻	Moll de la Fusta/ Port Vell/Barceloneta
❼	Beaches & Port Olímpic
❽	Old City Shopping
9️⃣	Bar del Pi

ℹ️ *Tourist Information*

Ⓜ *Metro Station*

After a very full first day in Barcelona, it's time for a more leisurely pace. Begin the day in the Gothic Quarter to get a feel for the city's ancient foundations before moving on to enjoy the revitalized waterfront, which since the 1992 Olympics has been a popular outdoor leisure destination. Stroll along the harbor, stop for lunch in the beachside district of Barceloneta, and hit the sands in the afternoon for sunbathing or a sunset cocktail, topped off by dinner at the new harbor, Port Olímpic. START: **Metro to Jaume I.**

① ★★ kids Conjunt Monumental de la Plaça del Rei. In one of the old quarter's most handsome squares, the stately Plaça del Rei, hemmed in by a remaining section of the old Roman city walls, are the fine **Museu d'Història de la Ciutat**—where the main attraction is underground walkways over the exposed foundations (1st c. B.C. to 7th c. A.D.) of Barcino, the ancient city of the Romans and Visigoths—and the **Palau Reial Major**, an 11th-century royal palace and the residence of the Kings of Catalonia and Aragón. According to legend, King Ferdinand and Queen Isabella received Columbus here when he returned from the New World. ⏱ 1½ hrs. Plaça del Rei s/n. ☎ 93-315-11-11. www. museuhistoria.bcn.es. Admission 4€ adults, 2.50€ students, free for children under 16. June–Sept Tues–Sat 10am–8pm; Oct–May Tues–Sat 10am–2pm and 4–8pm; year-round Sun 10am–3pm. Metro: Jaume I.

Portrait bust of the Roman Emperor Nerva at the Museu d'Història de la Ciutat.

②' ★★★ Mesón del Café. This tiny 100-year-old place is probably my favorite cafe in the world. Locals drop in at all hours for superb *café con leche, café solo, cortado,* or a mean *picardía* (coffee with layers of condensed milk and whiskey). And while the coffee's great, there's something just ineffably cool about the place. *Llibreteria, 16.* ☎ 93-315-07-54. $.

③ ★★ kids Museu Marítim. Barcelona's seafaring past comes to life in this rich maritime museum, located in the Reials Drassanes, or former Royal Shipyards, which includes a glorious replica of a massive 16th-century vessel, the *Galería Reial.* The medieval shipyards, a collection of evocative arches, columns, and vaults that was once at water's edge and today remains magnificently intact, is where the kingdom's ships were constructed, repaired, and dry-docked. ⏱ 1 hr. Av. de les Drassanes s/n. ☎ 93-342-99-20. Admission 6€ adults, 3€ children 7–16. Daily 10am–7pm. Metro: Drassanes.

See relics from Barcelona's seafaring past at the Museu Marítim.

View marine life galore at the Barcelona Aquarium.

4 **kids** **Monument à Colom.**
Though this monument to Christopher Columbus, built in 1888, has him pointing the wrong direction to the New World, it's a focal and meeting point, dividing the lower end of the Rambla from the waterfront. An elevator takes visitors inside to a mirador for nice panoramic views of the harbor. ⏱ *30 min. Portal de la Pau s/n.* ☎ *93-302-52-24. Admission 2.40€ adults, 1.40€ children 4–12, free for children under 4. June–Sept 9am–8:30pm; Oct–May 10am–6:30pm. Metro: Drassanes.*

5 **kids** ★★ **L'Aquàrium de Barcelona.** At Port Vell (the old port), and across the Rambla del

The Christopher Columbus monument.

Mar, a stylish drawbridge, is Europe's second-largest aquarium, with 21 glass tanks featuring different marine habitats. The highlight is a long, glass-enclosed tunnel, which produces the effect of fish, eels, and sharks swimming around and over wide-eyed visitors. ⏱ *1 hr. Moll d'Espanya-Port Vell.* ☎ *93-221-74-74. www.aquariumbcn.com. Admission 15.50€ adults, 12.50€ seniors, 10.50€ children 4–12 and students, free for children under 4. July–Aug daily 9:30am–11pm; Sept–June Mon–Fri 9:30am–9pm, Sat–Sun: 9:30am–9:30pm. Metro: Drassanes.*

6 ★ **kids** **Moll de la Fusta/ Port Vell/Barceloneta.** Moll de la Fusta, a very popular place for a *paseo,* or stroll, is a boardwalk and series of esplanades along Passeig Colom and the old harbor, beginning at the Columbus statue at the bottom of La Rambla and stretching to a giant Xavier Mariscal sculpture of a playful crayfish and colorful Pop-Art work, *Cap de Barcelona,* by the American artist Roy Lichtenstein. Continuing past the harbor and along Passeig Joan de Borbó takes you to Barceloneta, a colorful old beachfront neighborhood that got a controversial makeover for the '92 Olympics, displacing many longtime residents. It's still known for its longtime *chiringuitos,* or informal seafood restaurants, which makes it a perfect place to stop for lunch, especially on weekends. ⏲ *45 min. Metro: Drassanes or Barceloneta.*

7 ★★ kids **Barcelona's beaches & Port Olímpic.** It wasn't long ago that no self-respecting Barcelonan would venture down to the city's beaches, much less dream of wading into the polluted waters. Preparations for the 1992 Olympics dramatically reopened the city to the Mediterranean and cleaned up the urban beaches, vastly improving water quality. Today the long stretches of sand are a playground for city dwellers. The beaches (*platges*) are lined with palm trees, public sculptures, bars and restaurants, as well as paths for biking, in-line skating, and walking. The first major beach is Barceloneta, followed to the north by Nova Icària (the most popular beach, near the Port Olímpic marina and Vila Olímpica district), Bogatell, and Mar Bella (an unofficial nudist beach). ⏲ *2 hrs. Metro: Barceloneta or Ciutadella/Vila Olímpica.*

8 **Old City shopping.** Dozens of fashion boutiques, bars, and souvenir shops line bustling, pedestrian-only Carrer Ferran, while dark, atmospheric Carrer Banys Nous is home to some of the city's best antique shops. Shopaholics should continue across

Public sculptures can be found along Barcelona's beaches.

Vía Laetana to La Ribera and El Born, site of some of the chicest boutiques in old Barcelona. ⏲ *2 hrs. Metro: Liceu or Jaume I.*

9 ★ **Bar del Pi.** On one of the prettiest squares in the old city is one of the finest spots in town to linger at an outdoor cafe. Of the several cafes clustered around the square, Bar del Pi is the most traditional. People watching opportunities abound, and on weekends artists and artisans set up booths in the plaza. *Plaça Sant Josep Oriol.* ☎ *93-302-21-23. $.*

Xavier Mariscal's crayfish at the Moll de la Fusta.

The Best **in Three Days**

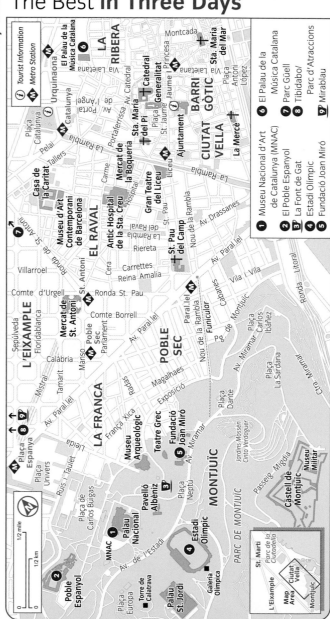

Key

- ℹ Tourist Information
- Ⓜ Metro Station

Locations on map:

- ❶ Museu Nacional d'Art de Catalunya (MNAC)
- ❷ El Poble Espanyol
- ❸ La Font de Gat
- ❹ Estadi Olímpic
- ❺ Fundació Joan Miró
- ❻ El Palau de la Música Catalana
- ❼ Parc Güell
- ❽ Tibidabo
- Parc d'Atraccions
- ❾ Mirablau

Map labels:

Montcada, LA RIBERA, El Palau de la Música Catalana, Urquinaona, Via Laietana, Sta. Maria del Mar, Plaça Antoni López, Catedral, Generalitat, BARRI GÒTIC, Plaça Catalunya, Pelai, La Rambla, Portaferrissa, Av. Catedral, Sta. Maria, Plaça del Pi, Sta. del Pi, Plaça St. Jaume, Jaume I Princesa, Av. Portal de l'Àngel, Ajuntament, CIUTAT VELLA, La Mercè, Casa de la Caritat, Carme, Mercat de la Boqueria, Museu d'Art Contemporani de Barcelona, EL RAVAL, Antic Hospital de la Sta. Creu, Hospital, Gran Teatre del Liceu, Liceu, St. Pau, Nou de la Rambla, La Rambla del Raval, Riereta, St. Pau del Camp, Av. Drassanes, Villarroel, Cera, Carrettes, Reina Amalia, Comte d'Urgell, St. Antoni, Ronda St. Pau, Nou de la Rambla, Av. Paral·lel, Mercat de St. Antoni, Comte Borrell, Paral·lel, Ronda de St. Antoni, L'EIXAMPLE, Sepúlveda, Floridablanca, Poble Sec, Parlament, POBLE SEC, Calàbria, Av. Paral·lel, Funicular, Vila i Vila, Cabanes, Ronda Litoral, Manso, Mistral, Tamarit, Pg. de Montjuïc, Plaça Carlos Ibáñez, Av. Miramar, Plaça La Sardana, Magalhaes, Exposició, Plaça Dante, LA FRANCA, França Xica, Radas, Museu Arqueològic, Teatre Grec, Fundació Joan Miró, Av. Miramar, Jardins Mossèn Cinto Verdaguer, Passeig Migdia, Museu Militar, Castell de Montjuïc, Ctra Miramar, Plaça Espanya, Plaça Univers, Plaça de Carlos Buïgas, Ruïs i Taulet, Leida, MONTJUÏC, Plaça Neptú, Pavelló Albéniz, Estadi Olímpic, PARC DE MONTJUÏC, St. Martí, Parc de la Ciutadella, Ciutat Vella, L'Eixample, Map Area, Montjuïc, Poble Espanyol, MNAC, Palau Nacional, Av. de l'Estadi, Estadi Olímpic, Palau St. Jordi, Galeria Olímpica, Torre de Calatrava, Plaça Europa

Scale: 0 — 1/2 mile / 0 — 1/2 km

This tour spends the morning on Montjuïc hill before making a brief stop in the Eixample district for one big *modernista* highlight, finishing the day with a gorgeous bird's-eye view of the city from Tibidabo. START: Metro to Espanya (though visitors who wish to take the aerial cable car from the port or funicular to Montjuïc should begin at Fundació Miró before working their way down to Poble Espanyol and MNAC).

❶ ★★★ Museu Nacional d'Art de Catalunya (MNAC). At the base of Montjuïc, within the domed Palau Nacional, this museum is anything but a stale repository of religious art. Its medieval collection, which includes Romanesque works salvaged from churches all over Catalonia, is unequaled; many of the superb altarpieces, polychromatic icons, and treasured frescoes are displayed in apses, just as they were in the country churches where they were found. Other highlights are paintings by some of Spain's most celebrated Old Masters, including Velázquez, Ribera, and Zurbarán. ⏱ *1½ hr. Palau Nacional, Parc de Montjuïc.* ☎ *93-622-03-60. www.mnac.es. Admission 8.50€ adults, 4€ students and youths 7–21, free for children 6 and under and first Thurs of month (also part of ArticketBCN joint admission). Temporary exhibits: 4.20€. Tues–Sat 10am–7pm; Sun 10am–2:30pm. Metro: Espanya.*

❷ ★ kids El Poble Espanyol. Erected for the 1929 Barcelona International Exhibition, this ambitious re-creation of a Spanish village presents more than 100 styles of emblematic architecture from across Spain, re-creating individual mansions, churches, streets, and squares, all reduced to scale. Though some adults and purists find it well-meaning kitsch, it's a fun and instructive place for families to visit and a great introduction to the country's architectural diversity for those who haven't had the opportunity to travel the breadth of Spain and see its whitewashed Andalusian alleyways, small-town plazas, or Renaissance palaces. ⏱ *1 hr. Av. Marqués de Comillas s/n (Parc de Montjuïc).* ☎ *93-508-63-00. www. poble-espanyol.com. Admission 7.50€ adults, 5.50€ children 7–12, free for children under 7; 15€ family ticket; 2€ guided tours. Mon 9am– 8pm; Tues–Thurs 9am–2am; Fri–Sat 9am–4am; Sun 9am–midnight.*

A piece from the Museu Nacional D'Art de Catalynya (MNAC).

Metro: Espanya, then 10-min walk uphill, or bus 13 or 50 from Plaça de Espanya.

3 **La Font de Gat.** This resurrected *modernista* cafe and restaurant, built by the acclaimed architect Puig i Cadalfach, is ensconced in gardens of the Montjuïc hillside and makes for a relaxing spot for a coffee or beer, or even an inexpensive fixed-priced lunch. *Passeig Sta. Madrona, 28.* ☎ *93-289-04-04. $.*

4 **Estadi Olímpic.** The setting for the majority of events during Barcelona's hosting of the 1992 Summer Olympics was Montjuïc, including the Olympic Stadium, originally built in 1929 for the World's Fair, and Arata Isozaki's sleek Palau d'Esports Sant Jordi, the indoor stadium that hosted gymnastics and volleyball events (and now also hosts concerts). Nearby are a small sports museum, Galería Olímpica, and the outdoor pool and diving pavilion, which overlooks the city below. ⏲ *30 min. Av. del Estadi, s/n (Parc de Montjuïc). Metro: Espanya (then take the escalator from Palau Nacional), bus 50 at Plaça d'Espanya, or Funicular de Montjuïc.*

5 **★★ Fundació Joan Miró.** Miró, a resolutely Catalan surrealist painter and sculptor, created a unique, whimsical artistic language—which to the uninitiated may look like colorful doodles—on his way to becoming one of the 20th century's most celebrated artists. In minimalist galleries bathed with natural light are several hundred of Miró's canvases, as well as a wealth of his drawings, graphics, and sculptures. A rooftop terrace and sculpture garden provides lovely views of Barcelona below. ⏲ *1½ hr. Parc de Montjuïc s/n.*

☎ *93-443-94-70. Admission 7.50€ adults, 4€ students, free for children under 14. Also part of ArticketBCN joint admission. July–Sept Tues–Wed and Fri–Sat 10am–8pm; Oct–June Tues–Wed and Fri–Sat 10am–7pm; year-round Thurs 10am–9:30pm and Sun 10am–2:30pm. Bus 50 at Plaça d'Espanya; or Funicular de Montjuïc.*

6 **★★★ El Palau de la Música Catalana.** Domènech i Montaner's magnificent 1908 music hall is over-the-top ornate but indisputably one of Barcelona's *modernista* masterpieces. The relatively sedate exterior is just a tease of what's inside: a riotous fantasy of ceramics, colored glass, and carved pumice, crowned by an enormous yellow, blue, and green stained-glass dome that looks like a swollen raindrop. It's surely the most exuberant music hall you'll ever see. A daytime guided tour addresses the architecture, but there's nothing like experiencing a concert here. ⏲ *1 hr. Carrer de Sant Francesc de Paula, 2.* ☎ *902-44-28-82 or 93-295-72-00 for information. http://home.palaumusica.org. Tour 8€ adults, 7€ students and*

Visit the rooftop terrace and sculpture garden at the Fundació Joan Miró.

Mosaics in the Palau de la Música Catalana.

seniors. Tickets can be bought up to 1 week in advance from the gift shop adjacent to the building. Guided tours daily, every half-hour 10am–3:30pm. Metro: Urquinaona.

7 ★★★ **kids** **Parc Güell.** Yet another of Gaudí's signature creations, this open-air park on the outskirts of the Eixample district is pure whimsy. Resembling an idiosyncratic theme park, it features a mosaic-covered lizard fountain, Hansel and Gretel pagodas, and undulating park benches swathed in broken pieces of ceramics, called *trencadís.* Gaudí carved part of the park out of a hillside, fashioning a forest of columns like tree trunks. A planned housing development that was never fully realized, the park is home to but a single house, now the Casa-Museu Gaudí, a small museum about Gaudí's life and work (where the ascetic architect lived while working on the project). On clear days, you can see much of Barcelona laid out beneath your feet, including the spires of La Sagrada Família and the twin towers on the beach. ⏱ 1 hr. Ctra. del Carmel 28. ☎ 93-424-38-09. Free admission to park; Casa-Museu Gaudí 4€. Daily 10am–sunset. Metro: Lesseps (then a 15-min. walk uphill). Bus: 24 or 28.

8 ★ **kids** **Tibidabo/Parc d'Atraccions.** High above Barcelona is Tibidabo Mountain, which has been a getaway destination for Barcelonans since the early 1800s for its cooler temperatures and panoramic views of the city and the ocean. The historic Tramvía

Casa-Museu Gaudí in the Parc Güell.

Tibidabo amusement park.

Blau, or Blue Tram, carries visitors to an overlook with bars and restaurants. Crowning Tibidabo is the odd juxtaposition of a neo-Gothic church and a 1950s-style amusement park, Parc d'Atraccions (the gentle swing ride is spectacular; it seems to suspend riders over the city). ⏱ *1–2 hrs. Plaça Tibidabo, 3.* ☎ *93-211-79-42. Parc d'Atraccions, 22€ for unlimited rides, 11€ 6 rides, 9€ children under 1.2m (4 ft.), free for children under 3. Summer daily noon–10pm; off season Sat–Sun noon–7pm. From Plaza Kennedy (Metro: Tibidabo), the tram* *connects with the Funicular Tibidabo, a cable car that completes the trek to the top of the mountain (mid-Sept to the end of Apr, weekends only); round-trip 3.30€.*

★ **Mirablau.** This bar perched on Tibidabo Mountain is sedate in the late afternoon and early evening, when it's perfect to relax and contemplate all of Barcelona, stretching out to the sea beneath you. *Plaça Doctor Andreu, 2.* ☎ *93-418-58-79. $$.* ●

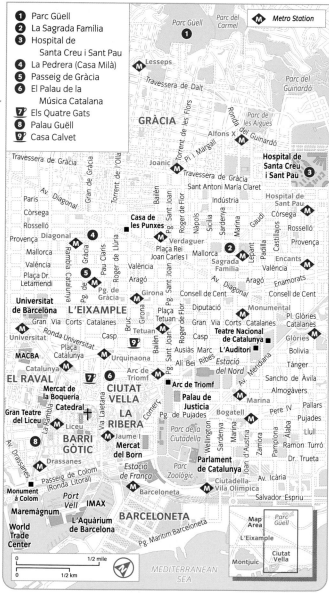

Modernista Barcelona

1 Parc Güell
2 La Sagrada Família
3 Hospital de
   Santa Creu i Sant Pau
4 La Pedrera (Casa Milà)
5 Passeig de Gràcia
6 El Palau de la
   Música Catalana
7 Els Quatre Gats
8 Palau Güell
9 Casa Calvet

M Metro Station

Parc Güell
Parc del Carmel
Parc del Guinardó
Lesseps
Travessera de Dalt
Parc de les Aigües
GRÀCIA
Alfons X
Ronda del Guinardó
Travessera de Gràcia
Joanic
Torrent de les Flors
Pi i Margall
Torrent de l'Olla
Gran de Gràcia
Hospital de Santa Creu i Sant Pau
Travessera de Gràcia
Sant Antoni Maria Claret
Paris
Av. Diagonal
Còrsega
Rosselló
Provença
Diagonal
Mallorca
València
Plaça Dr. Letamendi
Casa de les Punxes
Bailèn
Sant Joan
Roger de Flor
Nàpols
Sicília
Sardenya
Marina
Indústria
Hospital de Sant Pau
Còrsega
Rosselló
Gaudí
Castillejos
Padilla
Provença
València
Encants
Enamorats
Verdaguer
Plaça Rei Joan Carles I
Mallorca
Sagrada Família
Pau Claris
Roger de Llúria
Rambla Catalunya
Pg. de Gràcia
València
Aragó
Sant Joan
Aragó
Av. Diagonal
Consell de Cent
Girona
Universitat de Barcelona
L'EIXAMPLE
Gran Via Corts Catalanes
Bruc
Girona
Plaça Tetuan
Diputació
Roger de Flor
Monumental
Gran Via Corts Catalanes
Pl. Glòries Catalanes
Glòries
Bolívia
Universitat
Ronda Universitat
Casp
Tetuan
Bailèn
Sant Joan
Casp
Teatre Nacional de Catalunya
MACBA
Plaça Catalunya
Urquinaona
Ausiàs Marc
L'Auditori
Tànger
Sancho de Àvila
Catalunya
9 Casp
Ali Bei
Ribes
Estació del Nord
EL RAVAL
7
Arc de Triomf
Meridiana
Almogàvers
Mercat de la Boqueria
6
CIUTAT VELLA
Arc de Triomf
Palau de Justícia
Marina
Pere IV
Pallars
Gran Teatre del Liceu
Catedral
Comerç
Pg. de Pujades
Bogatell
Sardenya
Wellington
Marina
Joan d'Àustria
Zamora
Pamplona
Àlaba
Pujades
Llull
Liceu
La Rambla
Via Laietana
LA RIBERA
Jaume I
Ramon Turró
Dr. Trueta
BARRI GÒTIC
8
Mercat del Born
Parc de la Ciutadella
Drassanes
Estació de França
Parc Zoològic
Parlament de Catalunya
Av. Icària
Av. Drassanes
Passeig de Colom (Ronda Litoral)
Ciutadella-Vila Olímpica
Salvador Espriu
Monument á Colom
Port Vell
IMAX
Maremàgnum
L'Aquàrium de Barcelona
Barceloneta
BARCELONETA
World Trade Center
Pg. Marítim Barceloneta
MEDITERRANEAN SEA

0   1/2 mile
0   1/2 km

Map Area
Parc Güell
L'Eixample
Ciutat Vella
Montjuïc

Previous page: Antoni Gaudí's Casa Batlló.

Barcelona is renowned for the wildly original *modernisme*, or Catalan Art Nouveau, style of architecture that flourished in the late 19th and early 20th centuries. Best-known are the stunning works of Antoni Gaudí, but so many talented architects left their mark on Barcelona that it's a big task even to do a greatest hits tour in a single day. START: **Metro to Lessep, then a taxi or 15-min. walk uphill to Parc Güell, the first stop on the itinerary.**

❶ ★★★ kids Parc Güell. In 1900 Gaudí's life-long patron, the Catalan industrialist Eusebi Güell, envisioned a real estate development in a garden setting. Although never completed, the project bears Gaudí's visionary stamp and reflects the naturalism beginning to flower in his work. The architect set out to design every detail in the park, but much of the work was in fact completed by a disciple, Josep María Jujol, best known for the park's colorful splashes of *trencadís* (designs of broken shards of ceramics). Yet the unique man-made landscape is all Gaudí. At the main entrance are fairytale-like gatehouses, topped with chimneys resembling wild mushrooms. The covered marketplace, with an extraordinary tiled lizard fountain at the entrance, is supported by 86 Doric columns (not the 100 planned). But most famous are those sinuous, mosaic-covered benches that trace the perimeter of the plaza above. 🕑 *45 min. See p 53, bullet* ❺.

❷ ★★★ kids La Sagrada Família. Gaudí's most famous building is a work of unbridled ambition. He dedicated 4 decades of his life to it, and though the architect left behind no detailed plans, he expected that the cathedral—the world's largest if completed—would take several generations to finish. Gaudí envisioned 12 spires (one for each of the Apostles), a massive dome over the apse, and four additional, higher spires, as well as one central bell tower, representing the Virgin Mary. Portals in the dramatic Nativity facade represent Faith, Hope, and Charity, and Biblical elements, such as the Tree of Calgary, pack the dense surface. 🕑 *45 min. See p 5, bullet* ❼.

❸ ★★ Hospital de Santa Creu i Sant Pau. Just a few blocks' walk from La Sagrada Família, this hospital

Mosaic benches in the Parc Güell.

The modernista rooftops of Sant Pau.

campus reveals that Domènech i Montaner (1850–1923), like Gaudí, also thought in grand terms. Hospital Sant Pau, begun in 1902, was also left unfinished at the time of its architect's death, with just 18 of a planned 48 pavilions completed (12 of those are by Domènech i Montaner, and all are classified as World Heritage monuments). The fanciful brick-and-tile pavilions feature vaulted ceilings and decorative mosaics and sculpture, techniques that reach their apex in El Palau de la Música Catalana (see p 20). ⏱ *45 min. Sant Antoni María Claret 167–171.* ☎ *93-488-20-78. www. santpau.es. Free admission; guided tours as part of Ruta del Modernisme, 5€ adults, 3€ students, free for children under 15. Guided tours daily at 10:15am and 12:15pm in English, 1:15pm in Spanish. Metro: Hospital de San Pau or Sagrada Família (and 10-min. walk along Av. de Gaudí).*

④ ★★★ **kids La Pedrera (Casa Milà).** Gaudí's most inspired civic work, formally named for the patron who dreamed of creating a show-stopper on elegant Passeig de Gràcia,

this sinuous landmark apartment block is for many the pinnacle of *modernisme*. The rooftop chimneys (which some claim represent Christians and Moors battling for Spanish turf) are spectacular, but those with an interest in architecture will be fascinated by the museum (Espai Gaudí), which exposes the splendid arches of the attic and delves into the life, times, and techniques of the architect, while the restored original apartment (El Pis) shows off its peculiar shapes, handcrafted door-knobs, and period furniture, all of Gaudí's design. ⏱ *1 hr. See p 4, bullet ②.*

⑤ ★★★ **Passeig de Gràcia.** This elegant shopping boulevard is ground zero for *modernisme*. It's the one place to see a whole lot of *modernista* architecture without covering much distance. In fact, on a single block are pivotal buildings by Gaudí and the other two architects that make up the movement's great troika, Doménech i Montaner and Puig i Cadalfalch. The competing proximity of these landmarks earned the block the nickname "Manzana de la Discórdia" (Block of Discord). See mini-tour on following page.

The El Pis apartment is refurbished to its early 20th-century look.

5A Gaudí street tiles/ Falqués benches
5B Vinçon
5C Fundació Tàpies
5D Casa Batlló
5E Casa Amatller
5F Casa Lleó Morera

Passeig de Gràcia

i Tourist Information

M Metro Station

0   1/8 mile
0   1/8 km

At the foot of La Pedrera are some *modernista* surprises: **5A** The **street tiles** on the sidewalk (trumpeting nature and ocean themes) are by Gaudí, while the white **mosaic-covered benches** that flower into ornate, **wrought-iron lampposts** are by Pere Falqués. On the same block is the design shop **5B** **Vinçon** (see p 78), which occupies an elegant house built for the *modernista* painter Ramón Casas. Three blocks down is the famed **Manzana de la Discordia.** First take a peek at **5C** ★ **Fundació Tàpies** (p 37, bullet ❷), just off the boulevard at Aragó, 225, a museum dedicated to the Catalan artist Antoni Tàpies. Domènech i Montaner designed the erstwhile publishing headquarters in 1884.

Gaudí's spectacular **5D** ★★★ **Casa Batlló** (p 10, bullet ❹), open to the public since 2004, is as stunning inside as out; it features flowing staircases, a mushroom-shaped fire-place, and a gallery with bone-like columns. **5E** ★★ **Casa Amatller** (p 10, bullet ❺), Puig i Cadafalch's most famous building, was the first *modernista* building on the block. The exterior of carved stone is the work of a celebrated artisan, Eusebi Arnau. Domènech i Montaner's ornate **5F** ★ **Casa Lleó Morera** (p 10, bullet ❻) is less ground-breaking than its *modernista* companions on the block, but suffers even more in comparison since commercial tenants altered the ground floor and destroyed several magnificent sculptures.

The spectacular Palau de la Música Catalana.

6 ★★★ El Palau de la Música Catalana. Domènech i Montaner designed this audacious concert hall as a home for the Orfeó Catalán (Catalan Choral Society). The interior is hallucinatory: from colored-glass canisters on staircases and a ceiling dominated by a colossal teardrop of stained glass to a stage framed by pumice busts of the composers Bach, Beethoven, and Wagner by the sculptor Pau Gargallo. Long surrounded by apartment buildings, the Palau was given some breathing space when the noted Barcelona architect Oscar Tusquets completed a tasteful extension in 2003. ⏱ *45 min. See p 20, bullet* **6**.

7 ★★ Els Quatre Gats. A favorite hangout of Pablo Picasso, Ramón Casas, and other turn-of-the-century *modernista* bohemian intellectuals, this restaurant and cafe—one of the first commissions for the architect Puig i Cadalfalch and site of Picasso's first exhibition—is the perfect stop on a *modernisme* tour of Barcelona either for a late lunch or coffee and a pastry. *Carrer Montsió, 3.* ☎ *93-302-41-40. $–$$.*

8 ★★ Palau Güell. This 1888 mansion, not in the Eixample but in the much less fashionable district of El Raval, was Gaudí's first big

Ruta del Modernisme

You could easily spend days visiting *modernista* landmarks in Barcelona. If your appetite has been whetted, check out the **Ruta del Modernisme de Barcelona** (*modernisme* route) promoted by the city (www.rutadelmodernisme.com; ☎ 902-076-621; 12€– 18€). A self-guided tour of 115 sites, it offers discounted admissions of up to 50% at both major and lesser-known buildings—everything from palaces to pharmacies. Information and discount vouchers are available at a desk in the entry of the main tourist information office on Plaça de Catalunya. Besides the highlights listed in this chapter, several other of the Route's Top 30 sites are also included in the Eixample walking tour; see p 68.

Picasso was a regular at El Quatre Gats.

commission from Eusebi Güell, the textile magnate who would become a lifelong confidante and patron. It's heavier and less whimsical than Gaudí's later works—on the outside it looks like a fortress—but the architect's early genius is evident in the underground stables, interconnected floors, and Moorish-style decorative skylights. On the roof is the building's crowd-pleasing surprise, a preview of what would later come with La Pedrera: a small contingent of colorful, *trencadí*-covered chimneys. ⏱ *1 hr. carrer Nou de la Rambla 3–5.* ☎ *93-317-39-74.*

Admission 3€, free for children under 7. Mon–Sat 10am–6:15pm. Metro: Drassanes.

🔟 ★★ **Casa Calvet.** The best place to cap a day of touring *modernista* landmarks is dinner at this upscale restaurant, in one of Gaudí's earliest (and well-preserved) apartment buildings. The 1899 house features one of Barcelona's first elevators and elegant *modernista* details throughout, making for a unique dining experience. *Caspe, 48.* ☎ *93-412-40-12. $$$.*

Ciutat Vella: **Ancient Barcelona**

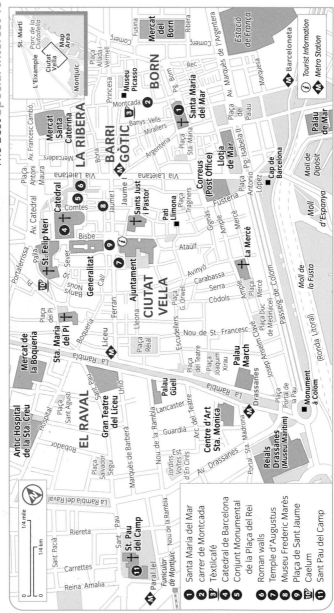

1 Santa Maria del Mar
2 carrer de Montcada
3 Tèxtilcafé
4 Catedral de Barcelona
5 Conjunt Monumental de la Plaça del Rei
6 Roman walls
7 Temple d'Augustus
8 Museu Frederic Marès
9 Plaça de Sant Jaume
10 Caelum
11 Sant Pau del Camp

(i) Tourist Information
M Metro Station

1/4 mile
1/4 km

Barcelona is one of Spain's most historic cities. Founded as Barcino by the Romans in 15 A.D., it expanded outside the ancient walls—sections of which still remain—in the 11th century. Much of medieval Barcelona lives on gloriously in the Ciutat Vella (old city) quarters of Barri Gòtic and La Ribera. See the Barri Gòtic walking tour (p 60) for additional details of the Roman and medieval city, including El Call, the old Jewish Quarter. START: **Metro to Jaume I.**

❶ ★★ Santa María del Mar. Designed by the architect Berenguer de Montagut in the mid-14th century and completed in just 5 decades, Santa María del Mar is a soaring Catalan Gothic church that once faced the Barcelona waterfront; its name ("St. Mary of the Sea") refers to its history as a place of worship for ship owners, merchants, and sailors (and wives left behind) who came to pray for safe returns. ⏱ *30 min. Plaça de Santa María.* ☎ *93-215-74-11. Free admission. Mon–Sat 9am–1:30pm and 4:30–8pm, Sun 9am–2pm and 5–8:30pm. Metro: Jaume I.*

❷ carrer de Montcada. At the back entrance to Santa María del Mar is this narrow, pedestrian-only lane through the La Ribera quarter, one of the most handsome medieval streets in Barcelona. From its origins in 1148, the street became an epicenter of commercial life. From the 14th to 17th centuries, Montcada's *palaus,* or mansions, were home to wealthy and noble families, many of whom were patrons of Santa Maria del Mar. While many palaus are private, a few are occupied by museums and galleries, giving visitors a chance to see their gorgeous courtyards and massive central stone staircases. ⏱ *45 min. Metro: Jaume I. See mini-tour on following page.*

Santa Maria del Mar is one of Barcelona's purest examples of Catalan Gothic architecture.

Carrer de Montcada   **LA RIBERA**

2A carrer de les Mosques
2B Palau dels Cervelló
2C Palau Dalmases
2D Palau Nadal
   (Museu Barbier-Mueller
   d'Art Precolombi)
2E Palau dels Marquesos de Lió
   (Museu Tèxtil i d'Indumentària)
2F Palau Aguilar
   (Museu Picasso)

Tiny 2A **carrer de les Mosques** ("street of the flies") is reputed to be the narrowest street in Barcelona; residents are able to reach out and touch the building across the street from their windows. The 15th-century 2B **Palau dels Cervelló (no. 25),** today home to a contemporary art gallery, maintains its original Gothic facade, while the 17th-century 2C **Palau Dalmases (no. 20)** retains a Gothic chapel and richly carved Renaissance staircase and elegant arches. 2D **Palau Nadal (no. 12–14),** home to the **Museu Barbier-Mueller d'Art Precolombi**—an excellent private

collection of pre-Colombian art— was constructed in the 15th and 16th centuries. Next door, the 13th—15th-century 2E **Palau dels Marquesos de Lió (no. 12)** houses the **Museu Tèxtil i d'Indumentària,** which features costumes, fabric, and lace-making techniques. The 15th-century 2F **Palau Aguilar (no. 15–23),** is today the site of the **Museu Picasso,** which it has been since 1963. Even if the art weren't inside, the museum would be worth visiting to see the extraordinary Gothic patios and staircases flanking superbly carved windows. *See p 13, bullet* 11.

3 **Tèxtilcafé.** This unexpected retreat, in the splendid medieval courtyard of the palace that houses the **Museu Tèxtil i d'Indumentària,** is a perfect relaxed spot either for coffee and a croissant at an outdoor table or a full, fixed-priced value lunch inside. *carrer de Montcada, 12–14.* ☎ *93-268-25-98. $.*

4 ★★★ **Catedral de Barcelona.** A Roman temple and later a mosque once stood on this site in the heart of the Gothic Quarter. The lush cloister, built between 1350 and 1448, continues to be home to white geese, which in the Middle Ages functioned as guard dogs, their squawks alerting priests to intruders. Beneath the ancient slabs of the stone floor lie the remains of members of the Barri Gòtic's ancient guilds. ⏱ *30 min. See p 12, bullet* **10**.

5 ★★★ **kids** **Conjunt Monumental de la Plaça del Rei.** Plaça del Rei abuts a remaining section of the old Roman walls, and in the 1930s, archaeologists unearthed ruins of Barcino, the old Roman city. (The subterranean ruins can be visited by the public.) The five-story tower Mirador del Rei Martí, which rises above the square, dates to 1555, when it was built as a lookout for foreign invasions and

Geese in the cloister of Catedral de Barcelona.

peasant uprisings. ⏱ *45 min. See p 15, bullet* **1**.

6 ★ **kids** **Roman walls.** Barcino was a small settlement, comprising just 10 hectares (25 acres) enclosed by walls 2 meters (6½ feet) thick. Several sections of the Roman walls, enlarged in the 3rd and 4th centuries A.D., remain; some of the best examples are on Plaça Ramon Berenguer, parallel to Via Laietana. To the right of the front entrance to the cathedral, the Portal de l'Angel's twin semicircular towers frame the entrance to carrer del Bisbe. ⏱ *15 min. Metro: Jaume I.*

Practical Matters: carrer de Montcada

Museu Barbier-Mueller d'Art Precolombí. carrer de Montcada 12–14. ☎ **93-310-45-16.** Admission 3€ adults, 1.50€ students, free for children under 16. Tues–Sat 10am–6pm; Sun 10am–3pm. Free on first Sunday of the month. Metro: Jaume I.

Museu d' Textil i d' Indumentària. carrer de Montcada 12. ☎ **93-319-76-03.** Admission 3.50€ adults, free for children under 16. Tues–Sat 10am–6pm; Sun 10am–3pm. Metro: Jaume I.

The Roman walls at night.

❼ ★ Temple d'Augustus.

Three massive Corinthian columns, the best-preserved relics of the Roman city, are all that remain of the Temple d'Augustus, the principal temple built in the 1st century B.C. Hidden from view and lower than Barcelona's modern street level, they are one of the Barri Gòtic's great secrets. The temple once formed part of the Roman Forum dedicated to the emperor Caesar Augustus. *carrer del Paradis, 10 (inside Centre Excursionista de*

The Temple d'Augustus columns date to the 1st century B.C.

Catalunya). ☎ *93-315-23-11. Free admission. June–Sept Tues–Sat 10am–8pm, Sun 10am–2pm, rest of year, Tues–Sat 10am–2pm and 4–8pm, Sunday 10am–2pm. Metro: Jaume 1.*

❽ ★★ Museu Frederic Marès.

Marès, a 20th-century sculptor and evidently obsessive collector, amassed one of Spain's finest private collections of medieval sculpture, from the pre-Roman to the Romanesque, Gothic, Baroque, and Renaissance eras. The collection is housed in a palace—itself worthy of study, with its handsome interior courtyards, carved stone, and expansive ceilings—just behind the cathedral. ⏱ *45 min. Plaça de Sant Iú 5–6.* ☎ *93-310-58-00. www. museumares.bcn.es. Admission 3€ adults, free for children under 12. Tues–Sat 10am–7pm, Sun 10am–3pm. Free Wed 3–7pm. Metro: Jaume I.*

❾ ★ Plaça de Sant Jaume. The

site of the city and regional governments, this stately plaza is also a popular gathering place for Barcelonans during holiday celebrations and political demonstrations. The **Palau de la Generalitat,** home to the autonomous Catalonian government, dates to the 15th century, while across the square, the 14th-century **Casa de la Ciutat,** built around a central courtyard, houses the municipal government. The **Saló de Cent** (Room of 100 Jurors) features immense arches, typical of the Catalan Gothic style. ⏱ *30 min. Casa de la Ciutat: Plaça de Sant Jaume s/n.* ☎ *93-402-70-00. Free admission. Sun 11am–3:30pm. Metro: Jaume I.*

10 ★ **Caelum.** On the surface this appears to be simply an appealing shop selling teas, jams, olive oil, sweets, and other products made by nuns and religious orders in Spain and Europe. But downstairs in the cafe (where you can have tea, coffee, pastries, and sandwiches), in a space referred to as "the crypt," is another treat altogether: the exposed foundations of

14th-century Jewish baths, or *mikves. carrer de la Palla, 8.* ☎ *93-302-69-93. $.*

⓫ ★★ **Sant Pau del Camp.** The oldest church in Barcelona, dating back to the 9th century, "Saint Paul of the Countryside" was once a rural church and part of a monastery, far beyond the city walls. It remains remarkably intact, with original Romanesque capitals and bases of the portal complementing sections from a rebuilding in the 11th and 12th centuries. The chapter house holds the tomb—which reads 912 A.D.—of Count Guifre Borrell, son of Wilfred the Hairy. ⏱ *30 min. carrer de Sant Pau, 99 (El Raval).* ☎ *93-441-00-01. Admission to cloister 2€. Mon–Fri noon–2pm, 5–8pm. Metro: Paral.lel.*

The (Hairy) Birth of a Nation

Although the Moors invaded Spain in 711 and would rule over much of its territory for 8 centuries, Catalonia only briefly succumbed to the invaders from North Africa. The Moors retreated after a defeat near the Pyrenees in 732, never establishing a lasting foothold in Catalonia. A 9th-century count with a descriptive name, Guifré el Pilós—Wilfred the Hairy—became a feudal lord and the founding father of Catalonia, unifying and then forging the region's independence. He founded a dynasty in 878 which ruled for nearly 500 years. Much of Spain remained under Moorish domination, but Barcelona and Catalonia were linked instead to northern Europe, a geo-political wrinkle that formed the basis for the fiercely independent and northward-looking Catalan character. The hero of Catalonia has been mythologized in the region's flag, which features four horizontal red stripes on a yellow field (and said to be the oldest still in use in Europe today). According to legend, the red bars were first etched in Wilfred's own blood on his golden shield (perhaps as he lay dying in battle). Scholars cast doubt on the veracity of the tale, but most Catalans believe it to be true.

Barcelona **for Art-Lovers**

- **1** Fundació Joan Miró
- **2** Fundació Antoni Tàpies
- **3** carrer Consell de Cent galleries
- **4** Bar Lobo
- **5** Museu d'Art Contemporani de Barcelona (MACBA)
- **6** Museu Picasso
- **7** El Xampanyet
- **8** Ciutat Vella galleries

(i) Tourist Information
Ⓜ Metro Station

Barcelona has a long tradition of embracing adventurous art and eccentric artists. Pablo Picasso began his career here, and the Catalans Joan Miró, Salvador Dalí, and Antoni Tàpies all made their marks in Barcelona before becoming international superstars. Barcelona's lively art scene of museums and galleries is especially appealing for anyone with a strong interest in contemporary and modern art, though this is a tour for those who also have the stamina to take in several museums back to back. START: **Metro to Espanya (or funicular to Montjuïc).**

1 ★★★ Fundació Joan Miró.
Miró, born in rural Catalonia in 1893, became one of the 20th century's most important artists. His whimsical and enigmatic abstract forms expressed complex themes, including sexuality, Catalan national identity, and opposition to the Spanish Civil War. Miró himself donated 11,000 works to this museum, constructed on Montjuïc hill in 1975. Pivotal works include the 1970s tapestry, *Tapis de la Fundació,* designed for the gallery in which it hangs; *L'Estel Matinal,* part of the Constellation Series; and 1940s and 1950s sculptures, including *Sun Bird* and *Moon Bird.* The museum's audioguide is especially insightful. ⏲ 1 hr. See p 20, bullet **5**.

2 ★ Fundació Antoni Tàpies.
One of Spain's great artists of the 20th century is the abstract expressionist Antoni Tàpies, born in Barcelona 1923. Tàpies is known for his collage and mixed-media "matter" paintings that incorporate earth, sand, and even pedestrian items such as socks into large canvasses. Much of his work is replete with politically charged and religious imagery, as well as graffiti-like words and insignias. Look for the works *Metal Shutter and Violin* (1956) and *Straw and Wood* (1969). The giant tangle of steel on the roof is the artist's once-controversial sculpture (now accepted by most Barcelonans) called *Cloud and Chair.* ⏲ 45

The sculpture Cloud and Chair *sits atop the Fundacío Antoni Tàpies.*

min. Aragó 255. ☎ 93-487-03-15. www.fundaciotapies.org. Admission 6€ adults, 4€ students. Tues–Sun 10am–8pm. Closed Mon; Dec 25–26 and Jan 1–6.

3 carrer Consell de Cent. This leafy Eixample street, between Passeig de Gràcia and Muntaner, is one of the most frequented in Barcelona for its contemporary art galleries featuring both Spanish and international artists. Among the galleries to keep an eye out for: **Sala Dalmau** (no. 349; ☎ 93-215-45-92); **Jordi**

The Carles Tache gallery.

Barnadas (no. 347; ☎ 93-215-63-65); **Senda** (no. 337; ☎ 93-487-67-59); **Galería René Metras** (no. 331; ☎ 93-487-58-74); **Galería Llucià Homs** (no. 315; ☎ 93-467-71-62); **Galería Carles Tache** (no. 290; ☎ 93-487-88-36); **Ambit** (no. 282. ☎ 93-488-18-00); and **Galería Eude** (no. 278; ☎ 93-487-93-86). ⏱ *1 hr. Metro: Passeig de Gràcia.*

4️⃣ Bar Lobo. This cool tapas bar is decorated with graffiti murals and the kind of concert posters and ads that usually litter city walls. It's great for lunchtime snacks or late-night drinks. *Pintor Fortuny, 3. ☎ 93-481-53-46. $–$$.*

5️⃣ ★ Museu d'Art Contemporani de Barcelona (MACBA). Although still best known for its gleaming white 1995 Richard Meier design, a stark contrast in the transitional Raval quarter, the Museum of Contemporary Art is continually expanding its permanent collection and refining its purpose. You'll find works by Calder, Basquiat, and Klee, as well as major Catalan artists such as Tàpies, Miquel Barceló, and the surrealist Joan Brossa. ⏱ *45 min. plaça dels Angels 1. ☎ 93-412-08-10. Admission 8.50€ adults, 6€ students, free for children under 14. Wed only 3€. Mon and Wed–Fri 11am–7:30pm; Sat 10am–8pm; Sun 10am–3pm. Metro: Catalunya or Universitat.*

6️⃣ ★★★ Museu Picasso. This museum is especially strong on the artist's early development, including his Blue and Rose periods. Picasso (1881–1973) donated 2,500 paintings and sculptures to the museum, the largest representation of his work in Spain, in 1970. The highlight is his playful series of 59 paintings based on Velázquez's seminal work *Las Meninas.* Also of note are *The Harlequin* and the young artist's sketch notebooks of Barcelona street scenes. Visitors more familiar with Picasso's later, convention-busting works may find his talents for traditional portraiture and figurative painting a revelation. ⏱ *1 hr. See p 13, bullet* 11️⃣.

7️⃣ El Xampanyet. A wonderful throwback, this classic and gregarious *cava* bar serves its sparkling wine (here, more a fizzy white wine than *cava*) in '50's-style glasses. An excellent selection of Catalan cheeses, salamis, and more are on offer. *carrer de Montcada, 22. ☎ 93-319-70-03. $.*

Sunlight provides brilliant, natural interior lighting at MACBA.

⑧ Ciutat Vella galleries.
Although the bulk of contemporary
and modern art galleries are in
L'Eixample, those in the old city
pose an interesting contrast to the
ancient surroundings. The Barri
Gòtic streets Petritxol and Palla mix
art galleries in with boutiques and
antiques dealers. Among galleries
worth seeking out are **Galería
Maeght** (carrer de Montcada, 25;
☎ 93-3142-45); **Artur Ramón
Espai Contemporani** (carrer de la
Palla, 10; ☎ 93-301-16-48); **Trama**
(Petritxol, 8; ☎ 93-317-48-77); and
the city's oldest gallery, **Sala Parés**
(Petritxol, 5; ☎ 93-318-70-08).
🕐 *1 hr. Metro: Jaume I.*

Inside the Museu Picasso.

Barcelona's Outdoor Sculpture

Not all of Barcelona's great art is behind museum doors. The
city is full of outdoor sculpture, much of it in heavily trafficked areas
you're likely to visit. If you arrive by air, you may first see Joan Miró's
giant **mosaic mural** (1970) outside Terminal B at the Barcelona
Airport. Look also for the great Basque sculptor Eduardo Chillida's
Topos V in Plaça del Rei; Roy Lichtenstein's *Cap de Barcelona*
(1992) at the intersection of Moll de la Fusta and Vía Laietana;
Antoni Tàpies's glass-enclosed *Homage to Picasso* (1983) on
Passeig Picasso, at
the entrance to Parc
de la Ciutadella; Miró's
Woman and Bird
(1982) in Parc Joan
Miró, near Estació de
Sants; *Pla de l'Ós*, the
Miró mosaic underfoot
on La Rambla (across
from the Teatre Liceu
opera house); and a
couple for the kids,
Xavier Mariscal's **giant
crayfish** on Moll de
la Fusta and Frank
Gehry's monumental
Fish sculpture on the
beach at Vila Olímpica.

Antoni Tàpies's Homage to Picasso.

Barcelona for Design & Architecture Fans

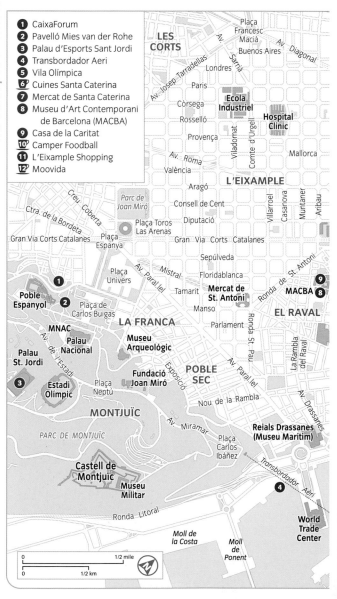

1 CaixaForum
2 Pavelló Mies van der Rohe
3 Palau d'Esports Sant Jordi
4 Transbordador Aeri
5 Vila Olímpica
6 Cuines Santa Caterina
7 Mercat de Santa Caterina
8 Museu d'Art Contemporani de Barcelona (MACBA)
9 Casa de la Caritat
10 Camper Foodball
11 L'Eixample Shopping
12 Moovida

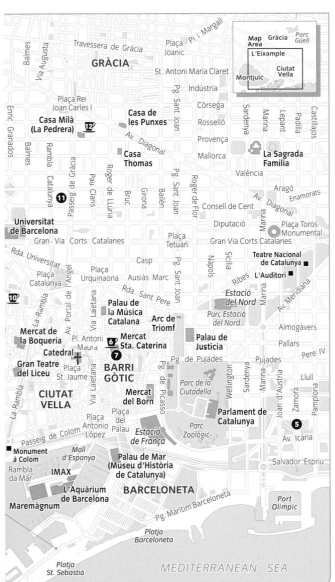

Travessera de Gràcia

Plaça Joanic

Pl. I. Margall

GRÀCIA

St. Antoni Maria Claret

Balmes

Via Augusta

Indústria

Pg. Sant Joan

Còrsega

Sardenya

Marina

Lepant

Padilla

Castillejos

Plaça Rei Joan Carles I

Enric Granados

Casa Milà (La Pedrera) 🔟²

Casa de les Punxes

Rosselló

Provença

Av. Diagonal

Balmes

Casa Thomas

Mallorca

La Sagrada Família

Rambla Catalunya

València

Passeig de Gràcia

Pau Claris

Roger de Llúria

Bruc

Girona

Bailèn

Pg. Sant Joan

Roger de Flor

Aragó

Enamorats

Av. Diagonal

🔟¹

Consell de Cent

Universitat de Barcelona

Diputació

Marina

Plaça Toros Monumental

Gran Via Corts Catalanes

Gran Via Corts Catalanes

Rda. Universitat

Plaça Catalunya

Plaça Tetuan

Casp

Pg. Sant Joan

Sicília

Nàpols

Teatre Nacional de Catalunya ■

Plaça Urquinaona

Ausiàs Marc

Ribes

L'Auditori ■

🔟⁰

La Rambla

Av. Portal de l'Àngel

Via Laietana

Rda. Sant Pere

Estació del Nord

Marina

Av. Meridiana

Palau de la Música Catalana

Parc Estació del Nord

Mercat de la Boqueria

Pl. Antoni Maura

Mercat Sta. Caterina 6️⃣

Arc de Triomf ■

Palau de Justícia

Almogàvers

Pallars

Pere IV

Catedral ✝

7️⃣

Pg. de Pujades

Pujades

Sardenya

Marina

Joan d'Àustria

Zamora

Pamplona

Llull

Gran Teatre del Liceu

Plaça St. Jaume

BARRI GÒTIC

Pg. de Picasso

Parc de la Ciutadella

CIUTAT VELLA

Via Laietana

Mercat del Born

La Rambla

Plaça Antonio López

Plaça del Palau

Estació de França

Parc Zoològic

Parlament de Catalunya

5️⃣

Av. Icària

Passeig de Colom

Monument á Colom ■

Moll d'Espanya

IMAX

Palau de Mar (Museu d'Història de Catalunya)

Salvador Espriu

Rambla da Mar

L'Aquàrium de Barcelona

BARCELONETA

Port Olímpic

Maremàgnum

Pg. Marítim Barceloneta

Platja Barceloneta

Platja St. Sebastià

MEDITERRANEAN SEA

Map Area: Gràcia, *Parc Güell*, L'Eixample, Montjuïc, Ciutat Vella

Though visitors flock to Barcelona for its *modernista* architecture and picturesque Gothic Quarter, the forward-looking Catalan capital is also a favorite with fans of contemporary architecture and design. The 1992 Summer Olympic Games provided a huge impetus for new, adventurous urban planning projects. Design pros or anyone with an appreciation for cutting-edge design will have a field day in Barcelona. As the Dean of Harvard's Graduate School of Design proclaimed, "Unlike many other cities, Barcelona seems to have chosen architecture and urbanism as its most conspicuous, long-lasting, and crowning glory." START: **Metro to Espanya.**

1 ★ CaixaForum. The 2002 conversion of a 1911 red-brick *modernista* textile factory (by Puig i Cadalfalch), by the Japanese architect Arata Isozaki and three others, transformed it into a brilliant new art exhibition space. It's a terrific synthesis of Barcelona's dominant design motifs—*modernista* and cutting-edge contemporary—and a terrace on the roof provides great views of the Palau Nacional, home to the Museu Nacional d'Art de Catalunya, and Montjuïc hill (see p 19, bullet **1**). ⏱ *30 min. Av. Marquès de Comillas 6–8.* ☎ *93-476-86-00. Free admission. Tues–Sun 10am–8pm. Metro: Espanya.*

2 ★★ Pavelló Mies van der Rohe. The famous minimalist German architect created this steel, glass, and marble structure as the German Pavilion for the 1929 World's Fair. Considered a classic of 20th-century design, it is recognized for its pure, precise lines. The interior holds little save van der Rohe's original Barcelona Chair, today a much-reproduced icon of modern design. The pavilion, unceremoniously banished from the city after the Fair, was returned to its original location in 1985 after prominent architects petitioned the city. ⏱ *30 min. Av. Marquès de Comillas s/n.* ☎ *93-423-40-16. Admission 3.50€ adults, free for children under 18. Daily 10am–8pm. Metro: Espanya.*

3 Palau d'Esports Sant Jordi. Arata Isozaki's sleek indoor sports stadium held gymnastic, volleyball, and basketball events during the '92 Olympics. When it was first opened to the public, some 50,000

The Pavelló Mies van der Rohe is considered a classic of 20th–century design.

Frank Gehry's Fish *sculpture at the Vila Olímpica.*

Barcelonans turned out to see the new addition to Montjuïc's Olympic Ring. Today it hosts both sporting events and concerts. Lording over it is the once-despised **Telefónica communications tower,** also built for the '92 Olympics, by the famed architect from Valencia, Santiago Calatrava. The tower's base is decorated with broken ceramic tiles, an homage to Gaudí. ⏱ *30 min. Av. del Estadi, s/n (Parc de Montjuïc). Metro: Espanya (then take the escalator from Palau Nacional); alternatively, take bus 50.*

❹ **kids Transbordador Aeri.** A great way to appreciate the layout of Barcelona, especially L'Eixample's grid designed by Ildefons Cerdà in 1859, is to take the aerial cable car from Montjuïc down to the port area and Barceloneta. The cable car runs every 15 minutes daily from 10:30am to 7pm. Cost is 6€ one-way, 7.20€ round-trip.

❺ ★ **Vila Olímpica.** The award-winning urban-design project that revamped the waterfront created an entirely new neighborhood of apartment buildings, gardens, and large public sculptures, by a host of both celebrated and young architects, designers, and artists. The apartment blocks first housed Olympic athletes before being turned over to private buyers, and in the years since, Vila Olímpica

has become a fashionable neighborhood. The waterfront's twin towers, among Barcelona's only skyscrapers (one is Hotel Arts, the other an office complex), were initially polemical, but their presence is now widely accepted. In front of Hotel Arts is Frank Gehry's massive, metal-lattice *Fish* sculpture, which appears to glow in the afternoon sun. ⏱ *45 min. Metro: Ciutadella/Vila Olímpica.*

❻ ★★ **Cuines Santa Caterina.** This cool tapas bar and restaurant makes the best of its privileged location inside the market and offers the freshest of seafood and vegetables, and inexpensive wines by the glass or carafe. It's a great spot for an array of small plates. *Av. Francesc Cambó s/n.* ☎ *93-268-99-18. $–$$.*

The Antoni Llena sculpture David and Goliath *in front of the Hotel Arts.*

The colorful, wave-like roof of Mercat de Santa Caterina.

⑦ ★★ Mercat de Santa Caterina. The 2005 remodeling of this 1848 city food market—the first covered market in Barcelona—is renowned for its colorful and undulating mosaic-tile roof. The project was the work of the celebrated firm of Enric Miralles and Benedetta Tagliabue. ⏱ *30 min. Av. Francesc Cambó s/n.*

⑧ ★ Museu d'Art Contemporani de Barcelona (MACBA). Much like the way that Frank Gehry's Guggenheim Bilbao stimulated the arts and urban development in that Basque city, Richard Meier's MACBA has been the impetus for updating and integrating the Raval district. Art galleries, boutiques, and restaurants, as well as new apartment buildings, have followed, displacing many longtime residents but overall making the northern section of the neighborhood safer and more attractive. ⏱ *45 min. See p 38, bullet ⑤.*

⑨ ★ Casa de la Caritat. One of the first projects undertaken in the revamping of the formerly marginal Raval district was the conversion of this 13th-century convent and charity hospital into an art and culture space. Two avant-garde Catalan architects, Albert Viaplana and Helio Piñón, gave the Centre de Cultura Contemporània de Barcelona (CCCB) an angled wall of glass that reflects neighborhood rooftops and the Mediterranean Sea. ⏱ *45 min. Carrer de Montalegre, 5–9. ☎ 93-306-41-00. Tues–Sun, 11am–8pm. Admission 6€, seniors and students 3.30€; free for children under 16 and 1st Wed of every month. Metro: Plaça de Catalunya or Universitat.*

⑩ ★ Camper Foodball. After visiting MACBA, take a break at a spot that highlights the artsy, modern direction in which the Raval district is headed. Camper, the funky, shoemaker, has opened a funky, small hotel in the neighborhood as well as this hipster take on tapas. It uses rice balls as a base, to which one adds a host of vegetarian ingredients, much like toppings on a sundae, for inventive, tasty snacks. *carrer Elisabets, 9. ☎ 93-270-13-63. $.*

⑪ ★ L'Eixample Shopping. A day of design for the fashion-conscious would be senseless without at least a couple of stops at Barcelona's renowned design emporiums. Vinçon (Passeig de Gràcia, 96) is a local institution for

Architecture Superstars

For design-crazy sorts who can't get enough, a number of relatively recent contributions to Barcelona's urban landscape are by celebrated architects in the zone north of Vila Olímpica, near Plaça de les Glòries. Pritzker prizewinner Rafael Moneo built the sleek white concert hall **L'Auditori** (Lepant, 150), while nearby the glass-fronted **Teatre Nacional de Catalunya** (Pl. de les Arts, 1) is by Barcelona native Ricardo Bofill. The most talked-about recent building in Barcelona is Jean Nouvel's **Torre Agbar (**Avda. Diagonal 209–211), a tall (142 m/465 ft.), phallic skyscraper that's illuminated at night with the colors of Barça, the local *fútbol* (soccer) team. Several blocks west (along Ronda St. Martí at Felip II) is Santiago Calatrava's **Pont Bac de Roda,** a white, arching bridge and work of stellar engineering by the man who has quickly become Spain's most famous architect, with projects in place across the globe.

housewares, lamps, and furniture, all selected for their innovative design. Also visit the shops of Catalan fashion designers **Josep Font** (Provença, 304), **Antonio Miró** (Consell de Cent, 349), and **Armand Basi** (Passeig de Gràcia, 49), three of the hippest clothiers in town.
🕐 *45 min. Metro: Passeig de Gràcia or Provença. See chapter 4, "The Best Shopping," p 71.*

12 ★ **Moovida.** On the third floor of the high-design Hotel Omm, a hotspot with fashionable types, is the informal and less pricey cousin to Moo, the ultra-hip restaurant of the Roca brothers. It won't break the bank, and you can just have a drink or order a few tapas if you want. *Rosselló, 265–269.* ☎ *93-445-40-00. $$.*

The Richard Meier-designed Museu d'Art Contemporani de Barcelona (MACBA).

Gourmet Barcelona

1. El Quim de la Boqueria
2. Mercat de la Boqueria
3. Escribà
4. Pastis
5. Granja Viader
6. Colmado Quílez
7. Cacao Sampaka
8. Queviures J. Murrià
9. Mercat Santa Caterina
10. Museu de la Xocolata
11. E & A Gispert
12. Tot Formatge
13. Origen 99,9%
14. Vila Viniteca

With its rise as a foodie capital in the last decade, Barcelona now rivals San Sebastián as one of the top eating cities in Europe. In addition to haute-cuisine restaurants and chef-driven tapas bars, there are scores of both old-school and innovative *colmados* (grocery stores), chocolatiers, and wine shops. Don't worry, this isn't a day-long tasting menu unless you choose to make it one! Note that Monday isn't the best day for this tour, as several shops are closed. START: **Metro to Liceu.**

1️⃣ ★★★ El Quim de la Boquería. Quim has been at the helm of this bustling kiosk bar (*taburete*) within La Boquería food market for the last 21 years. Prized by fellow chefs and foodies-in-the-know, it's a place for fresh grilled seafood and tapas of the highest order. My favorite is breakfast at the counter; try the fried eggs topped by a heaping pile of *chipirones* (baby squid). *Mercat de la Boquería, parada no. 584/585.* ☎ *93-301-98-20. $$.*

2️⃣ ★★★ Mercat de la Boquería. Spain's largest food market is a gastronomic paradise. The market, just off La Rambla, dates to 1840; today it has more than 300 stalls stocked with eye-popping displays of salted fish, exotic fruits, wild mushrooms (*ceps* and *bolets*), and more. You can eat, too, at El Quim, Bar Pintxo, and a couple of restaurants in the back. Buffet & Ambigú (parada no. 437), a shop toward the rear, features cookbooks of some of Spain's best-known chefs. 🕐 *1 hr. See p 11, bullet 8️⃣.*

A few of the bountiful offerings at La Boquería.

3️⃣ ★ Escribà. Talk about eye candy. One of Barcelona's oldest and best-known chocolatiers is this little shop on La Rambla with a shimmering *modernista* exterior (of colorful broken glazed tiles, a la Gaudí) and tea salon within. Its traditional chocolates now have lots of competition from designer chocolate shops such as Oriol Balaguer and the small chains Xocoa and Cacao Sampaka, but a stop here is essential. 🕐 *20 min. La Rambla 83.* ☎ *93-221-07-29. Metro: Liceu or Plaça de Catalunya.*

4️⃣ Pastis. Another venerable chocolate seller in *modernista* surroundings, this place began as a

Gourmet Tip

For more information on where to buy and eat your favorite gourmet items, check "The Best Shopping," p. 72, and "The Best Dining," p. 94.

coffee roaster, Cafés Garriga, in 1890. Formerly a branch of the small chain Xocoa, it has now gone independent. Check out the lovely stained-glass design at the rear of the shop and elegant carved-wood ceiling. ⏱ *20 min. carrer Carme, 3.* ☎ *93-304-23-60. Metro: Liceu or Plaça de Catalunya.*

5 ★ **Granja Viader.** Although the old neighborhood of El Raval has seen a huge amount of upheaval, this place with marble-topped tables has resisted change. A gloriously authentic *granja,* or "milkbar," (the oldest in Barcelona, since 1870), it's known for thick chocolate drinks such as *xocolata desfeta* and the original *cacaolat,* a bottled chocolate drink famous throughout Spain. *Carrer Xuclà, 4–6.* ☎ *93-318-34-86. $.*

6 ★★ **Colmado Quílez.** Another charming throwback is this 1908 grocery store and wine shop, the most famous *colmado* in Barcelona. Its floor-to-ceiling shelves are stocked with gourmet packaged goods, while back rooms stock wines from across Spain and even 300 types of beer. ⏱ *30 min. Rambla de Catalunya, 63.* ☎ *93-215-23-56 Metro: Passeig de Gràcia.*

Colmado Quilez is an old-school Barcelona grocery store.

Cheeses, wines, and cured meats are all on offer at Queviures J. Murrià.

7 **Cacao Sampaka.** The pastry-chef brother of Ferran Adrià, the world-famous chef of El Bulli, started this hip shop that features both traditional and avant-garde chocolates, as well as a cafe-restaurant (menu items are both sweet and savory). With great packaging, the chocolates here make great gifts. ⏱ *20 min. Consell de Cent, 292.* ☎ *93-272-08-33. Metro: Passeig de Gràcia.*

8 ★★ **Queviures J. Murrià.** Even older and more old-school than Quílez, this food-and-wine shop has been in the same family since the late-19th century. Its handsome exterior, the work of the *modernista* artist Ramón Casas, is only a prelude to the 200 types of cheese, 300 wines, Iberian *jamón* (ham), and canned goods inside. ⏱ *30 min. carrer Roger de Llúria, 85.* ☎ *93-215-57-89. Metro: Passeig de Gràcia.*

9 ★★ **Mercat Santa Caterina.** This gorgeously redesigned covered food market has a nice casual restaurant, Cuines de Santa Caterina, tucked inside. See p 44, bullet **7**.

10 kids **Museu de la Xocolata.** A small chocolate museum, with exhibits about the history of chocolate and chocolate-making classes. The large-scale chocolate sculptures of cartoon figures and Barcelona landmarks, including Gaudí's La Sagrada Familia and La Pedrera, are fun. ⏱ 30 min. carrer del Comerç, 32. ☎ 93-268-78-78. Admission 3.80€ adults, 3.20€ seniors and children. Mon and Tues–Sat 10am–7pm; Sun 10am–3pm. Metro: Arc de Triomphe.

11 ★★ **E & A Gispert.** One of the oldest continuously running shops in Barcelona (since 1851) sells coffee and teas, dried fruits and nuts, honey and jams, and traditional Catalan torron desserts, as well as gift baskets and other artisanal and organic products. One of the most redolent places you'll ever poke your nose into, the shop retains the original one-piece counter and wood shelves and still uses a spectacular 150-year-old, wood-burning nut roaster—the only one of its kind in Europe. ⏱ 30 min. c/dels Sombrerers, 23. ☎ 93-319-73-35.

12 ★ **Tot Formatge.** This cute little cheese shop (the name means "All

Cheeses of all kinds tempt the senses at Tot Formatge.

The characters from Chicken Run *made out of chocolate at the Museu de la Xocolata.*

Things Cheese") on stylish Passeig del Born is another place to overwhelm your nose. ⏱ 15 min. Passeig del Born, 13. ☎ 93-319-53-75.

13 **Origen 99,9%.** Through the door on one street it's an intimate shop specializing in Catalan gastronomy, with local olive oils and cheeses, while through another, facing Santa Maria del Mar, it's a busy, informal eating space promoting popular and traditional Catalan recipes. Try the torradas and cocas (toasted open-face sandwiches), as well as the nice selection of Catalan wines. ⏱ 30 min. carrer de Vidriera, 6–8. ☎ 93-310-75-31. Metro: Jaume I.

14 **Vila Viniteca.** From cult wines like Pingus to small-yield Priorats, including plenty of bottles you can't get outside Spain, this is Barcelona's wine temple, with more than 6,000 choices. Check out scheduled catas (wine tastings) at www.vilaviniteca. es. ⏱ 30 min. Agullers, 7. ☎ 93-268-32-27. Metro: Jaume I.

Barcelona **for Kids**

1. La Rambla
2. Waterfront
3. Parc Zoològic/
   La Ciutadella
4. Agua
5. Parc Güell
6. CosmoCaixa
   (Museu de la Ciència)
7. Parc d'Atraccions/
   Tibidabo
8. Font Màgica
9. IMAX Port Vell
10. FC Barcelona/Camp Nou

↑ Parc d'Atraccions
Tibidabo
Plaça
Francesc
Macià

LES
CORTS

Av. Diagonal

Av. Josep Tarradellas

Av. Sarrià

Londres

Paris

Còrsega

Ecola
Industrial

Rosselló

Hospital
Clinic

Provença

Av. Roma

Mallorca

Vilamari

Llançà

València

L'EIXAMPLE

Viladomat

Comte d'Urgell

Aragó

Villarroel

Casanova

Muntaner

Aribau

↖ Camp Nou
(FC Barcelona) 10

Ctra. de la Bordeta

Tarragona

Parc de
Joan Miró

Consell de Cent

Diputació

Gran Via Cors Catalanes

Plaça
Espanya

Plaça Toros
Las Arenas

Gran Via Corts Catalanes

Sepúlveda

Poble
Espanyol

Plaça
Univers

Av. Paral·lel

Mistral

Floridablanca

Ronda de St. Antoni

MACBA

8 Font
Màgica

Tamarit

Mercat de
St. Antoni

EL RAVAL

Plaça de
Carlos Buigas

LA FRANCA

Manso

Parlament

Ronda St. Pau

MNAC

Palau
Nacional

Museu
Arqueològic

La Rambla
del Raval

Palau
St. Jordi

Fundació
Joan Miró

Exposició

POBLE
SEC

Av. Paral·lel

Av. Drassanes

Estadi
Olímpic

Plaça
Neptú

Nou de la Rambla

MONTJUÏC

Av. de l'Estadi

PARC DE MONTJUÏC

Av. Miramar

Plaça
Carlos
Ibáñez

Reials Drassanes
(Museu Marítim)

Transbordador Aéri

Castell de
Montjuïc

Museu
Militar

Ronda Litoral

Moll de
la Costa

Moll
de
Ponent

World
Trade
Center

0 ——— 1/2 mile
0 ——— 1/2 km

Map Area: Gràcia, Parc Güell, L'Eixample, Montjuïc, Ciutat Vella

GRÀCIA

Travessera de Gràcia

Plaça Joanic

Pi i Margall

St. Antoni Maria Claret

Indústria

Còrsega

Rosselló

Provença

Mallorca

València

Aragó

Consell de Cent

Diputació

Gran Via Corts Catalanes

Casp

Ausiàs Marc

Rda. Sant Pere

Via Augusta

Balmes

Via Augusta

Plaça Rei Joan Carles I

Casa Milà (La Pedrera)

Casa de les Punxes

Av. Diagonal

Casa Thomas

Enric Granados

Balmes

Rambla Catalunya

Passeig de Gràcia

Pau Claris

Roger de Llúria

Bruc

Girona

Bailèn

Roger de Flor

Pg. Sant Joan

Pg. Sant Joan

Pg. Sant Joan

Sardenya

Marina

Lepant

Padilla

Castillejos

La Sagrada Família

Enamorats

Av. Diagonal

Plaça Toros Monumental

Sicília

Nàpols

Ribes

Teatre Nacional de Catalunya ■

L'Auditori ■

Marina

Av. Meridiana

Universitat de Barcelona

Gran Via Corts Catalanes

Rda. Universitari

Plaça Catalunya

Plaça Urquinaona

Plaça Tetuan

Rda. Universitat

Av. Portal de l'Àngel

Via Laietana

La Rambla

La Rambla

Estació del Nord

Parc Estació del Nord

Almogàvers

Pallars

Pere IV

Pujades

Llull

Joan d'Àustria

Zamora

Pamplona

❶ **Mercat de la Boqueria**

✝ **Catedral**

Gran Teatre del Liceu

CIUTAT VELLA

Pl. Antoni Maura

Plaça St. Jaume

BARRI GÒTIC

Mercat Sta. Caterina

Palau de la Música Catalana

Arc de Triomf

Palau de Justicia

Pg. de Pujades

Pg. de Picasso

Pg. de Picasso

Mercat del Born

Plaça del Palau

Parc de la Ciutadella

❸

Parlament de Catalunya

Wellington

Sardenya

Mar na

Av. Icària

Salvador Espriu

Plaça Antonio López

Estació de França

Parc Zoològic

Passeig de Colom

■ **Monument á Colom** ❷

Moll d'Espanya

Rambla da Mar

IMAX ❾

L'Aquàrium de Barcelona

Maremàgnum

Palau de Mar (Musèu d'Història de Catalunya)

BARCELONETA

Pg. Marítim Barceloneta

❹

Port Olímpic

Platja Barceloneta

Platja St. Sebastià

MEDITERRANEAN SEA

With its sophisticated architecture, design, and foodie appeal, Barcelona might seem like a city just for grownups, but it has plenty to offer children of all ages. Much of the fun is outdoors, from the amusing mimes on La Rambla to the family-oriented waterfront and zoo in the city's largest park. Even transportation can be exciting: Kids are sure to love the aerial cable car from the port to Montjuïc and the antique Blue Tram that climbs the hill to Tibidabo. **START: Metro to Plaça de Catalunya.**

1 ★★★ **La Rambla.** Though you'll need to watch your kids closely among the throngs that crowd La Rambla, children are sure to be amused by the human statues who spring to life for a coin or two and the kiosks with all kinds of squawking birds for sale. ⏱ *30 min. See p 11, bullet* **7**.

2 ★★ **Waterfront.** Past the sailboats in the harbor and on the other side of the pedestrian-only **Rambla del Mar** drawbridge are several excellent options for families: **L'Aquarium,** a large and well-designed aquarium that lets you get up close and personal with sharks, eels, and other aquatic creatures that appear to be swimming above and around you; a traditional-styled **carousel** for younger children; and **Maremàgnum** shopping mall with lots of shops geared toward kids. You can also board double-decker swallow boats, **Las Golondrinas,** that cruise the harbor, or stroll along the **Moll de la Fusta** boardwalk from the old port towards the Barceloneta district; there's a sculpture of a giant, cartoon-like crayfish waiting for kids at the end. ⏱ *1½ hrs. See p 88.*

3 ★★ **Parc Zoològic/La Ciutadella.** Barcelona's largest city park is a great place for kids to unwind, with plenty of green space, a large pond and rowboats, a massive Gaudí-designed fountain, and a cool old greenhouse. But it's the zoo that will probably be first on most kids' to-do lists. Although its star attraction, an albino gorilla named Copito de Nieve (Snowflake), passed on a couple years ago, several of his (non-albino) offspring are here, as well as llamas, lions, bears, hippos, and a large primate community—most of whom are not behind bars, but are kept in their "enclosures" by a slightly more humane moat. There are more than 4,000 animals in all. ⏱ *1 hr. Parc de la Ciutadella.* ☎ *93-225-67-80. www.zoobarcelona.com Admission 15€ adults, 9€ students and children 3–12. Summer daily 10am–7pm; off season daily 10am–5pm. Metro: Ciutadella or Arc de Triomf.*

A performer on La Rambla.

Parc de la Ciutadella is one of Barcelona's most popular green spaces.

4️⃣ Agua. Near Port Olímpic is this informal and good-value restaurant with outdoor tables overlooking the beach. The Mediterranean menu features seafood and risottos (cooked over coals), but there are plenty of items for the kids, and you can just get some small plates and drinks and feast on the beach, too. *Passeig Marítim de la Barceloneta, 30.* ☎ *93-225-12-72. $–$$.*

5️⃣ ★★★ Parc Güell. Gaudí's imaginative park is mostly playground, and kids love it. Stone columns look like trees, gatehouses look transported from Hansel and Gretel, and the gurgling, mosaic-covered lizard fountain simply looks adorable. It's a great place for hide-and-seek. And if it's a clear day, the views of Barcelona all the way to the beach—past the spires of La Sagrada Familia—are terrific. ⏱ *1 hr. Ctra. del*

Cheetah Girls in Barcelona

The hugely popular **Cheetah Girls,** the teen girl vocal group that stars in two Disney movies, go to Barcelona for a musical competition in *Cheetah Girls 2*. The entire movie was shot on location in the city, which plays a starring role. The girls—Galleria, Dorinda, Aquanetta, and Chanel—hop from spot to spot, fudging the geography but making the most of the city. If your daughter is begging to see all the places where the Cheetahs danced, sang, and romanced Spanish boys, you'll have to hop around a bit, too. Major sites include: Montjuïc; textilcafé, in the courtyard of the Textile museum; Passeig del Born; carrer Montcada; Parc Güell; El Palau de la Música (site of rehearsal); Estació de França; and, for the grand finale and open-air concert, Plaça del Rei. Big surprise, though: no strutting on La Rambla.

Carmel 28. ☎ *93-424-38-09. Free admission to park; Casa-Museu Gaudí 4€. Daily 10am–sunset. Metro: Lesseps (then a 15-min. walk uphill). Bus: 24 or 28.*

6 ★★★ CosmoCaixa (Museu de la Ciència). One of the largest and finest science museums anywhere, this recently revamped learning center is high-tech and hands-on, and a blast for kids. It's in an original *modernista* building (now ingeniously updated), to boot. With a daring underground extension and renovation of the original edifice, the museum offers 3,700 sq. m. (39,826 sq. ft.) of exhibition space. "The Flooded Forest," an exhibit of a living Amazonian rain forest inside the museum with over 100 species of animal and plant life, is thrilling; kids are encouraged to pick up and touch rats, frogs, spiders, and other fauna. The 3D planetarium and cool Geological Wall are also big draws. ◷ 1½ hrs. *Teodor Roviralta 55.* ☎ *93-212-60-50. 3€*

Ronaldinho (right) is Barcelona's biggest soccer star.

Planetarium and other activities, 2€ supplement. First Sun every month free admission. Tues–Sun 10am–8pm. FGC: Av. Tibidabo (then 10-min. walk). Bus: 17, 22, 58, or 73. ●

Evening Entertainment for Families

If kids and parents are both raring to go at night, consider these options:

The old-school **Parc d'Atraccions Tibidabo 7,** the nostalgic amusement park with a magnificent chair ride that appears to dangle you high above the city below. See p 21; bullet **8**.

Font Màgica 8, the colorful, dancing fountains set to pop tunes at the base of Montjuïc. Plaça Carles Buïgas 1. May–Oct, Thurs–Sun every half hour between 9:30 and 11:30pm. Oct–Sept, Fri–Sat every half hour between 7 and 8:30pm. Free admission. Metro: Espanya.

IMAX Port Vell 9 theatre at the waterfront. Moll de Espanya. ☎ 93-225-11-11. Admission 7€.

A match of Barcelona's hugely popular *fútbol,* or soccer, team, "Barça" at **FC Barcelona/Camp Nou 10.** Aristides Maillol, s/n. ☎ 93-496-36-00. www.fcbarcelona.com. Tickets start at 24€. Visits to the Camp Nou stadium and museum are also available, 7€–11€. Metro: Collblanc.

La Rambla

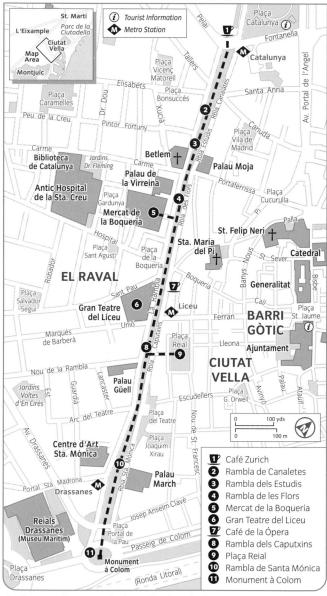

St. Martí

L'Eixample   Parc de la
            Ciutadella

Map Area   Ciutat
            Vella

Montjuïc

Plaça
Caramelles

(i) Tourist Information
(M) Metro Station

Plaça
Catalunya   *(i)*

Fontanella

Peral

Tallers

Plaça
Vicenç
Matorell

Elisabets

Plaça
Bonsuccés

Xuclà

Santa Anna

Rbla. Canaletes

Av. Portal de l'Angel

Catalunya

Peu de la Creu

Dr. Dou

Pintor Fortuny

Canuda

Plaça
Vila de
Madrid

Rbla. Estudis

Carme

Biblioteca
de Catalunya

Jardins
Dr. Fleming

Carme

Betlem ✝

Palau de
la Virreina

Antic Hospital
de la Sta. Creu

Plaça
Gardunya

Mercat de
la Boquería

Palau Moja

Portaferrissa   Plaça
                Cucurulla

Rbla. des Flors

Pl.
Palla

St. Felip Neri ✝

Catedral

Hospital

Plaça
Sant Agusti

Robador

Plaça
Salvador
Seguí

EL RAVAL

Sant Pau

Plaça
de la
Boquería

Sta. Maria
del Pi ✝

Boquería

St.-Sever

Banys Nous

Bisbe

Generalitat

La Rambla

Gran Teatre
del Liceu

Unió

Marquès
de Barberà

Nou de la Rambla

Jardins
Voltes
d'En Cirès

Av. Drassanes

Est

Guardia

Lancaster

Liceu *(M)*

Caputxins

Plaça
Reial

Rbla.

Ferran

Call

Cali

BARRI
GÒTIC

Plaça
St. Jaume   *(i)*

Lleona

Ajuntament

CIUTAT
VELLA

Plaça
G. Orwell

Avinyó

Palau

Ataülf

Palau
Güell

Arc del Teatre

Escudellers

Plaça
del Teatre

Nou de St. Francesc

Plaça
Joaquim
Xirau

0   100 yds
0   100 m

Centre d'Art
Sta. Mònica

Rbla. Sta. Mònica

Portal Sta. Madrona

Drassanes *(M)*

Palau
March

Josep Anselm Clavé

Reials
Drassanes
(Museu Marítim)

Plaça
Portal de
la Pau

Passeig de Colom

Plaça
Drassanes

Monument
á Colom

(Ronda Litoral)

1' Café Zurich
2 Rambla de Canaletes
3 Rambla dels Estudis
4 Rambla de les Flors
5 Mercat de la Boquería
6 Gran Teatre del Liceu
7' Café de la Ópera
8 Rambla dels Caputxins
9 Plaça Reial
10 Rambla de Santa Mónica
11 Monument à Colom

Previous page: A woman walks along a Barcelona street.

Is there a finer boulevard for strolling in the world? Not in my book. Victor Hugo proclaimed La Rambla "the most beautiful street in the world," while the Spanish poet Federico García Lorca said it was the "only street he wished would never end." The tree-shaded, pedestrian-only promenade stretches nearly 2 km (1.2 miles) down a gentle slope from the city's hub, Plaça de Catalunya, to the waterfront. To the left (as you walk down it) is the Barri Gòtic; to the right is El Raval. START: **Metro to Plaça de Catalunya.**

1 Café Zurich. At the very top of La Rambla, to the west of Plaça de Catalunya (and at the base of El Triangle shopping mall), is this terrace cafe, the best spot in the city for people-watching and a jolt of coffee before you start your stroll. The cafe was much more atmospheric before it was rebuilt and sanitized a few years back (the mall's to blame), but it remains a pivotal reference point in Barcelona. *Pl. Catalunya, 1.* ☎ *93-317-91-53. $.*

The Font de Canaletes.

2 Rambla de Canaletes. The beginning of La Rambla usually swarms with people, particularly on game days of Barça, the local football (soccer) club. Kiosks sell foreign newspapers and magazines, and the first of La Rambla's celebrated mimes, or "human statues," begin to appear. The rotating cast of flamboyant characters includes opera singers, bearded nuns, and Roman

A crowd gathers around an entertainer on La Rambla.

soldiers, all vying for a few coins. The 19th-century Font (fountain) de Canaletes is said to convert anyone who drinks from it into a lifelong resident of Barcelona.

3 ★★ kids Rambla dels Estudis. Hear that squawking? Popularly called Rambla dels Ocells ("of the birds"), this section becomes an outdoor aviary, with parakeets, parrots, and other winged creatures in cages for sale. At the end of the day, vendors simply board up the stalls, and the birds remain overnight.

4 ★★ kids Rambla de les Flors. Birds are replaced by flowers in this section, officially La Rambla de Sant Josep. Keep an eye out, to your right, for the *modernista* chocolate shop, **Escribà** (Antiga Casa Figueres, La Rambla, 83), one of the oldest chocolatiers in Barcelona. Another notable *modernista* building to look

A vendor clips her flowers on La Rambla de les Flors.

for is the **Farmacia Genové** (no. 77). **Palau de la Virreina** (no. 99), a grand, late 18th-century palace built for the widow of the viceroy of colonial Peru and today a museum hosting rotating contemporary art exhibits, is also worth a look.

⑤ ★★★ La Boquería. Set back from La Rambla, on the right side, is a constant in the life of Barcelonans: Mercat de Sant Josep, better known as La Boquería. This bustling 19th-century covered market overflows with gastronomic delights.

Longtime shoppers and merchants greet each other by name and shout across the aisles. The market opens before dawn, and the best shoppers know to arrive early. *La Rambla, 91–101.* ☎ *93-318-25-84.*

⑥ ★★ Gran Teatre del Liceu. The midpoint and heart of the Ramblas is the bustling intersection Pla de la Boquería, with a **Joan Miró mosaic** underfoot. One of Europe's great opera houses, the **Liceu** (lee-say-oo), is to the right. Since 1874 it has been home to all the Catalan greats, including Montserrat Caballé and Josep Carreras. Gutted by fire in 1994 (its third), it reopened after a restoration added high-tech improvements but preserved its soul. *La Rambla 51–59.* ☎ *93-485-99-14. Guided tours, including the private Cercle del Liceu, daily at 10am. Admission 8.50€, free for children under 10. Shorter tours (no entry to the Cercle del Liceu) daily at 11:30am, noon, and 1pm. Admission 3.50€, free for children under 10.*

The Hotel Oriente was Hemingway's favorite Barcelona hotel.

La Rambla? Les Rambles? Las Ramblas?

The name La Rambla is derived from Arabic, signifying a dry riverbed—which is what this spot was until the 14th century, when Barcelonans began to populate the area. The stream was soon paved over, and it developed into a pedestrian-only boulevard. Some call it by the plural name, Les Rambles (Las Ramblas in Spanish), since in fact it comprises five distinct sections with individual names. However, they all blend together so seamlessly that most Barcelonans call the whole stretch by the singular, La Rambla. It's most crowded just before the lunch hour and in the early evening, but it's never deserted. In the wee hours it's the haunt of a sometimes motley mix of early-morning newspaper sellers, street sweepers, and party animals stumbling back to their apartments and hotels.

A view up La Rambla from Rambla de Santa Mónica.

7 ★ **Café de la Ópera.** This Belle Epoque cafe is a longtime gathering spot for opera-goers and literary types and now a hangout for young people, tourists, gays, and old-timers. A good spot for coffee, beers, and snacks during the day, it gets more animated at night. *La Rambla, 74.* ☎ *93-317-75-85. $.*

8 ★ **Rambla dels Caputxins.** As the Rambla descends down a slight incline, so does its reputation. But you'll also find some of the Rambla's best entertainment—jugglers, tarot-card readers, more mimes, and street artists whipping out portraits and caricatures. On the right is **Hotel Oriente;** it was Hemingway's favorite place to stay in Barcelona. Nearby is **Palau Güell,** a Gaudi-designed mansion built in 1885. The high-Gothic palace can and should be visited; make sure to see the impressive tiled chimneys on the rooftop.

9 ★ **Plaça Reial.** Across La Rambla and down a short passage is a pretty, arcaded square with a central fountain and soaring palm trees. Once home to a convent and later the haunt of junkies and thieves, today it is greatly cleaned up, and full of bars, cafes, and restaurants pushing legal stimulants.

10 ★ **Rambla de Santa Mónica.** The final section leads down to the harbor. Though the sleek **Centre d'Art Santa Mònica**

hosts contemporary art exhibits, this zone is the least savory part of La Rambla (the maze of small and still-scruffy streets to the right, or west, comprise Barcelona's once-notorious Barri Xino, or Chinatown). The **Drassanes Reials,** beautifully vaulted medieval shipyards and home to the excellent **Museu Marítim,** are the highlight of La Rambla before you arrive at the waterfront. *See p 15, bullet* **3**.

11 **Monument à Colom.** Marking the end of the Rambla and the start of the waterfront is a statue honoring Christopher Columbus. Though he is ostensibly indicating the way to the New World, snarky observers like to point out that Columbus is actually looking towards Mallorca rather than the Americas. Columbus is reputed to have come to Barcelona after his maiden journey to the Americas to meet with the Catholic monarchs Isabel and Ferdinand.

Plaça Reial is a great place to sit at a cafe and people-watch.

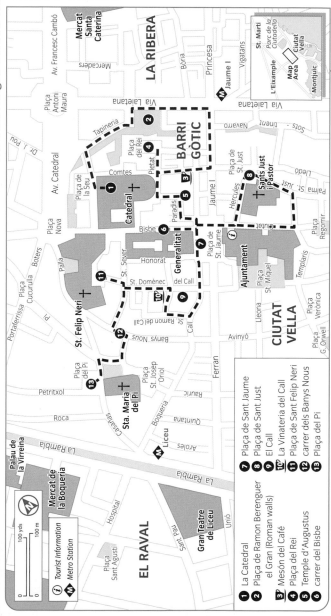

Barri Gòtic

Mercat Santa Caterina

Av. Francesc Cambó

LA RIBERA

Mercaders

Bòria

Princesa

Vigatans

St. Martí

Parc de la Ciutadella

Ciutat Vella

Map Area

L'Eixample

Montjuïc

Plaça Antoni Maura

Tapineria

Via Laietana

Jaume I

Via Laietana

Sots - Tinent Navarro

Dr. J. Pou

Av. Catedral

Plaça del Rei

Pietat

BARRI GÒTIC

Plaça de St. Just

Palma St. Just

Lledó

Comtes

Plaça de la Seu

Catedral

Paradís

Jaume I

Hercules

Sagts Just i Pastor

Regomir

Plaça Nova

Bisbe

Generalitat

Plaça de St. Jaume

Ciutat

Templers

Palla

Boters

St. Sever

Honorat

Ajuntament

Plaça St. Miquel

Plaça Verònica

Plaça Cucurulla

St. Domènec

del Call

CIUTAT VELLA

Plaça G. Orwell

Portaferrissa

Pl

St. Felip Neri

St. Ramon del Call

Call

Lleona

Avinyó

Ferran

Petritxol

Plaça del Pi

Plaça St. Josep Oriol

Sta. Maria del Pi

Rauric

Quintana

Boqueria

Roca

Casares

Liceu

Aròles

La Rambla

Palau de la Virreina

Mercat de la Boqueria

Hospital

Sant Pau

Unió

EL RAVAL

Gran Teatre de Liceu

Plaça Sant Agustí

Banys Nous

Tourist Information

Metro Station

100 yds

100 m

① La Catedral
② Plaça de Ramon Berenguer el Gran (Roman walls)
③ Mesón del Café
④ Plaça del Rei
⑤ Temple d'Augustus
⑥ carrer del Bisbe
⑦ Plaça de Sant Jaume
⑧ Plaça de Sant Just
⑨ El Call
⑩ La Vinateria del Call
⑪⑫ carrer dels Banys Nous
⑬ Plaça del Pi

The Gothic Quarter, which includes remnants of the medieval Jewish district, El Call, as well as Barcelona's 2,000-year-old Roman past, is a joy to wander. Its labyrinth of narrow, cobblestone streets are lined with both important monuments—including palaces, convents, and churches—and smaller, lesser-known attractions.

START: Metro to Jaume I.

① ★★ **La Catedral.** The Barri Gòtic has long been known as the "Cathedral Quarter," so this is the logical place to start. Locals gather at the **Plaça Nova** ("new square," dating from 1358!) in front of the cathedral to perform the *sardana*, a Catalan folk dance (Sunday mornings and national holidays). To the right of the main entrance to the cathedral is the **Portal de Bisbe,** semicircular twin towers and one of three gateways to the walled settlement of Roman Barcino (4th c. A.D.). *See p 12, bullet* **⑩**.

② ★★ **Plaça de Ramon Berenguer el Gran.** In this square is one of largest surviving sections of the second Roman wall, dating to the fourth century A.D. The equestrian statue is of the 12th-century Catalan hero who gives the square its name. Rising above the wall are the 14th-century Palau Reial Major (Royal Palace), Santa Àgata chapel, and a

Mirador del Rei Martí (King Martin's Watchtower) rises above the Plaça del Rei.

Plaça Ramon Berenguer.

Gothic tower. These are all best seen from Plaça del Rei, which you'll visit shortly. *Via Laietana s/n*

③ ★★ **Mesón del Café.** A tiny, charming cafe that dates back to 1909, this is the kind of good-vibes spot where some neighborhood folks stop by every day for some of the city's best coffee. Belly up to the bar or see if you can score a table in back. *carrer Llibreteria, 16.* ☎ 93-315-07-54. $.

④ ★★★ **Plaça del Rei.** This noble and austere square is the most beautiful part of the Barri Gòtic. Here you'll find subterranean Roman ruins and the medieval Royal Palace where the Catholic Monarchs are said to have received Columbus on his return from the New World in 1493. The sculpture in the square, *Topos V,* is by the Basque sculptor Eduardo Chillida, one of Spain's great 20th-century artists. *See p 15, bullet* ❶.

❺ ★★ **Temple d'Augustus.** *See p 34, bullet* ❼.

❻ ★★ **carrer del Bisbe.** One of the loveliest streets in the Gothic Quarter, the former principal artery of the Roman city connects the cathedral to Plaça Sant Jaume. On one side are the **Cases dels Canonges,** a series of 14th-century Gothic palaces. On the other is the **Palau de la Generalitat,** home to

A bike rider in the Barri Gòtic.

The walkway above carrer del Bisbe was added in 1928.

the Regional Government of Catalonia. Notice the rooftop gargoyles watching over the street action below. Arching over the lane is a bridge of carved stone, which only looks Gothic; it was added in 1928.

❼ ★ **Plaça de Sant Jaume.** An important crossroads during the Roman era, this broad square has been the political epicenter of Barcelona for more than 5 centuries. On one side is the Palau de la Generalitat. Across from it is the 14th-century **Ajuntament,** Barcelona's Town Hall. *See p 34, bullet* ❾.

❽ ★★ **Plaça de Sant Just.** This quiet, diminutive square is one of the most representative and unadulterated of medieval Barcelona. The **Església dels Sants Just i Pastor,** a church begun in 1342, features a single nave in the Catalan Gothic style. It's usually open only for

El Caganer in a Manger

Barcelona's annual nativity crafts fair and Christmas market in the square in front of the cathedral features one traditional folkloric figure that in recent years has taken on all kinds of modern permutations. It is *el caganer.* Placed in nativity scenes, the small figure, traditionally donning a red peasant's cap, is depicted squatting and defecating. El caganer symbolizes Catalans' ties to the land and the hope for continued fertility. With an eye toward young consumers and tourists, today el caganer is not limited to peasant figures. You'll also see figurines of priests, nuns, Bart Simpson, local and international politicians, and more—all squatting and fertilizing the earth.

Sunday Mass. The Gothic fountain in the square dates to 1367. **Palau Moxó,** a seigniorial mansion across the square, was added in 1700.

9 ★ **El Call.** Carrer del Call leads into the warren of small streets that once comprised the Call, or Jewish Quarter, in medieval Barcelona (until the Jews were expelled from Spain in 1492). Only a few important vestiges of the community remain. The **Sinagoga Medieval de Barcelona** claims to be the oldest synagogue in Spain (based on a royal document from 1267). A nearby medieval Hebrew inscription marking a death in 692 A.D. reads, "Rabbi Samuel Hassareri, may his life never cease." *carrer Marlet, 5.* ☎ *93-317-07-90. www.calldebarcelona.org. Admission 2€. Mon–Sat 11am–6pm; Sun 11am–3pm.*

10 **La Vinateria del Call.** This romantic little spot in the heart of the old Jewish Quarter serves up local wines and Catalan tapas, such as cured meats and cheese. *carrer de Sant Domènec del Call, 9.* ☎ *93-302-60-92. $.*

11 ★★★ **Plaça de Sant Felip Neri.** Down a tiny passageway off carrer Sant Sever is one of the most tranquil and poetic spots in the

Plaça de Sant Felip Neri, a quiet spot in the Barri Gòtic.

A relic from Barcelona's El Call (Jewish Quarter).

Ciutat Vella. It was once the site of a cemetery and the specter of the dead lingers. Behind the gurgling fountain is a reminder of Spain's not-too-distant violence: The walls of the 17th-century church are scarred by Civil War bombs that killed 42 people in 1938.

12 ★ **carrer dels Banys Nous.** This atmospheric street (named for the location of the "new baths," dating from the 12th century) follows the line of the old Roman wall and today is known as *el carrer dels antiquaris*—the street of antiques dealers.

13 ★★ **Plaça del Pi.** A trio of pretty, contiguous plazas surrounds the 15th-century church **Santa Maria del Pi,** known for its rose window. **Plaça de Sant Josep Oriol** adjoins Plaça del Pi and, behind the church, tiny **Placeta del Pi.** The squares are recognized for the unusual *sgraffito* decorative technique on the plaster facades of several buildings, an 18th-century style imported from Italy. But the leafy squares are most popular for the weekend artisans' market and open-air cafe-bars, making this an excellent place to while away the hours and finish a walking tour.

La Ribera

Metro Station

Ortigosa
Trafalgar

0   100 yds
0   100 m

Comtal

El Palau de la
Música Catalana **15**

St. Pere Més Alt

Sant Pere de
les Puel.les **14** ✝

Arc de Triomf Ⓜ

Arc de
Triomf

Plaça
Lluis Millet

Montsió

Verdaguer

St. Pere Mitjà

Plaça
de St. Pere

Rec Comtal

Lluis Companys

Dr. J. Nou

Via Laietana

St. Pere Més Baix

St. Jaume Giralt

Plaça
Marquilles

Portal Nou

Plaça
Antoni
Maura

Av. Francesc Cambó

Pg. de Picasso

Av.
Catedral

Mercader

Mercat
Santa
Caterina **13**

Plaça
St. Augustí
Vell

Comerç

LA RIBERA

Corders

Plaça
Allada i
Vermell

Museu
Zoologia

Plaça
del
Rei

Via Laietana

Bòria

Assaonadors

12

Museu de
la Xocolata

Princesa

7

Museu
Geologia

Jaume I

Princesa

Jaume I Ⓜ

1

11

Montcada

Museu
Picasso

Rec

8

Fusina

6

**CIUTAT
VELLA**

Argenteria

Banys Vells
Miralles

9

BORN

Comerç

Mercat
del Born **5**

Passeig de Picasso

Santa Maria
del Mar ✝

10

Mosques

2

Pg. Born

4

Jardins de
Fontserè
i Mestre

Plaça
Sta. Maria

3

Esparteria

Rec

Ribera

Gignàs

Fustería

Correus
(Post Office)

Llotja
de Mar

Plaça
del Palau

Av. Marquès de l'Argentera

Passeig de Circumval.lació

Zoo de
Barcelona

Parc
Zoològic

Estació
de França

Marquesa

1 carrer de l'Argenteria
2 Santa Maria del Mar
3 Fossar de les Moreres
4 Passeig del Born
5 Antic Mercat del Born
6 Passeig de Picasso
7 carrer del Comerç
8 Montiel
9 carrer de Montcada
10 carrer dels Sombrerers
11 La Ribera fashion boutiques
12 Capella del Marcús
13 Mercat Santa Caterina
14 Sant Pere de les Puel.les
15 El Palau de la
    Música Catalana

Barceloneta Ⓜ

Plaça
Pau Vila

Ronda Litoral

Balboa

Ginebra

BARCELONETA

La Maquinista

St. Martí

L'Eixample

Parc de la
Ciutadella

Ciutat
Vella

Map
Area

Montjuïc

As maritime commerce grew in the 13th and 14th centuries, Barri de la Ribera ("neighborhood of the waterfront," reflecting a time when the shoreline reached this far), became a populous residential neighborhood for the merchant class. Until recently the quarter was known principally for its great church, Santa María del Mar, and the much-frequented Museu Picasso. But in the last decade, La Ribera (and particularly the zone within it called "El Born") has become the city's most fashionable district, exploding with chic bars, restaurants, and boutiques. Though it can get rowdy late at night, it still retains its medieval character. **START: Metro to Jaume I.**

❶ carrer de l'Argenteria. Leave behind the congestion of Vía Laeitana, a thoroughfare cut through the Ciutat Vella in the 1930s, for the foot traffic of the "street of silversmiths," a name dating to the 16th century. Fashion boutiques, bars, tapas restaurants, and hotels have taken over, but take a detour onto carrer Grunyí or Rosic, for example, and you'll glimpse the old Ribera district.

❷ ★★★ Santa María del Mar. I am powerless to pass by without taking at least a quick spin through—for the thousandth time—this extraordinarily graceful 14th-century Catalan Gothic church. It's the kind of contemplative place that should clear your head before you continue through this bustling neighborhood. *See p 13, bullet* ❿.

❸ Fossar de les Moreres. An eternal flame burns on a small square around the right side of the main entrance to Santa María del Mar. It commemorates the royal sacking of Barcelona on September 11, 1714, which marked the end to the Spanish War of Succession. The king, Felipe V, then outlawed Catalan culture and its institutions, including the Catalan language. The date, 9/11 (or 11/9 in Spain), is now celebrated as the National Day of Catalonia. From here, duck into the tiny passageway carrer de Malcuinat (literally, "poorly cooked") and walk out to **Plaça de les Olles** and back

to Passeig del Born, along carrer de la Vidreria, just to get a feel for this part of the quarter that leads to the waterfront.

❹ ★★ Passeig del Born. This wide and elegant tree-lined promenade, with its stone benches, is a good place for a breather. Once the site of medieval jousting tournaments, it became the main square and heart of the city during

Santa María del Mar.

A bustling scene on the Passeig del Born.

Barcelona's seafaring heyday (13th–18th centuries). Today apartment dwellers in its Gothic mansions are more commonly up in arms against the busy boutiques, outdoor cafes, and bars that populate the ground floors and every side street leading off the *passeig*.

⑤ Antic Mercat del Born. At the end of Passeig del Born is the old Ribera covered market, with its distinctive wrought-iron roof. Constructed in 1876, it has been abandoned for years, as authorities have deliberated its potential uses. However, since it was found to sit on medieval archaeological remains, it's most likely that it will soon become a museum and/or cultural center.

⑥ Passeig de Picasso. This avenue borders the western edge of Parc de la Ciutadella, the largest green space in downtown Barcelona. Here you'll find Antoni Tàpies's 1981 sculpture, *Homenatge a Picasso,* a glass cube containing a Cubist-like assemblage of running water and furniture. A bit farther up are the Museu de Geologia and Museu Zoologia (Museums of Geology and Zoology; see p 86, bullet ②), the latter designed by Domènech i Montaner, and the L'Hivernacle, a 19th-century greenhouse.

⑦ carrer del Comerç. This street, bending around the edges of La Ribera, is one of many that have been inundated with shops and restaurants—not surprisingly, given its name, Commerce Street. The **Museu de la Xocolata** (see p 49, bullet ⑩) is found at Comerç, 36. The street parallel to Comerç, **carrer del Rec,** is flush with designer clothing and furniture boutiques.

Archeological remains in the Mercat del Born.

The carrer de les Mosques.

8 ★ **Montiel.** This attractive little gourmet food store–cum–informal restaurant serves Catalan and Spanish standards, including *jamón de Jabugo* (Iberian ham), *pa amb tomaquet* (peasant bread with rubbed tomatoes and olive oil), Catalan sausages, and local wines. Have a selection of tapas or the inexpensive fixed-price lunch. *carrer Flassaders, 19.* ☎ *93-268-37-29. $.*

9 ★★★ **carrer de Montcada.** Famous for its collection of stately Gothic mansions and Museu Picasso, this elegant avenue is a joy to stroll. Don't miss the narrow and poetically named carrer de les Mosques ("street of the flies"). *See p 31, bullet* **2**.

10 **carrer dels Sombrerers.** Just off carrer de Montcada, and flanking Santa María del Mar, is this small street, formally named "St. Anthony of the Hat Makers." **E&A Gispert** (see p 49, bullet **11**), at no. 23, is a wonderful old epicurean shop with a 150-year-old roasting oven.

11 ★ **La Ribera fashion boutiques.** Off carrer de la Princesa is a series of alleyways that have given over to a handful of chic designer boutiques, typifying the neighborhood's stunning transformation. Make a brief detour along carrers Carassa and Vigatans before returning to Princesa.

12 ★ **Capella del Marcús.** Worth a look is this small Romanesque chapel, built in 1166 next to what was once the main thoroughfare in and out of the Roman city (today carrer dels Carders). *Pl. Marcús, s/n.*

13 ★★ **Mercat Santa Caterina.** This colorfully reimagined covered market has become a hit with foodies and architecture fans. *See p 44, bullet* **7**.

14 **Sant Pere de les Puel.les.** Little remains of the original pre-Romanesque church and Benedictine monastery, although you can still see a section of the 10th-century Greek-cross floorplan, Romanesque bell tower, and a few Corinthian capitals beneath the 12th-century dome. *carrer Lluís el Piadós, 1.* ☎ *93-268-07-42. Free admission. Mon–Fri 8:30am–1pm and 5–7:30pm; Sat 8:30am–1pm and 4:30–6:30pm; Sun 10am–2pm.*

15 ★★★ **El Palau de la Música Catalana.** If you haven't already had a chance to tour this extraordinary concert hall, Domènch i Montaner's masterpiece, this would be the time to do it. *See p 20, bullet* **6**.

The stained glass ceiling in El Palau de la Música Catalana.

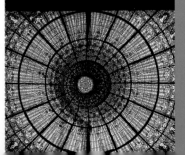

L'Eixample

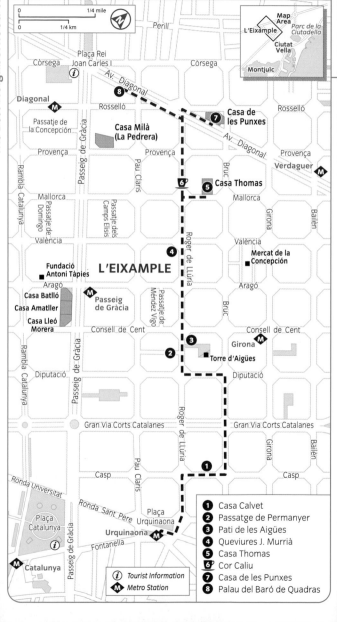

Map Area
L'Eixample
Ciutat Vella
Parc de la Ciutadella
Montjuïc

1 Casa Calvet
2 Passatge de Permanyer
3 Pati de les Aigües
4 Queviures J. Murrià
5 Casa Thomas
6' Cor Caliu
7 Casa de les Punxes
8 Palau del Baró de Quadras

ⓘ Tourist Information
Ⓜ Metro Station

L'Eixample is an area best known for its extraordinary collection of late 19th and early 20th century *modernista* (Catalan Art Nouveau) buildings, which earned it the nickname El Quadrat d'Or (the Golden Square). This tour takes you off the Eixample's well-trodden path. If you have time and energy at the end of this tour, you should tack on a stroll down Passeig de Gràcia or Rambla de Catalunya. **START: Metro to Urquinaona.**

❶ Casa Calvet. Antoni Gaudí's 1899 apartment building, one of his first commissions, is an understated work, best appreciated for its wrought-iron and sculptural details. The building saw the installation of Barcelona's first elevator, which has an impressively embellished cupola. A top-flight restaurant, Casa Calvet, inhabits the first floor—originally a textile shop designed by Gaudí—allowing architectural and gastronomic enthusiasts an enticing look up-close at an important early work of Gaudí. *carrer Caspe, 48. See p 29, bullet* ❾.

Dinner at Casa Calvet allows for a sneak peak inside the remarkable building.

❷ ★ Passatge de Permanyer. This inner courtyard, with a brick water tower in the center, is now open to the public. You'll find this lovely side street off Roger de Llúria, between Diputació and Consell de Cent. It is home to a small community of impeccable townhouses and English-style gardens, tucked behind an engraved iron gate. It is perhaps the finest example of what Ildefons Cerdà, who designed L'Eixample, had in mind for the district.

❸ Pati de les Aigües. In the next block along Diputació, between Roger de Llúria and Bruc, this inner courtyard with a brick water tower in the center has been reclaimed and opened to the public. It's one of the few opportunities to view the central courtyards of the original Eixample apartment buildings as Cerdà intended—as open, green public spaces. Most have been built over or otherwise appropriated by private interests. *carrer Roger de Llúria, 56.* ☎ *93-424-38-09.*

The charming Passatge de Permanyer.

Palau de Baró de Quadras was designed by Puig i Cadafalch.

❹ ★★ Queviures J. Murrià. This wonderful, old-school *colmado* (grocery or packaged-goods store) has remained in the same family for 150 years. The decorative storefront is the work of *modernista* painter Ramón Casas. *carrer Roger de Llúria, 85.* ☎ *93-215-57-89.*

❺ ★★ Casa Thomas. Just down carrer Mallorca is this spectacular house (1895–98) by Domènech i Muntaner. Originally just two floors, it was expanded in 1912. Until recently it was home to the chic B. D. Ediciones de Diseño, famous for its high-design modern furnishings and Gaudí reproductions. A slightly less distinguished furniture store, Favorita, took over in 2006. Feel free to enter and wander among the two floors of this important building. *carrer Mallorca, 291–293.* ☎ *93-476-57-21.*

❻ Cor Caliu. An attractive corner restaurant-bar, this surprisingly elegant spot is perfect for coffee, a beer, or tapas in the front bar, or a full meal in the restaurant at back. It's a longtime neighborhood favorite. *carrer Roger de Llúria 102.* ☎ *93-208-20-29. $$.*

❼ Casa de les Punxes. Also called Casa Terrades, or "House of Spikes," for its sharp turrets, this massive and eccentric 1905 house is one of Josep Puig i Cadafalch's and *modernisme's* most prized buildings. It's a neo-Gothic, fairytale- and castlelike mansion with distinctive features, such as three separate entrances (built for each of the family's daughters), outer walls facing all four points of the compass, and patriotic ceramic motifs. *Av. Diagonal, 416–420.*

❽ Palau de Baró de Quadras. This 1904–06 mansion, also by Puig i Cadafalch, is a great example of this architect's creativity. Formerly the Museu de la Música until 2003, when it was acquired by Casa Asia, an Asian cultural foundation, it is open to visitors. Although the imported Asian themes, incense, and modern light fixtures seem out of place, the interior, with its Moorish-style ceiling, carved wood, and leaded glass, is extremely handsome. From the top-floor terrace are terrific views of Casa de les Punxes, echoing the spires of La Sagrada Família in the background. *Av. Diagonal, 373.* ☎ *93-368-73-37. www.casaasia.es. Free admission. Mon–Sat 10am–8pm; Sun 10am–2pm.* ●

The castle-like Casa de les Punxes is hard to miss.

Shopping Best Bets

Best **Dreamy Antiques**
★★★ L' Arca de l'Aviva, *c/ Banys Nous 20*

Best **Hip Designer Clothing (Men's)**
★★ Antonio Miró, *c/ Consell de Cent 349*

Best **Drop-Dead-Gorgeous Designer Clothing (Women's)**
★★★ Josep Font, *c/ Provença 304*

Best **Creative Leather Goods**
★★★ Lupo Barcelona, *c/ Mallorca 257, bajos*

Best **Shop for Slaves to Design**
★★★ Vinçon, *Pg. de Gràcia 96*

Best **Barcelona Souvenirs**
Vaho Works, *c/ Cotoners, 8*

Best-**Smelling Gourmet Foods**
★★★ E & A Gispert, *c/ dels Sombrerers, 23*

Best **Wine Cellar Fantasy** Shop
★★★ Vila Viniteca, *c/ Agullers, 7*

Best **Dip into Old-World Barcelona**
★★ Herbolisteria del Rei, *c/ del Vidre 1*

Best **Cookbooks**
★ Buffet y Ambigú Mercat de la Boqueria, *La Rambla, 91, parada 437*

Best **One-Stop Shopping**
El Corte Inglés, *Plaça de Catalunya, 14*

Best **Old-City Spot for an Antiques Stroll**
★★ Carrer de la Palla
★★ Carrer Banys Nous

Best **Mall for Kids**
Maremàgnum, *Moll d'Espanya, 5*

Most **Theatrical Clothing Boutique**
★★★ Natalie Capell Atelier de Moda, *Carassa, 2*

Best **Products by Nuns & Priests (or: Best Archaeological Surprise in a Store)**
★★ Caelum, *c/ de la Palla, 8*

Best **Catalan Goodies for Foodies**
★★ Origen 99.9%, *c/ Vidreria, 6–8*

Best **Unpronounceable T-Shirt Shop**
★★ Kukuxumusu, *c/ L'Argenteria, 69*

Previous page: A display at Heritage. This page: Fresh roasted nuts at E&A Gispert.

L'Eixample Shopping

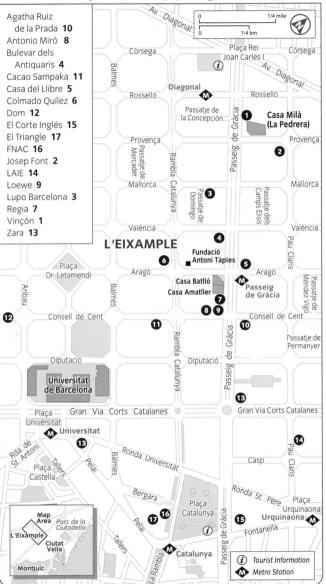

Agatha Ruiz
de la Prada **10**
Antonio Miró **8**
Bulevar dels
Antiquaris **4**
Cacao Sampaka **11**
Casa del Llibre **5**
Colmado Quílez **6**
Dom **12**
El Corte Inglés **15**
El Triangle **17**
FNAC **16**
Josep Font **2**
LAIE **14**
Loewe **9**
Lupo Barcelona **3**
Regia **7**
Vinçón **1**
Zara **13**

Av. Diagonal

Còrsega

Plaça Rei
Joan Carles I

Còrsega

Av. Diagonal

Diagonal

Rosselló

Rosselló

Balmes

Passatge de
la Concepció

❶ Casa Milà
(La Pedrera)

Provença

Passatge de
Mercader

Passatge de
Domingo

Provença

❷

Mallorca

❸

Mallorca

Rambla Catalunya

Passeig de Gràcia

Passatge dels
Camps Elisis

Passatge dels

València

❹

València

Pau Claris

L'EIXAMPLE

❻

Fundació
■ Antoni Tàpies

❺

Plaça
Dr. Letamendi

Aragó

Aragó

Ⓜ

Passeig
de Gràcia

Passatge de
Mèndez Vigo

Aribau

Balmes

Casa Batlló
Casa Amatller

❼
❽ **❾**

Ⓜ

Consell de Cent

⓬

Consell de Cent

⓫

❿

Passatge de
Permanyer

Diputació

Rambla Catalunya

Diputació

Passeig de Gràcia

**Universitat
de Barcelona**

Plaça
Universitat

Gran Via Corts Catalanes

Gran Via Corts Catalanes

Ⓜ **Universitat**

Rda. de
St. Antoni

Plaça
Castella

⓭

Balmes

Pelai

Ronda Universitat

Casp

⓮

Pau Claris

Bergara

Ronda St. Pere

Plaça
Urquinaona

Tallers

Pelai

⓱ **⓰**

Plaça
Catalunya

Passeig de Gràcia

⓯

Ⓜ **Urquinaona**

Fontanella

Map
Area

Parc de la
Ciutadella

L'Eixample

Ciutat
Vella

Montjuïc

La Rambla

Ⓜ
Catalunya

ⓘ

ⓘ *Tourist Information*
Ⓜ *Metro Station*

0   1/4 mile
0   1/4 km

Ciutat Vella & Waterfront
Shopping

BCN Original Shops **17**
Beardsley **7**
Buffet y Ambigú **6**
Caelum **9**
Camper **2**
Casas **5**
Cereria Subira **16**
Custo Barcelona **31**
Demasié **23**
Discos Castelló **4**
E & A Gispert **27**
Etxart & Panno **30**
Forvm Ferlandina **1**
Ganiveteria Roca **8**
Giménez & Zuazo **3**
Herbolisteria del Rei **14**
Heritage **12**
Ici Et Là **35**
Itaca **15**
Ivo & Co. **24**
Jocomomola de Sybilla **20**
Kukuxumusu **26**
L'Arca de l'Aviva **11**
La Galería de
  Santa María Novella **34**
Maremàgnum **36**
Natalie Capell Atelier
  de Moda **21**
Origen 99,9% **32**
Platamundi **22**
Rafa Teja Atelier **33**
Sala d'Art Artur Ramón **10**
1748 Artesana i Coses **28**
Sombrerería Obach **13**
Tot Formatge **29**
Vaho Works **19**
Verd Poma **18**
Vila Viniteca **25**

Casa de la Caritat

Museu d'Art Contemporani de Barcelona

Tallers

Pelai

Plaça Caramelles

Elisabets

Xuclà

Pintor Fortuny

La Rambla

Carme

Betlem

Palau Moja

Antic Hospital de la Sta. Creu

Mercat de la Boqueria

Plaça del Pi

Hospital

Robador

Plaça Sant Agustí

Sta. Maria del Pi

La Rambla del Raval

EL RAVAL

Boqueria

Plaça Salvador Seguí

Sant Pau

Liceu

Gran Teatre del Liceu

Ferran

Unió

Marquès de Barberà

Lleona

Plaça Reial

Nou de la Rambla

Palau Güell

Jardins Voltes d'En Cirés

Est

Guardia

Lancaster

Escudellers

Arc del Teatre

Plaça del Teatre

Nou de St. Francesc

Av. Drassanes

Centre d'Art Sta. Mònica

Plaça Joaquim Xirau

Palau March

Portal Sta. Madrona

La Rambla

Drassanes

Josep Anselm Clavé

Plaça Duc de Medinaceli

Reials Drassanes (Museu Marítim)

Plaça Drassanes

Plaça Portal de la Pau

Monument á Colom

(Ronda Litoral)

Golondrinas

Rambla da Mar

Moll de Barcelona

Dàrsena Nacional

Maremagnum

St. Martí

Parc de la Ciutadella

L'Eixample

Ciutat Vella

Montjuïc

Map Area

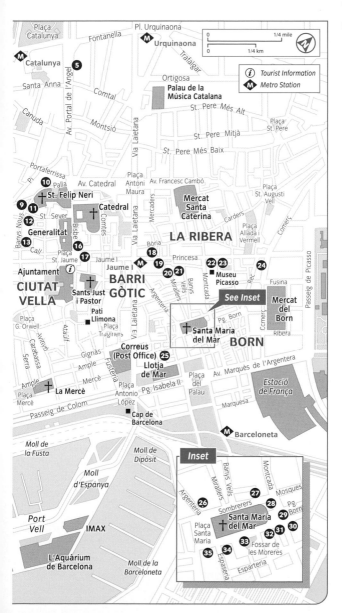

Barcelona **Shopping A to Z**

Antiques & Art

★ **Bulevar dels Antiquaris** L'EIX-AMPLE   An indoor mall containing some 70 small shops of art, antiques, and bric-a-brac. Unfortunately, stall owners set their own hours, which can be wildly inconsistent. *Pg. de Gràcia 55.* ☎ *93-215-44-99. www. bulevardelsantiquaris.com. Metro: Passeig de Gràcia. Map p 73.*

★ **Heritage** BARRI GOTIC   A thea-trical-looking shop, stuffed with old costumes, jewelry, and Spanish shawls. You have to buzz to be let in, but it's worth it to snoop around a bit under the proprietor's watchful eye. *c/ Banys Nous, 14.* ☎ *93-317-85-15. MC, V. Metro: Jaume I. Map p 74.*

★★ **L' Arca de l'Avia** BARRI GOTIC   Antique lace, linens, and curtains, as well as handkerchiefs, and other textiles from the 18th to early 20th centuries are found at this uniquely lovely shop, where some of the period clothing for

Theatrical treasures abound at Heritage.

the movie *Titanic* was purchased. *c/ Banys Nous 20.* ☎ *93-302-15-98. www.larcadelavia.com. MC, V. Metro: Liceu. Map p 74.*

★★ **Sala d'Art Artur Ramón** BARRI GOTIC   A top antiques and art dealer and longtime family gallery known for its 19th- and 20th-century painting, sculpture, engrav-ings, and decorative arts. *c/ de la Palla 23.* ☎ *93-302-59-70. AE, DC, MC, V. Metro: Jaume I. Map p 74.*

Books

★ **Buffet y Ambigú** LA RAMBLA At the back of La Boqueria food mar-ket is this small book shop with cook-books by Spain's star chefs, as well as those touting tapas recipes and regional dishes. Many books are in English. *Mercat de la Boqueria, La Rambla, 91, parada 437.* ☎ *93-317-13-36. MC, V. Metro: Liceu. Map p 74.*

Casa del Llibre L'EIXAMPLE   A large book shop covering the gamut of titles, including English and foreign-language books. *Pg. de Gràcia 62.* ☎ *93-272-34-80. MC, V. Metro: Pas-seig de Gràcia. Map p 73.*

★★ **LAIE** L'EIXAMPLE   With a cafe and nice stock of English-language books, including literature, travel maps, and guides, LAIE's a favorite with foreigners resident in Barcelona. *c/ Pau Claris 85.* ☎ *93-318-1739. MC, V. Metro: Catalunya or Urquinaona. Map p 73.*

Ceramics & Pottery

1748 Artesana i Coses EL BORN Near Museu Picasso, this crowded ceramics shop stocks largely inex-pensive pottery and porcelain from all over Spain (and Portugal). *Placeta de Montcada 2.* ☎ *93-319-54-13. AE, MC, V. Metro: Jaume I. Map p 74.*

★ **Itaca** BARRI GOTIC   On hand is handmade pottery from Spain, Portugal, Mexico, and Morocco. Pieces are simple but well conceived, and there are a number of Gaudiesque objects fashioned with *trencadis* (broken ceramic tile). *c/ Ferran 26.* ☎ *93-301-30-44. MC, V Metro: Liceu. Map p 74.*

Cosmetics

★★ **La Galeria de Santa Maria Novella** LA RIBERA   This is the Barcelona outlet of a famed apothecary in Florence, the oldest in the world. The perfumes and soaps are extraordinary, and the packaging delightfully antiquated. *c/ Espaseria 4–8.* ☎ *93-268-02-37. MC, V. Metro: Jaume I or Barceloneta. Map p 74.*

★ **Regia** L'EIXAMPLE   This high-end cosmetics shop has a treat: a museum (free admission) with 5,000 examples of perfume bottles and flasks dating back as far as ancient Greece, including a cool bottle by Salvador Dalí. *Pg. de Gràcia 39.* ☎ *93-216-01-21. AE, MC, V. Metro: Passeig de Gràcia. Map p 73.*

Ceramics, like these at 1748 Artesana i Coses, make great souvenirs and gifts.

Department Stores/ Shopping Centers

El Corte Inglés PLAÇA DE CATALUNYA   Spain's largest department store chain sells everything from wine and music to furnishings and fashion. You'll also find a restaurant, travel agent, and excellent supermarket (Plaça Catalunya branch only). *Plaça de Catalunya, 14.*

Prime Shopping Zones

Barcelona's elegant **Passeig de Gràcia** is home to some of the most fashionable and expensive retail space in Spain. **La Rambla de Catalunya,** which runs parallel to Passeig de Gràcia, is like an open mall of stores, perfect for strolling, and the cross streets between the two are loaded with interesting shops of all kinds—particularly València, Provença, and Consell de Cent, the last known for its art galleries. The long boulevard **Diagonal** is the site of many high-end furnishings and fashion boutiques. In the **Ciutat Vella,** the main streets Portal d'Angel, Portaferrisa, and Ferrán are packed with clothing stores and young shoppers. Small boutiques and one-of-a-kind retailers are tucked in the neighborhoods **El Born** and **Barri Gòtic,** and increasingly in **El Raval.** Antiques dealers, meanwhile, are largely clustered around the labyrinth of streets near carrer de la Palla, Banys Nous, and Plaça del Pi in the **Barri Gòtic.**

The Maremàgnum mall at the waterfront.

☎ *93-306-38-00. AE, DC, MC, V. www.
elcorteingles.es. Metro: Catalunya.
Map p 73.*

El Triangle PLAÇA DE CATALUNYA
This large white elephant occupies a
good chunk of Plaça de Catalunya at
the head of La Rambla. It may stick
out, but it's convenient for hitting
shops like Sephora, FNAC, Camper,
and Habitat. *c/ Pelai, 39.* ☎ *93-318-
01-08. Metro: Plaça de Catalunya.
Map p 73.*

Maremàgnum WATERFRONT
This mall is perched out in the old
harbor, near L'Aquarium. It has
plenty for the whole family, from toy
stores to high-end fashion. *Moll
d'Espanya, 5.* ☎ *93-225-81-00.
Metro: Drassanes. Map p 74.*

Designer Home Goods & Furnishings
Dom L'EIXAMPLE Funky, eclectic,
kitschy, and inexpensive, this shop is
all things pop. Housewares include
beaded curtains, toys, bubble furniture, chrome lamps, and kitchen-
ware in bold colors. *c/ Consell de
Cent, 248.* ☎ *93-452-17-68. MC, V.
Metro: Pg. de Gràcia. Other branch:
Avinyó, 7 (*☎ *93-342-55-91; Metro:
Jaume I). Map p 73.*

★ **Ici Et Là** LA RIBERA A good indi-
cation of Barcelona's individualistic,

design-crazy personality is this stylish
shop. You'll find quirky and limited
editions by local artists and designers, as well as interesting "world"
pieces, such as African baskets, or
Indian textiles. *Plaça de Sant Maria, 2.*
☎ *93-268-11-67. MC, V. Metro: Jaume
I or Barceloneta. Map p 74.*

★★★ **Vinçón** L'EIXAMPLE Fernando Amat's temple of good
design, Vinçón features more than
10,000 products—everything from
household items to the finest Catalan and Spanish contemporary furnishings. Housed in the former
home of modernista painter Ramón
Casas. The singular window displays
alone are always a conversation
piece. *Pg. de Gràcia 96.* ☎ *93-215-
60-50. AE, MC, V. Metro: Diagonal or
Passeig de Gràcia. Map p 73.*

Fashion & Accessories
★★ **Antonio Miró** L'EIXAMPLE
The designs of the Catalan Antonio
Miró are chic and sleek, with a retro
edge. Men's and women's clothing,
including a less-expensive Miró
Jeans line. *c/ Consell de Cent 349.*
☎ *93-487-06-70. AE, MC, V. Metro:
Passeig de Gràcia. Map p 73.*

★ **Agatha Ruiz de la Prada**
L'EIXAMPLE The playful, brightly

*Antonio Miró designs chic clothes for
men and women.*

colored, almost childlike fashions of this Madrid designer have hit the big time, and she now has shops in Paris, Milan, and New York. *c/ Consell de Cent, 314-316.* ☎ *93-215-52-88. AE, MC, V. Metro: Passeig de Gràcia. Map p 73.*

Custo-Barcelona LA RIBERA Custo's emblematic tops and tees, skirts, and pants are emblazoned with wildly colored retro-cool motifs. Seen on Hollywood starlets and in the fashion pages, these now-international pieces aren't cheap, but they are distinctive. *Plaça de les Olles, 6.* ☎ *93-268-78-93. MC, V. Metro Jaume I or Barceloneta. Map p 74. Other location: c/ Ferran, 36 (*☎ *93-342-66-98; Metro: Jaume I).*

★★ Etxart & Panno EL BORN Unabashedly sexy fashions for women with style and money to burn, in a cool little shop in the heart of the chic Born district. *Pg. del Born, 14.* ☎ *93-310-37-24. MC, V. Metro: Jaume I or Barceloneta. Map p 74.*

★★ Giménez & Zuazo EL RAVAL These quirky and cutting-edge creations with audacious prints, interesting fabrics, and contrasting cross-stitches represent Barcelona at its most fashion-conscious. *c/ Elisabets, 20.* ☎ *93-412-33-81. AE, MC, V. Metro: Plaça de Catalunya or Liceu. Map p 74. A second location is at c/ Rec, 42 in El Born.*

★★ Jocomomola de Sybilla EL BORN The brightly colored, informal women's fashions from this Madrileña designer have a retro bent and look as though they might have dressed Amelie, the heroine of the funky French film of a few years ago. *c/ Vigatans, 6 (off Princesa).* ☎ *93-310-66-66. AE, MC, V. Metro: Jaume I. Map p 74.*

★★★ Josep Font L'EIXAMPLE This original Catalan designer, whose

Custo-Barcelona.

gorgeous shop shows off *modernista* details, creates women's clothes that are timeless, sleek, and bold, with a dramatic feel for luxurious materials. *c/ Provença, 30.* ☎ *93-487-21-10. MC, V. Metro: Passeig de Gràcia. Map p 73.*

★★★ Natalie Capell Atelier de Moda EL BORN Timeless, handmade, high-fashion designs for women in a dark boutique that looks like a theater set. *Carassa, 2 (off Princesa).* ☎ *93-319-92-19. MC, V. Metro: Jaume I Map p 74.*

★ Rafa Teja Atelier EL BORN Terrific, colorful scarves and shawls from India, Asia, and Spain, as well as embroidered jackets and sumptuous fabrics. *Sta. María, 18.* ☎ *93-310-27-85. MC, V. Metro: Jaume I or Barceloneta. Map p 74.*

Verd Poma LA RIBERA If you love the designs of Custo-Barcelona but find the prices extreme, this tiny closet of a shop is the place for you. Wildly colored pop-art tees and tops. *c/ Princesa, 5.* ☎ *93-319-01-01. MC, V. Metro: Jaume I. Map p 74.*

Zara BARRI GOTIC This ubiquitous shop makes men's, women's, and kid's fashions (and now home design) accessible. For trendy, seasonal items, it's tough to beat Zara (pronounced "*thah*-duh"). *c/ Pelayo, 58.* ☎ *93-301-09-78. Metro: Plaça de Catalunya. Many other locations, including Pg. de Gràcia, 16.* ☎ *93-318-76-75; Metro: Passeig de Gràcia. Map p 73.*

Gourmet Food Shops

★ **Cacao Sampaka** L'EIXAMPLE Best described as designer chocolate, with items categorized into "collections," such as "flowers and herbs," etc. Repair to the bar/cafe for delicious hot chocolate, pastries, and sandwiches. *c/ Consell de Cent, 292.* ☎ *93-272-08-33. AE, DC, MC, V. Metro: Passeig de Gràcia. Map p 73.*

★★ **Caelum** BARRI GOTIC Clositered nuns and religious orders produce everything in this shop, including jams and preserved fruit, biscuits, marzipan, and liquors, all handsomely packaged. In the cafe downstairs are the remains of ancient Jewish baths. *c/ de la Palla 8.* ☎ *93-302-69-93. MC, V. Metro: Jaume I. Map p 74.*

★★★ **Colmado Quilez** L'EIXAMPLE An old-school *colmado,* or packaged goods store, with great

Stop by for a wine tasting and leave with a bottle or two from Vila Viniteca.

Catalan and Spanish cheeses, canned goods, and a huge selection of wines. A real throwback. *Rambla de Catalunya, 63.* ☎ *93-215-23-56. MC, V. Metro: Passeig de Gràcia. Map p 73.*

Demasié LA RIBERA A gourmet cookie shop with all kinds of treats both sweet and savory, including expected and very unusual cookies (black tea, Roquefort and nuts, mustard, curry). *c/ Princesa, 28.* ☎ *93-310-42-95. MC, V. Metro: Jaume I or Barceloneta. Map p 74.*

★★★ **E & A Gispert** LA RIBERA Follow your nose to this fantastic, century-old food shop, where coffee and nuts are roasted daily (in a 150-year-old oven). Also: dried fruit, olive oils, and much more. *c/ dels Sombrerers, 23.* ☎ *93-319-75-35. MC, V. Metro: Jaume I. Map p 74.*

★★ **Origen 99,9%** LA RIBERA This small shop has a restaurant on one side and on the other sells gourmet products from Catalonia. Perfect for knowledgeable and curious foodies. *c/ Vidrería 6–8.* ☎ *93-310-75-31. MC, V. Metro: Jaume I or Barceloneta. Map p 74.*

★ **Tot Formatge** EL BORN Cheesehounds should beeline to this cute little shop, with terrific smells and a cornucopia of cheeses from Catalonia and across Spain. *Pg. de born, 13.* ☎ *93-319-53-75. MC, V. Metro: Jaume I or Barceloneta. Map p 74.*

★★★ **Vila Viniteca** LA RIBERA Barcelona's best wine shop started as a food shop in 1932, and it maintains a gourmet locale just across the alley. Connoisseurs of Spanish wines will be in heaven, especially because among its 4,000-plus wines the shop stocks a number of hard-to-find, small-production bottles, several not available outside Spain. *c/ Agullers, 7.* ☎ *902-32-77-77. AE, MC, V. Metro: Jaume I or Barceloneta. Map p 74.*

Gifts

★ **BCN Original Shops** BARRI GOTIC If you're after particularly Barcelona-themed gifts and souvenirs, this is your place. Art and architecture books, mugs, ceramics, jewelry, T-shirts, notebooks, and more. *Citutat, 2.* ☎ *93-270-24-29. AE, MC, V. Metro: Jaume I. Map p 74.*

★ **Beardsley** BARRI GOTIC This classic Barcelona shop is seductive-looking, featuring home goods, candles, great glassware, chandeliers and lighting, paper products, and much more. *c/ Petritxol, 12.* ☎ *93-301-05-76. AE, MC, V. Metro: Liceu or Jaume I. Map p 74.*

★ **Ivo & Co.** EL BORN Cool kitchen utensils, housewares, journals, candles, and books in this invitingly retro-looking shop. *c/ Rec, 20 baixos.* ☎ *93-268-33-31. MC, V. Metro: Arc de Triomf. Map p 74.*

★★ **Kukuxumusu** LA RIBERA Don't even try to pronounce the name of this shop, originally from Navarra but now all over Spain. Do pop by for witty, hip T-shirts and accessories. With a fun take on Spanish cultural traditions, they make great souvenirs. *L'Argenteria, 69.* ☎ *93-310-36-47. AE, MC, V. Metro: Jaume I. Map p 74.*

★★ **Vaho Works** EL BORN This funky bag maker uses recycled heavy-duty PVC culture posters (used as cultural advertising by the city and regional governments) to create unique messenger bags and purses (which they call "trashion"). A unique souvenir from Barcelona for eco- and fashion-conscious sorts. *c/ Cotoners, 8.* ☎ *93-310-66-66. AE, MC, V. Metro: Jaume I. Map p 74.*

Jewelry

★★ **Forvm Ferlandina** PLAÇA DE CATALUNYA The unique works of several dozen contemporary jewelry

Rings on display at Platamundi.

designers are on view in this gallery-like shop. *c/ Ferlandia 31.* ☎ *93-441-80-18. AE, DC, MC, V. Metro: Liceu and Catalunya. Map p 74.*

Platamundi LA RIBERA This small chain of affordable stores features nicely designed silver pieces by local and international artisans. *c/ Montcada, 11.* ☎ *93-317-13-89. MC, V. Metro: Jaume I. Other branches: Plaça Santa María 7 (Metro: Jaume I) and Portaferrisa 22 (Metro: Liceu). Map p 74.*

Leather Goods

★★ **Loewe** L'EIXAMPLE This prestigious Spanish leather-goods and luxury fashion chain occupies the ground floor of a splendid *modernista* building on Passeig de Gràcia. Chic and expensive, this is where the elite shop. Clothing lines are now up to par with the leather items. *Pg. de Gràcia, 35.* ☎ *93-216-04-00. AE, DC, MC, V. Metro: Passeig de Gràcia. Map p 73.*

★★★ **Lupo Barcelona** L'EIXAMPLE Hipper and skewing younger than Loewe, Lupo is the hottest name in stylish leather goods. Bags

The old-fashioned hat shop Sombrereria Obach.

and belts mold and fold leather into unexpected shapes and feature vivid colors. *c/ Mallorca 257, bajos.* ☎ *93-487-80-50. AE, DC, MC, V. Metro: Pg. de Gràcia. Map p 73.*

Music

Discos Castelló EL RAVAL   This chain of CD shops has three locations on one street alone, a corridor replete with music and vinyl shops. The flagship store at no. 7 is mainly pop rock. Next door, you'll find jazz, Spanish, and world music. *c/ Calle Tallers.* ☎ *93-318-20-41. MC, V. Metro: Plaça de Catalunya. Map p 74.*

FNAC PLAÇA DE CATALUNYA   The FNAC megastore is full of mainstream choices, with a nice selection of Spanish music and flamenco. *Plaça de Catalunya, 4.* ☎ *93-344-18-00. AE, DC, MC, V. Metro: Plaça de Catalunya. Map p 73.*

Old World Emporiums

★★ Cereria Subira BARRI GOTIC   The oldest continuous shop in

Barcelona, this iconic store specializes in candles, from those used at Mass to more creative and colorful numbers. *Baixada de Llibreteria, 7.* ☎ *93-315-26-06. MC, V. Metro: Jaume I. Map p 74.*

★ Ganiveteria Roca BARRI GOTIC   A specialty shop dealing exclusively in sharp objects: knives, blades, scissors, and other cutting instruments. *Plaça del Pi, 3.* ☎ *93-302-12-41. AE, MC, V. Metro: Jaume I. Map p 74.*

★★ Herbolisteria del Rei EL RAVAL   A purveyor of herbs, natural remedies, cosmetics, and teas since 1823, this atmospheric shop looks the part. *c/ del Vidre 1.* ☎ *93-318-05-12. MC, V. Metro: Plaça de Catalunya or Liceu. Map p 74.*

★ Sombrereria Obach BARRI GOTIC   Proudly old-fashioned, this shop in the old Jewish quarter sells nothing but hats, including classic Spanish berets (*boinas*). *c/ del Call 2.* ☎ *93-318-40-94. MC, V. Metro: Jaume I. Map p 74.*

Shoes

★★ Camper EL RAVAL   Camper shoes, originally from Mallorca, are now famous across the globe. You can get the latest models of this hipster shoemaker, in unusual colors and shapes, in Barcelona. Shop interiors are quirky, just like the shoes. *Plaça dels*

The classic Camper shoe design.

Àngels, 4. ☎ *93-342-41-41. AE, DISC, MC, V. Metro: Universitat. Map p 74.*

★ Casas BARRI GOTIC   Stocking the top Spanish brands of footwear as well as Italian and other imports, this is as close to one-stop shoe shopping as you'll find. *Portal de l'Angel, 40.* ☎ *93-302-11-12. AE, MC, V. Metro: Catalunya or Liceu. Map p 74.* ●

5 The Best of the **Outdoors**

Montjuïc

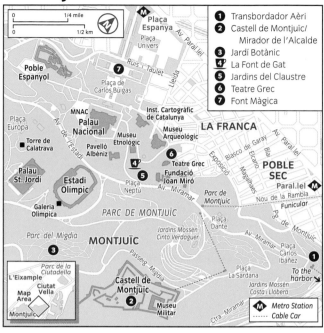

1. Transbordador Aèri
2. Castell de Montjuïc/ Mirador de l'Alcalde
3. Jardí Botànic
4. La Font de Gat
5. Jardins del Claustre
6. Teatre Grec
7. Font Màgica

The largest green space in Barcelona, this gentle hill overlooking the city and the Mediterranean is treasured by locals for its serene parkland—popular with families on weekends—as well as its museums and cultural attractions. First settled by Iberian Celtic peoples and then used by the Romans for ceremonies, Montjuïc has continued to play a central role in modern celebrations in Barcelona, including the 1929 International Exhibition and the 1992 Olympic Games. For other attractions in Montjuïc, see "The Best in Three Days," p 19. START: **Aerial cablecar or funicular to Montjuïc.**

1 ★ kids **Transbordador Aèri.** The best way to get to the great expanse of Montjuïc is to soar over the city in this aerial cable car that travels from the harbor up to the hill (dropping you off among the pine trees and cactus gardens of **Costa i Llobera**). See p 43, bullet 4.

Previous page: Getting out on the water in the Parc de la Ciutadella.

2 **Castell de Montjuïc.** Pass the Plaça de la Sardana (marked by a sculpture of the folkloric Catalan group dance) and through the Miramar and Mirador gardens in Parc de Montjuïc. Then head up Ctra. Montjuïc to **Mirador de l'Alcalde,** a viewpoint overlooking the sea. Just beyond is a *castell* (fortress) built in the 18th century to defend

The fortress (castell) at Monjuïc.

Barcelona. The courtyard is open to the public, and inside the castle is a military museum. The views of the sea, though, are the star attraction. *Parc de Montjuïc, s/n.* ☎ *93-239-86-13.*

❸ ★ kids Jardí Botànic. The Botanic Gardens of Barcelona, originally inaugurated in 1930, reopened as a new and improved, and beautifully landscaped, green space in 1999. The gardens show off Mediterranean-climate plants from all over the globe, including Africa, Australia, California, the Canary Islands, and Chile. The 71 zones are connected by paths and feature walkways over ponds. *Dr. Font i Quer, s/n (Parc de Montjuïc).* ☎ *93-426-49-35. Oct–Mar, daily 10am–5pm; Apr, May, and Sept, Mon–Fri 10am–6pm, Sat–Sun 10am–8pm; June–Aug, daily 10am–8pm. Admission 3€, seniors and students 1.50€; under 16, free. Free admission the last Sun of every month.*

❹ Font de Gat. Down a path from the Fundació Miró (see p 20, bullet ❺) is this historic *modernista* cafe, now revived as a cafe and restaurant surrounded by gardens. It's a nice, open-air spot for a breather and refreshments, which might even be a fixed-price lunch. *Passeig de Sta. Madrona, 28.* ☎ *93-289-04-04. $*

❺ Jardins del Claustre. The Cloister Garden is one of the prettiest spots on Montjuïc, with a tree-lined pond, pergola, and sculpture by the Catalan artist Antoni Alsina for the 1929 International Exposition.

❻ Teatre Grec. This replica of a bowl-shaped Greek theater, built for the 1929 World's Fair, continues to host open-air concerts and dance performances. It's a focal point of the **Festival Grec** summer music and arts festival held every summer. *Passeig de Sta. Madrona, 36.* ☎ *93-413-24-00.*

❼ ★ kids Font Màgica. The waters of the Magic Fountain dance to a light and pop-music show at the center of a plaza in front of the Palau Nacional. *See p 54, bullet ❽.*

Font Màgica.

Parc de la Ciutadella

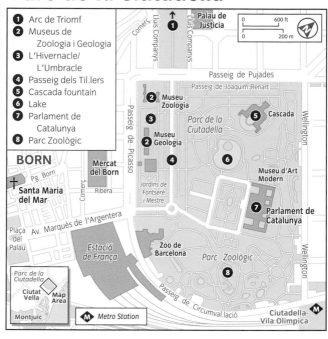

1. Arc de Triomf
2. Museus de Zoologia i Geologia
3. L'Hivernacle/ L'Umbracle
4. Passeig dels Til.lers
5. Cascada fountain
6. Lake
7. Parlament de Catalunya
8. Parc Zoològic

In a dense city with few green spaces, Barcelona's largest urban oasis is this 30-hectacre (74-acre) park between the old city and waterfront. Although curiously underutilized, the park makes for an ideal respite from the city, with the Barcelona Zoo, a massive waterfall fountain, lake, sculptures, and monuments, and wide promenades and tree-lined trails for strolling or cycling. The park has a peculiar history: After the end of the Spanish War of Succession in 1714, King Felipe V ordered the neighborhood "of traitors" razed, and he built a citadel, which later functioned as a prison for political opponents, in its place. Local authorities demolished the citadel and in 1872 built a large park, which hosted the 1888 World's Fair. The park is open daily, sunrise to sunset. START: Arc de Triomf.

1 ★ **Arc de Triomf.** The formal gate to Parc de la Ciutadella is this massive red-brick triumphal arch, built in 1888. The wide avenue Passeig de Lluís Campanys, lined with large palm trees and ornate pale-blue iron lampposts, leads into the park. *Pg. de Lluís Campanys, s/n.*

2 **Museus de Zoologia i Geologia.** The Zoology Museum occupies a Moorish-influenced brick building (popularly called the "Castle of Three Dragons") designed by Domènech i Montaner for the 1888 Universal Exhibition. Next door is the 1878 Geology Museum. *Pg. de Picasso s/n, Parc de la Ciutadella.* ☎ *93-319-69-12.*

3 kids **L'Hivernacle/L'Umbracle.** The *Hivernacle,* located between the two museums, is an iron-and-glass greenhouse designed in 1884. Today it occasionally hosts concerts. On the other side of the Geology Museum is the *Umbracle,* a peaceful spot full of tropical plants and palm trees under its tall nave.

4 **Passeig dels Til.lers.** The wide "Avenue of Lime Trees" is marked at the southern end by an equestrian statue of General Prim, who ordered the old fortress demolished. Although the original statue was melted down during the Civil War, a replacement was commissioned from the sculptor Frederic Marès in 1940.

5 ★ kids **Cascada fountain.** This massive ornamental fountain, featuring Aurora's chariot, is the work of Josep Fontserè, although much of its recognition is due to the contributions of his young apprentice, Antoni Gaudí, who was just a student at the time. Gaudí added the decorative lampposts and other details.

A bear in the Parc Zoològic.

6 kids **Lake.** In the center of the park is this tree-ringed lake, with rowboats for rent, just as they were at the end of the 19th century.

7 **Parlament de Catalunya.** Home to the regional parliament since 1932, this grand building, once the arsenal of the citadel, faces a pond and the 1903 *modernista* sculpture, *El Desconsol* (Grief), by Josep Llimona.

8 ★★ kids **Parc Zoològic.** The Barcelona Zoo, which has been in Ciutadella park since 1892, features a garden-like setting that occupies nearly half the park's expanse, with 4,000 animals kept, not in cages, but behind moats. *See p 52, bullet* **3**.

The Arc de Triomf marks the entrance to Parc de la Ciutadella.

The **Waterfront**

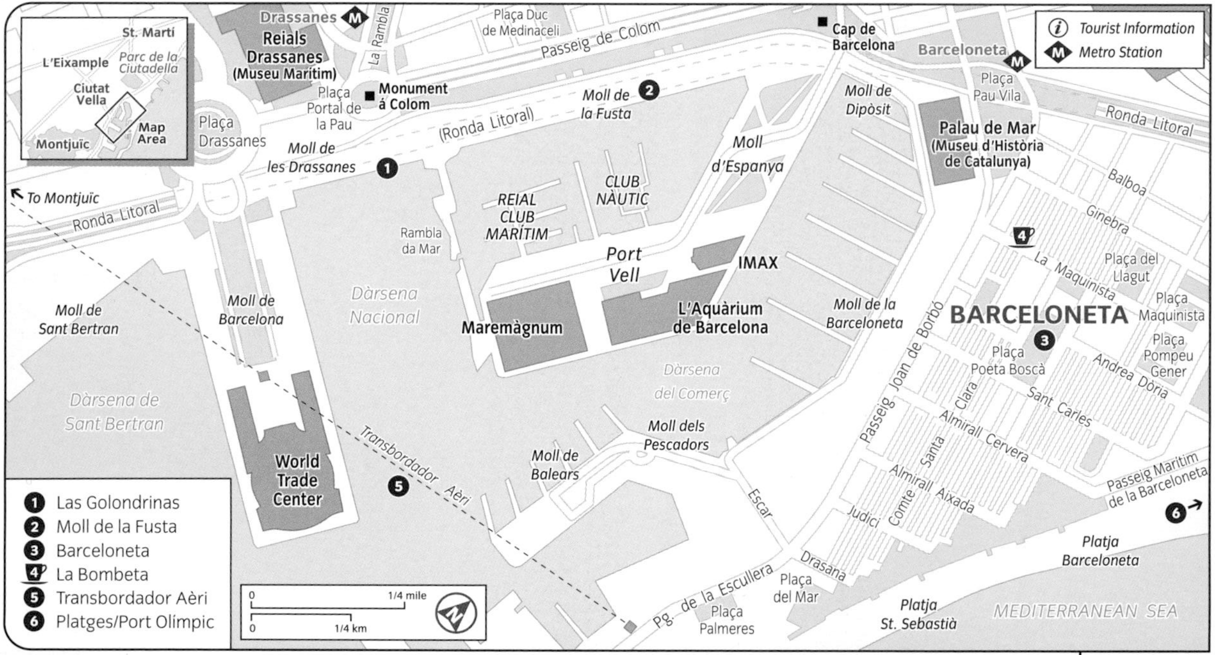
Tourist Information
Metro Station
St. Martí
L'Eixample
Parc de la Ciutadella
Ciutat Vella
Montjuïc
Map Area
Drassanes
Reials Drassanes (Museu Marítim)
La Rambla
Plaça Duc de Medinaceli
Passeig de Colom
Cap de Barcelona
Barceloneta
Plaça Pau Vila
Ronda Litoral
Plaça Portal de la Pau
Monument á Colom
Plaça Drassanes
Moll de les Drassanes
(Ronda Litoral)
Moll de la Fusta
Moll de Dipòsit
Palau de Mar (Museu d'Història de Catalunya)
Moll d'Espanya
CLUB NÀUTIC
REIAL CLUB MARÍTIM
Rambla da Mar
Port Vell
IMAX
Maremàgnum
L'Aquàrium de Barcelona
To Montjuïc
Ronda Litoral
Moll de Sant Bertran
Moll de Barcelona
Dàrsena Nacional
Dàrsena de Sant Bertran
World Trade Center
Transbordador Aèri
Dàrsena del Comerç
Moll dels Pescadors
Moll de Balears
Moll de la Barceloneta
Passeig Joan de Borbó
BARCELONETA
Balboa
Ginebra
La Maquinista
Plaça del Llagut
Plaça Maquinista
Plaça Pompeu Gener
Andrea Dòria
Plaça Poeta Boscà
Sant Carles
Clara
Santa
Almirall Cervera
Almirall Aixada
Comte
Judici
Drasana
Escar
Passeig Marítim de la Barceloneta
Platja Barceloneta
Platja St. Sebastià
MEDITERRANEAN SEA
Plaça del Mar
Pg. de la Escullera
Plaça Palmeres
0 1/4 mile
0 1/4 km
1 Las Golondrinas
2 Moll de la Fusta
3 Barceloneta
4 La Bombeta
5 Transbordador Aèri
6 Platges/Port Olímpic

For much of the 20th century, Barcelona's Mediterranean waterfront was a polluted, industrial, and marginalized sector. But Barcelona took advantage of the 1992 Olympic Games to completely revamp the old port and beaches and create new areas for leisure. Today it's Barcelona's outdoor playground, an essential part of the city. START: Metro to Drassanes.

1 kids **Las Golondrinas.** You'll see these double-decker "swallow boats" lined up across from the Mirador de Colom, boarding passengers for 35-minute cruises around the old harbor. *Weekdays 11:45am–7pm; weekends and holidays 11am–6pm. 5€ adults, 2.50€ children ages 4–14. Plaça Portal de la Pau, s/n.* ☎ *93-442-31-06; www.lasgolondrinas.com.*

2 **Moll de la Fusta.** The tree-lined boardwalk in front of Port Vell (the old port) extends from the Golondrinas to the Barceloneta district. It's popular with locals on weekend strolls. At the eastern end of the promenade are massive pop-art sculptures of a giant crayfish and a head by Roy Lichtenstein.

3 ★ **Barceloneta.** Barcelona's fishermen and their families inhabited this picturesque beachfront neighborhood for decades before it received a stylistic makeover in 1992. It was a traditional haunt for low-key seafood restaurants called *chiringuitos*, several of which have survived.

4 ★ **La Bombeta.** This authentic tapas joint serves great seafood snacks like mussels and fried calamari. The *bombas* are the house take on *patatas bravas* (fried potatoes with a spicy sauce). *c/ Maquinsta, 3.* ☎ *93-319-94-45. $–$$*

5 ★ kids **Transbordador Aèri.** The aerial cable car that climbs from the port to Montjuïc starts out at Passeig de Joan de Borbó in Barceloneta. It stops at the World Trade Center and soars above the harbor. See p 43, bullet **4**.

6 ★★ kids **Platges and Port Olímpic.** Barcelona's urban beaches (*platges*) have been amazingly transformed, and the water quality is now excellent. Popular with families, topless sunbathers, and surfers, the beaches are lined with public sculptures, bars and restaurants, and paths for biking, in-line skating, and walking. In order: Barceloneta, Nova Icària, Bogatell, and Mar Bella (unofficially the most popular, the best spot for people-watching and with the most bars and restaurants in easy reach, while Bogatell and Mar Bella are even prettier and less populated. The Port Olímpic marina between the first two beaches is full of chic sailboats and trendy restaurants and bars.

The beach at Barceloneta.

Barcelona **by Bike**

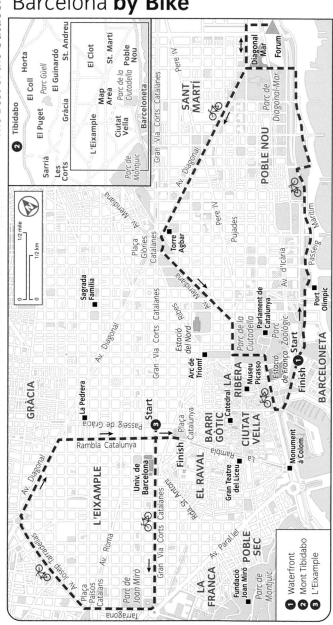

1 Waterfront
2 Mont Tibidabo
3 L'Eixample

Although the old city and L'Eixample aren't the most conducive to bike riding, given the preponderance of cars and *motos*, several other areas are perfect for hopping on a bike, getting some exercise, and seeing Barcelona from two wheels. The best areas are the Waterfront and Tibidabo, both of which have designated bike paths.

❶ ★★ Waterfront. Starting out at Barceloneta, take Passeig Maritim and head northeast along the beach, to Port Olímpic and Vila Olímpica, where you can ride around the wide avenues of the former Olympic Village. Cycle along the paths that line the beaches (Nova Icària, Bogatell, and Mar Bella, a favorite of nudist sunbathers). You can continue as far north as Fòrum Park. For an easy ride, return to Barceloneta along the same path. Or opt for a more ambitious ride: Travel west along Av. Diagonal to Plaça de les Glòries and then head south along Av. Meridiana, which leads right to Parc de la Ciutadella. Within the park, you can bike around wide unpaved avenues with no worry about cars. From here, it's a short distance back to Barceloneta.

❷ ★ Mont Tibidabo. Winding across the hillside of Mt. Tibidabo is the *Carretera de les Aigües*, a cycling

A bike rider on the beach at Barceloneta.

Modernisme & L'Eixample

The *modernisme* movement, although a cousin to the late 19th-century styles French *Art Nouveau* and German and Austrian *Jugendstil,* reached new heights in Catalonia. From the late 19th century until the 1930s, an entire school of *modernista* architects thrived in Barcelona, building hundreds of private houses and public works. Although Gaudí and his cohorts also designed a handful of structures to be built outside of Barcelona, the movement reached its apogee in little more than 10 square blocks of the Catalan capital's L'Eixample quarter. A geometric grid, the dryly named "Extension", provided for the enlargement of the city northward from its medieval core. Curiously, *modernisme* prospered in that hyper-rationalist district, transforming it into what is commonly, and accurately, called the *Quadrat d'Or* (Golden Square).

Carretera de les Aigües, on Mont Tibidabo, is a scenic bike path.

and jogging path that's a favorite of locals on weekends. The 8km (5-mile) unpaved path has drinking fountains at regular intervals and splendid views of Barcelona spread out below. The beginning of the route is about 1km (.6 miles) from Avinguda del Tibidabo; take the Tramvia Blau (see p 21, bullet **8**) there and walk. You'll find a bicycle rental outfit at the beginning of the path.

3 L'Eixample. Although much of the city is clogged with traffic, there are several major thoroughfares with safe biking lanes. Avinguda Diagonal, Gran Via de les Corts Cata-lanes, and Rambla de Catalunya all provide clearly marked lanes on medians. Taking a ride in this neigh-borhood is a great way to see some of the Eixample's *modernista* archi-tecture (see p 25). ●

Practical Matters: Barcelona by Bike

City bike lanes are indicated on the CicloBus Barcelona map, available at the Tourist Information Office (Plaça de Catalunya, 17; underground) or at most bike rental shops. On average, bike rental rates are about 5€ per hour or 15€ to18€ per day.

    Barcelona Bici: ☎ 93-285-38-32; rental points at Plaça de Catalunya; Mirador de Colom; and Pg. Joan de Borbó.

    Un Cotxe Menys ("One Less Car")/**Bike Tours Barcelona:** c/ Espaseria, 3; ☎ 93-268-21-05; www.bicicletabarcelona.com; Mon to Fri 10am to 2pm; Sat 10am to 7pm; Sun 10am to 2pm. Rentals and guided bike tours of the old city and harbor (departures Sat–Sun 10am).

    Classic Bikes Barcelona: c/ Tallers, 45; ☎ 93-317-19-70; www. barcelonarentbikes.com; Daily 9:30am to 2pm and 3:30 to 8pm; guided cyclotours and rentals of folding and Dutch bikes.

    Biciclot: Pg. Marítim, 33; ☎ 93-221-97-78; www.biciclot.net; Daily 10am to 7pm.

    Scenic: c/ Balboa, 3; ☎ 93-319-28-35; www.scenicbcn.com; Mon to Fri 10am to 8pm; rentals and daily routes of the Gothic Quarter and waterfront.

Dining Best Bets

Best **Old-School Catalan Dining**
★★ Agut d'Avignon $$$ *c/ Trinitat 3*
(p 98)

Best **Wine List**
★★ Àbac $$$$ *c/ del Rec, 79 (p 98)*

Best **Desserts**
★★ Espai Sucre $$ *c/ de la*
Princesa, 53 (p 102)

Best **Worth the Wait**
★★★ Cal Pep $$ *Plaça des les*
Olles, 8 (p 100)

Best for **Foodies & Design**
Freaks
★★★ Moo $$$$ *c/ Rosselló 265*
(p 104)

Best **Hushed Foodie Dining**
Temple
★★★ Àbac $$$$ *Rec, 79–89 (p 98)*

Best **Comfort Food**
★ Senyor Parellada $$ *c/ L'Argente-*
ria, 37 (p 105)

Best **Designer Tapas**
★★★ Comerç 24 $$$ *c/ Comerç, 24*
(p 101)

Best **Classic Tapas**
★ Inopia $ *c/ Tamarit, 104 (p 103)*

★ Taller de Tapas $ *Plaça Sant*
Josep Oriol, 9 (p 106)

Best **Seaside Dining**
★★ Can Majó $$$ *c/ Almirall*
Aixada, 23 (p 100)

Best **Seafood**
★★ Els Pescadors $$$ *Plaça Prim, 1*
(p 101)

★★★ Botafumeiro $$$$ *Gran de*
Gràcia, 81 (p 100)

Best for **Nice Family Meal**
★★ 7 Portes $$ *Pg. d'Isabel II, 14*
(p 105)

Best *Modernista* **Digs**
★★ Casa Calvet $$$ *c/ Casp 48*
(p 101)

Best **Lunch Deal**
★ Café de L'Acadèmia $ *c/ Lledó, 1*
(p 100)

Best **Relaxed Beachfront**
Dining
★ Agua $$ *Ps. Marítim de la*
Barceloneta, 30 (p 98)

Best **Hotel Restaurant**
★★★ Moo $$$$ *Hotel Omm,*
c/ Rosselló 265 (p 104)

★★★ Lasarte $$$$ *Hotel Condes*
de Barcelona, c/ Mallorca, 259
(p 103)

Best **Upstart Foodie**
Destination
★★ Cinc Sentits $$$ *c/ Aribau, 58*
(p 101)

Best-**Value Foodie Restaurant**
★★ Hisop $$ *Ptge. Marimón, 9*
(p 102)

Best **Cooking-School Eatery**
★★ Hofmann $$$ *c/ L'Argenteria,*
74–78 (p 102)

Best **Mammoth Portions/The**
Antithesis of Tapas
★★ 7 Portes $$ *Pg. d'Isabel II, 14*
(p 105)

Best **Unsung French Bistro**
★ La Dentellière $$ *c/ Ample, 26*
(p 103)

Best **Outdoor Dining**
★ Café de L'Acadèmia $ *c/ Lledó, 1*
(p 100)

Best for **Impatient Kids**
La Paradeta $$ *c/ Comercial, 7*
(p 103)

Previous page: A menu board at Tapaç 24.

L'Eixample Dining

Casa Calvet **6**
Cinc Sentits **4**
El Japonés **1**
Inopia **7**
Lasarte **3**
Moo **2**
tapaç 24 **5**

Av. Diagonal

Paris
Còrsega
Rosselló
Provença
Mallorca
València
Aragó
Consell de Cent
Diputació
Gran Via Corts Catalanes

Plaça Rei
Joan Carles I

Plaça Universitat

Aribau
Balmes
Enric Granados
Passatje de Mercader
Rambla Catalunya
Passatje de Domingo
Passeig de Gràcia
Passatje dels Camps Elisis
Pau Claris
Passatje de Méndez Vigo
Roger de Llúria

Diagonal

Passatje de la Concepció

L'EIXAMPLE

Fundació
Antoni Tàpies

Plaça
Dr. Letamendi

Casa Batlló
Casa Amatller
Casa Lleó
Morera

Passeig
de Gràcia

Casa de
les Punxes

Casa Milà
(La Pedrera)

Casa Thomas

Universitat
de Barcelona

Passatje de
Permanyer

Torre
d'Aigües

Rda. de St. Antoni
Universitat
Balmes
Ronda Universitat
Pelai
Pg. de Gràcia
Casp
Pau Claris
Roger de Llúria

Plaça
Castella

Tallers
Bergara
Plaça
Catalunya
Ronda St. Pere

Casa de la
Caritat

Pelai
Plaça
Urquinaona
Urquinaona

Map
Area

L'Eixample
Ciutat
Vella

Parc de la
Ciutadella

Tallers
Catalunya
La Rambla
Sta. Anna
Canuda

Av. Portal de l'Àngel
Estruc
Moles
Fontanella
Via Laietana
Jonqueres
Ortigosa

Montjuïc

ⓘ Tourist Information
Ⓜ Metro Station

0   1/4 mile
0   1/4 km

Ciutat Vella & Waterfront Dining

L'EIXAMPLE

Universitat de Barcelona

Plaça Gran Via Corts Catalanes
Universitat
Universitat M
Plaça Castella
Rda. de St. Antoni
Ronda Universitat
Tallers
Balmes
Pelai
Bergara
Rambla Catalunya
Pg. de Gràcia
Casp

Plaça Catalunya (i)

Plaça Urquinaona
Urquinaona M
Fontanella

Bruc
Girona

Casa de la Caritat
Elisabets
Pintor Fortuny
Xuclà

Catalunya M

Santa Anna
La Rambla
Canuda
Comtal
Av. Portal de l'Angel

1 Montsió

Ronda Sant Pere
Trafalgar

Museu d'Art Contemporani de Barcelona
Plaça Caramelles

Palau de la Música Catalana
St. Pere Més Alt

Carme
2 Betlem

LA RIBERA
St. Pere Més Baix

Antic Hospital de la Sta. Creu
Hospital
Plaça Sant Agustí

Palau de la Virreina
Mercat de la Boqueria
Portaferrissa
Palau Moja

Via Laietana

St. Felip Neri
Sta. Maria del Pi

3
EL RAVAL
La Rambla del Raval

Liceu M
Gran Teatre del Liceu

Boqueria
4
5
Ferran
Cali
Plaça St. Jaume

Plaça Catedral Antoni Maura
Av. Catedral
Av. Francesc Cambó

Mercat Santa Caterina
Plaça Allada i Vermell

Catedral †
Generalitat
BARRI GÒTIC
(i)

Bòria
Mercaders
Jaume I M Princesa

Plaça

Marquès de Barberà
Nou de la Rambla

6
Plaça Reial
7
Lleona

CIUTAT VELLA

11
10
Av. Laietana
12
Argenteria
Banys Vells
13
Montcada
Museu Picasso
17
18
Pg. Born
Comerç

Palau Güell
Arc del Teatre

Escudellers
8
Còdols
Carabassa
Ataülf

Santa Maria del Mar †
15
16

Centre d'Art Sta. Mònica
Portal Sta. Madrona

Palau March
9
Mercè
Gignàs
Ample

Plaça Antonio López
La Mercè

Llotja de Mar
14
Plaça del Palau
Marquesa

Reials Drassanes (Museu Marítim)
Plaça Portal de la Pau

Drassanes M

Passeig de Colom (Ronda Litoral)
Cap de Barcelona

Barceloneta M
Plaça Pau Vila

Monument á Colom
Golondrinas

Moll de la Fusta
Moll d'Espanya

Moll de Dipòsit
Palau de Mar (Museu d'Història de Catalunya)
Ginebra

Moll de les Drassanes

Plaça Drassanes

Rambla de Mar

World Trade Center

Transbordador Aeri

Moll de Barcelona

Port Vell

IMAX
L'Aquàrium de Barcelona

Maremàgnum

Moll dels Pescadors
Moll de Balears

Moll de la Barceloneta

La Maquinista

BARCELONETA
19
Plaça Poeta Boscà
Sant Carles
Passeig Joan de Borbó
Comte Sta. Clara
Almirall Cervera
Almirall Aixada

20
Judici

Platja St. Sebastià
Plaça Palmeres
Plaça del Mar
Pg. de l'Escullera
Drasana

L'Eixample

St. Martí
Parc de la Ciutadella

Ciutat Vella
Map Area

Montjuïc

(i) *Tourist Information*

M *Metro Station*

Àbac **17**

Agua **25**

Agut d'Avignon **7**

Arola **27**

Bestial **26**

Café de
L'Academia **11**

Cal Pep **16**

Can Costa **19**

Can Culleretes **5**

Can Majó **20**

Comerç 24 **21**

Els Pescadors **29**

Els Quatre Gats **1**

Espai Sucre **23**

Gente de Pasta **22**

Hofmann **12**

La Dentellière **9**

La Paradeta **24**

Les Quinze Nits **6**

Lonja de Tapas **15**

Los Caracoles **8**

Organic **3**

Pla **10**

Senyor Parellada **13**

7 Portes **14**

Sikkim **18**

Talaia Mar **28**

Taller de Tapas **4**

Umita **2**

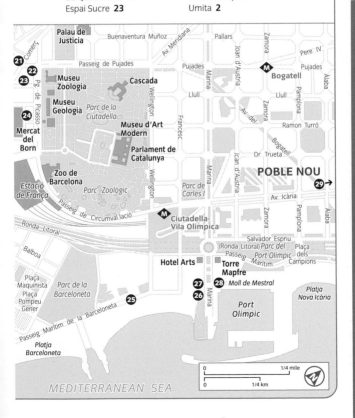

Barrios Altos Dining

Botafumeiro **1**
Flash-Flash Tortillería **3**
Hisop **2**
Oli e un Llum **4**

Barcelona **Dining A to Z**

Dining Hours Tip

Catalans generally have lunch between 2 and 4pm and dinner after 9pm. Most kitchens stay open until 11:30pm.

★★ **Àbac** LA RIBERA (EL BORN) *CATALAN/INTERNATIONAL*   A favorite with foodies, Àbac is slick, hushed, and confident, and chef Xavier Pellicer's menu, which emphasizes color and texture, is innovative to the point of being experimental. *c/ del Rec, 79. ☎ 93-319-66-00. Entrees 25€–38€; tasting menu 85€. AE, DC, MC, V. Lunch & dinner, Tues–Sat, dinner only Mon.*

Closed Aug. Metro: Jaume I or Arc de Triomf. Map p 96.

★ **kids Agua** WATERFRONT (VILA OLÍMPICA) *MEDITERRANEAN*   A casually cool spot with great beach views, Agua is popular for simply prepared fresh fish, rice dishes, and vegetarian items. It's a great spot for families with boisterous and picky young ones. *Pg. Marítim de la Barceloneta, 30. ☎ 93-225-12-72. Entrees 8€–19€. AE, DC, MC, V. Lunch & dinner daily. Metro: Ciutadella. Map p 96.*

★★ **Agut d'Avignon** BARRI GOTIC *CATALAN*   A classic revered among locals for its consistently

Arola, in the Hotel Arts.

3 weeks in Aug. Metro: Jaume I or Liceu. Map p 96.

★★ Arola WATERFRONT (VILA OLIMPICA) *CATALAN/SPANISH* Amid colorful, pop-art decor, Arola does a modern take on *pica-pica* ("nibbles") and adds bursts of flavor to Mediterranean standards such as steamed mussels with citrus juice and saffron, and Gorgonzola cheese croquettes. *Hotel Arts, Marina, 19–21.* ☎ *93-483-80-90. Entrees 10€–32€; tasting menu 48€. AE, DC, MC, V. Lunch only Wed, lunch & dinner Tues–Sun. Closed Jan. Metro: Ciutadella/Vila Olímpica. Map p 96.*

kids Bestial WATERFRONT (VILA OLIMPICA) *MEDITERRANEAN/ ITALIAN* This cool, futuristic spot is hip but relaxed, with large picture windows looking out to a very attractive outdoor space and views of the beach. The Mediterranean menu has an Italian bent, offering pastas, risottos, and individual pizzas with fresh ingredients. *c/ Ramón*

fine, traditional Catalan cooking, this rustic spot is one of my favorite places in the city to sample the down-to-earth ingredients of *cuina catalana* such as duck with figs and langostinos (prawns) ali-oli. *c/ Trinitat 3 (alley off Avinyó 8).* ☎ *93-302-60-34. Entrees 19€–44€. MC, V. Lunch & dinner daily. Closed last*

Bestial's Waterfront location is ideal for alfresco dining.

Trias Fargas, 2–4 (Vila Olímpica). ☎ *93-224-04-07. Entrees 9€–20€. AE, DC, MC, V. Lunch & dinner daily. Metro: Ciutadella–Vila Olímpica. Map p 96.*

★★★ Botafumeiro GRACIA
SEAFOOD Among seafood restaurants, none has more pedigree than this perennial favorite, which has entertained Barcelona's business elite and the king of Spain for years. Much of the incredibly fresh seafood is flown in daily from Galicia. The long seafood bar has repeatedly been named the best in Spain. *Gran de Gràcia, 81.* ☎ *93-218-42-30. Entrees 24€–60€. AE, DC, MC, V. Lunch & dinner daily. Closed last 3 weeks in Aug. Metro: Fontana or Diagonal. Map p 98.*

★ Café de L'Academia
BARRI GOTIC CATALAN This dark, ancient-looking little restaurant sits on a lovely medieval square and is usually packed for lunch, when it offers a superb fixed-price menu. In warm weather, tables are set out on the terrace, a perfect place to drink in this quintessential Barri Gòtic corner. *c/ Lledó, 1.* ☎ *93-315-00-26. Entrees 10€–16€. AE, MC, V. Lunch & dinner Mon–Fri. Metro: Jaume I. Map p 96.*

★★ Cal Pep LA RIBERA/WATER-
FRONT SEAFOOD This tiny place used to be a secret, but local foodies and those from abroad now know that it serves some of the most succulent seafood in town. Cal Pep doesn't take reservations, so you have to wait until a seat at the counter opens up. There's no menu, either, but Pep and his boys will set you up with the works. *Plaça des les*

An innovative dish at Cinc Sentits.

Olles 8. ☎ *93-310-79-61. Entrees 14€–20€. AE, DC, MC, V. Dinner Mon; lunch & dinner Tues–Sat. Closed Aug. Metro: Barceloneta or Jaume I. Map p 96.*

★ Can Costa WATERFRONT
(BARCELONETA) SEAFOOD Since the 1930s this has been one of the most dependable restaurants in Barcelona. Although there's no harbor view, the freshly prepared seafood makes up for it. Longtime admirers claim the sautéed baby squid is unequalled. I love the *fideuà de peix,* similar to a shellfish paella but made with thin, dark noodles rather than rice. *Pg. de Joan de Borbón, 70.* ☎ *93-221-59-03. Entrees 16€–35€. AE, DC, MC, V. Lunch & dinner Mon–Tues and Thurs–Sat; lunch only Sun. Closed Wed. Metro: Barceloneta. Map p 96.*

Can Culleretes BARRI GOTIC CATA-
LAN Barcelona's oldest restaurant has been serving traditional Catalan cooking since 1786. It's down-home and old-school, a good place to try standards like *espinacas a la catalana* (spinach with pine nuts and raisins) and *butifarra* (white sausage). *c/ Quintana, 5.* ☎ *93-317-64-85. Entrees 8€–16€; fixed-price menu 15€. MC, V. Lunch & dinner Tues–Sat, lunch only Sun. Closed August. Metro: Liceu. Map p 96.*

★★ Can Majó WATERFRONT (PORT
VELL) SEAFOOD Insiders know that this tavern-style, harborfront restaurant is one of the top seafood places in Barcelona. Try the excellent *sopa*

de pescado y marisco (fish and shell-fish soup), sautéed squid, or paellas. *c/ Almirall Aixada, 23.* ☎ *93-221-58-18. AE, DC, MC, V. Lunch & dinner Tues–Sat; lunch only Sun. Metro: Barceloneta. Map p 96.*

★★ **Casa Calvet** L'EIXAMPLE *CATALAN/MEDITERRANEAN* Casa Calvet is housed within one of Antoni Gaudí's first *modernista* apartment buildings, with a gorgeous white-brick and stained-glass decor. The contemporary Catalan cuisine doesn't take a back seat to the surroundings. *c/ Casp 48.* ☎ *93-412-40-12. Entrees 20€–32€; tasting menu 50€. AE, DC, MC, V. Lunch & dinner Mon–Sat. Closed last 2 weeks in Aug. Metro: Passeig de Gràcia. Map p 95.*

★★ **Cinc Sentits** L'EIXAMPLE *MEDITERRANEAN* Haute cuisine, but also family-run—this recent arrival is a unique synthesis of the Barcelona dining scene. Chef Jordi Artal's innovative fusion cuisine is best sampled on the "Gourmet" tasting menu. Prepare yourself for monkfish sprinkled with bacon "dust" or a soft poached egg with tomato jam. *c/ Aribau, 58.* ☎ *93-323-94-90. Entrees 14€–32€; tasting menu 40€ & 55€.*

The minimalist design at Comerç 24.

AE, DC, MC, V. Lunch Mon; lunch & dinner Tues–Sat. Closed Easter week and Aug 8–31. Metro: Passeig de Gràcia. Map p 95.

★★★ **Comerç 24** LA RIBERA (EL BORN) *CATALAN/INTERNATIONAL* The small plates of celebrity chef Carles Abellán are so creative that it's a disservice to call them tapas. The theatrical dishes offer a visionary take on Catalan classics. *c/ Comerç, 24.* ☎ *93-319-21-02. Entrees 11€–25€; tasting menu 48€. AE, DC, MC, V. Lunch & dinner Tues–Sat. Closed Christmas week & last 3 weeks in Aug. Metro: Jaume I. Map p 96.*

★ **El Japonés** L'EIXAMPLE *JAPANESE* Tucked away in a rare alleyway in L'Eixample, this a perfect place for a quick lunch break. It focuses on *kushiyaki* (brochettes), as well as tempura and sushi. *Pje. de la Concepció, 2.* ☎ *93-487-25-92. Entrees 8€–22€. AE, DC, MC, V. Lunch & dinner daily. Metro: Diagonal. Map p 95.*

★★ **Els Pescadors** WATERFRONT (POBLE NOU) *SEAFOOD* Family-run, "the Fishermen" focuses, naturally, on providing superb fresh fish and seafood, with just a hint of new-school preparations. *Plaça Prim, 1.* ☎ *93-225-20-18. Entrees 15€–35€. AE, DC, MC, V. Lunch & dinner daily. Closed Easter week. Metro: Poble Nou. Map p 96.*

★ **Els Quatre Gats** BARRI GOTIC *CATALAN* A cafe that's become legend, this place was the turn-of-the-20th century hangout of Picasso and other bohemian intellectuals. The "Four Cats" today is on the *modernista* tourist circuit, but it's a surprisingly good spot for simple, homey Catalan fare using fresh market ingredients. *c/ Montsió, 3.* ☎ *93-302-41-40. Entrees 14€–22€; fixed-price lunch menu 14€. AE, DC, MC, V. Breakfast, lunch & dinner daily. Metro: Plaça de Catalunya. Map p 96.*

★★ Espai Sucre LA RIBERA *DESSERTS* Were Willy Wonka a restaurateur, this might be his temple. Yes, this tiny, minimalist restaurant ("Sugar Space") exclusively serves dessert, but the tasting menus of dessert courses actually work as (more or less) balanced dinner menus. For those fearful of sugar overload, you can add a savory dish, such as magret of duck or ginger couscous. *c/ de la Princesa, 53.* ☎ *93-268-16-30. Entrees 10€–12€; tasting menus 28€–35€. MC, V. Dinner, Tues–Sat. Closed mid-Aug & Christmas week. Metro: Arc de Triomf. Map p 96.*

★ kids Flash-Flash Tortilleria GRÀCIA *OMELETS/HAMBURGERS* With its monochrome mid-70s glam look and vibe, this place is a longtime favorite of young and old alike. In addition to a roster of 70 types of tortillas (omelets), there are tasty, bunless hamburgers (almost always cooked very rare), steaks, and salads. *La Granada de Penedès, 25.* ☎ *93-237-09–90. Entrees 9€–25€. AE, DC, MC, V. Lunch & dinner daily. Metro/FGC: Gràcia. Map p 98.*

kids Gente de Pasta LA RIBERA *ITALIAN* It looks more like a warehouse than a *trattoria,* and the place can get loud, but it shouldn't be hard to find something the kids will eat, including risottos, basic pastas, and salads. *Pg. de Picasso, 10.* ☎ *93-268-70-17. Entrees 7€–18€. AE, MC, V. Lunch & dinner daily. Metro: Jaume 1 or Barceloneta. Map p 96.*

★★ Hisop GRACIA *COMTEMPO-RARY CATALAN* Less intimidating than some of Barcelona's chicest restaurants featuring *cocina de autor* (creative haute cuisine), Hisop is small, inviting, and dynamic. Although difficult to find on a tiny side street just north of the Diagonal boulevard, it's worth the hunt for subtly complex dishes, such as scallops with figs and Jabugo ham, and scrumptious desserts. *Ptge. Marimón, 9.* ☎ *93-141-32-33. Entrees 21€–29 €; tasting menu 48€. AE, DC, MC, V. Lunch & dinner Tues–Sat. Closed last 2 weeks in August. Metro: Hospital Clinic. Map p 98.*

★★ Hofmann LA RIBERA *CATA-LAN/FRENCH* Now with a Michelin

The interior of Flash-Flash hasn't been altered since it opened in 1970.

A delightful dessert at Hofmann.

star to add to its fame, this restaurant is connected to a respected culinary school. Menu items are a delicious mix of French and Catalan dishes, such as foie gras wrapped in puff pastry, or filet steak cooked in red wine and served with shallot confit and potato gratin. *c/ L'Argenteria, 74–78.* ☎ *93-319-58-89. Entrees 16€–40€; tasting menu 35€. AE, DC, MC, V. Lunch & dinner Mon–Fri. Closed Aug & Christmas week. Metro: Jaume I. Map p 96.*

★ **Inopia** L'EIXAMPLE (ESQUERRA) *TAPAS* People hear that this tapas joint is by the brother of the legendary chef Ferran Adrià and expect all kinds of funky foams. But it's a classic tapas bar serving up superb Spanish and Catalan tapas. The standards, such as *patatas bravas* (spicy fried potatoes) and *croquetas de jamón ibérico* (croquettes stuffed with Spanish ham), are rarely this tasty elsewhere. *c/ Tamarit, 104.* ☎ *93-424-52-31. Tapas 3€–9€. MC, V. Dinner Tues–Fri, lunch & dinner Sat. Metro: Poble Sec. Map p 95.*

★ **La Dentellière** BARRI GOTIC *FRENCH* This friendly, rustic restaurant has the kind of natural charm you'd find at a neighborhood spot in a small French village. Look for the *carpaccio* of filet of beef with pistachios, lemon juice, vinaigrette, and Parmesan cheese, or enjoy the inexpensive three-course meal with homemade dessert. *c/ Ample, 26.* ☎ *93-218-74-79. Entrees 8€–16€. MC, V. Dinner Tues–Sat. Metro: Drassanes. Map p 96.*

kids La Paradeta LA RIBERA *SEAFOOD* You can pick your own seafood and *mariscos* (shellfish) from large plastic tubs; it's then weighed and served on a platter. Kids should love it, and parents can accompany dinner with a nice selection of wines. *c/ Comercial, 7.* ☎ *93-268-19-39. Entrees (cost is per kilo) 12€–20€. No credit cards. Dinner Tues–Sat. Closed Dec 22–Jan 22. Metro: Arc de Triomf. Map p 96.*

★★★ **Lasarte** L'EIXAMPLE *BASQUE* Opened by Michelin three-star chef Martin Berasategui in 2006, this venture is an elegant, minimalist temple to his avant-garde cooking. If you've never had the luxury of haute Basque cuisine, Lasarte's expensive but exquisite tasting menu is a great place to start. *Hotel Condes de Barcelona, c/ Mallorca, 259.* ☎ *93-445-32-42.*

A lively scene at Inopia.

Entrees 32€–50€. AE, DC, MC, V. Dinner daily. Metro: Passeig de Gràcia. Map p 95.

Les Quinze Nits LA RAMBLA/BARRI GOTIC *MEDITERRANEAN* This attractive, bargain-priced restaurant, with a few tables under the arches on Plaça Reial, draws long lines of people looking for a solid meal and great deal. The Catalan and Mediterranean dishes are simple and straightforward, but surprisingly well prepared. *Plaça Reial 6.* ☎ *93-317-30-75. Entrees 5€–12 €. MC, V. Lunch & dinner daily. Metro: Liceu. Map p 96.*

Lonja de Tapas WATERFRONT *TAPAS* A bright and easygoing tapas restaurant, in a good-looking space, this new place is solid, especially if you're just in the mood for grazing or don't quite know what you want. Tapas cover the Spanish standards, from Iberian ham and steamed cockles to paellas and monkfish with wild mushrooms. *Pla del Palau, 7.* ☎ *93-268-72-58. Tapas 3€–20€; tasting menu 26€. AE, DC, MC, V. Lunch & dinner daily. Metro: Barceloneta or Jaume I. Map p 96.*

Los Caracoles BARRI GOTIC *CATALAN* Popular with tourists, this restaurant is one of those only-in-Spain places. You're first greeted by an open spit roasting chickens; inside is an ancient, atmospheric labyrinth of cluttered dining rooms. "The Snails" is all about Catalan comfort food, such as *arroz negre* (rice cooked in squid ink), grilled squid, and roast chicken. *c/ Escudellers, 14.* ☎ *93-302-31-85. Entrees 8€–28€. AE, DC, MC, V. Lunch & dinner daily. Metro: Liceu or Drassanes. Map p 96.*

★★★ Moo L'EIXAMPLE *MODERN MEDITERRANEAN* You can't get much more mod than Hotel Omm, home to this exquisite restaurant.

The very mod Moo.

Unusually, all the dishes are available in half-size portions, so you can design your own *menú de degustación.* Or just saddle up for the "Joan Roca" tasting menu: five gourmet dishes served with well-chosen wines. Desserts are earth-shaking. *c/ Rosselló 265.* ☎ *93-445-40-00. Entrees 18€–30€; midday menu 45€; tasting menu (with wine pairing) 85€. AE, DC, MC, V. Lunch & dinner daily. Metro: Diagonal. Map p 95.*

★ kids Oli e un Llum SARRIÀ (BARRIOS ALTOS) *SANDWICHES/SNACKS* This hip-looking bar is an unusual venture, serving up some of the most delectable *bocadillos,* or sandwiches, you've ever dreamed of. Many have a distinctly Catalan angle. *c/ Bon Pastor, 6 bis.* ☎ *93-201-73-97. Entrees 7€–17€. MC, V. Dinner daily. Metro/FGC: Gràcia. Map p 98.*

★ Organic RAVAL *VEGETARIAN* It's taken a while for vegetarian restaurants to catch on, but this cool, laid-back place with large communal tables really fills a void. There's a help-yourself soup and salad bar, and main courses that include vegetarian pizza, pasta, and stir-fries. *c/ Junta de Comerç 11.* ☎ *93-301-09-02. Main*

courses 6€–12€. AE, DC, MC, V.
Lunch & dinner daily. Metro: Liceu.
Map p 96.

★ **Pla** BARRI GOTIC *MEDITER-
RANEAN* Popular with locals and
visitors alike for its well-prepared
dishes at exceedingly fair prices, this
attractive restaurant serves excellent
carpaccios, tasty salads, and gently
exotic main courses, such as
Thai curry or Moroccan
couscous. c/ Bellafila, 5.
☎ 93-412-65-52.
Entrees 7€–17€. DC,
MC, V. Dinner daily.
Closed Dec 25–27.
Metro: Jaume I.
Map p 96.

★ **Senyor Parel-
lada** LA
RIBERA *CATA-
LAN/MEDITER-
RANEAN* One
of the best val-
ues in Barcelona
is this cheery,

PARELLADA

A sign outside Senyor Parellada.

stylish restaurant carved out of an
old mansion. The colorful dining
rooms look photo ready, so it's a surprise to get such dependably exe-
cuted, fresh preparations of
authentic Catalan fare as baked
monkfish with mustard and garlic

sauce, at bargain prices. c/ L'Argenteria, 37. ☎ 93-310-50-94. Entrees
8€–21€. AE, DC, MC, V. Lunch &
dinner daily. Metro: Jaume I. Map
p 96.

★★ **kids** **7 Portes** WATERFRONT
CATALAN A favorite of large dining
parties since 1836, this elegant but
unassuming place really does have
seven doors under porticoes (hence
the name). It's famous for its
rice dishes, such as black
rice with squid in its
own ink; portions are
enormous and
reasonably priced.
Pg. d'Isabel II, 14.
☎ 93-319-30-33.
Entrees 18€–
35€. AE, DC,
MC, V. Lunch &
dinner daily.
Metro:
Barceloneta
or Drassanes.
Map p 96.

Sikkim LA RIBERA *INDIAN/
TURKISH* A sexy, dark cave lighted
by candles and overflowing with all
kinds of glowing Buddha statues,
this is the antithesis of the minimalist aesthetic Barcelona is so fond of.
And the rich spices of Indian and

7 Portes.

Turkish items, including Himalayan barbecue and sea bass with cous cous, are a welcome change. *Plaça Comercial, 1.* ☎ *93-268-43-13. Entrees 9€–20€. AE, DC, MC, V. Lunch & dinner daily. Metro: Arc de Triomf. Map p 96.*

★★ **Talaia Mar** WATERFRONT (PORT OLIMPIC) *MEDITERRANEAN* The Olympic Port teems with restaurants, but none of them is as good as this one. The innovative chef has created a seafood-dominated menu, featuring grilled fresh fish and more audacious dishes that tempt the senses, including barnacles with a sea water sorbet. *Marina, 16.* ☎ *93-221-90-90. Entrees 18€–28€; fixed-price menu 55€. AE, DC, MC, V. Lunch & dinner, Tues–Sun. Metro: Ciutadella–Vila Olímpica. Map p 96.*

★ **Taller de Tapas** BARRI GOTIC *TAPAS* This pleasant, modern "Tapas Workshop" simplifies the ordering of tapas, which are prepared fresh in an open kitchen. You'll find delightful small dishes from across Spain: marinated anchovies, prawns with scrambled eggs, and sizzling *chorizo* cooked in cider. *Plaça Sant Josep Oriol, 9.* ☎ *93-301-80-20. Tapas 3€–11€. AE, DC, MC, V. Lunch & dinner daily. Metro: Liceu. There's a second location at c/ L'Argentaria 51.* ☎ *93-268-85-5; Metro: Jaume I; map p 96.*

★★ **Tapaç 24** L'EIXAMPLE *CRE-ATIVE TAPAS* Ultra-cool Comerç 24 does upscale tapas, while this below-street-level bar is the more informal off-shoot. But it shares an interest in fresh ingredients and just the right touch of creativity. *c/ Diputació, 269.* ☎ *93-488-09-77. Tapas 2.50€–14€. MC, V. Lunch & dinner Mon–Sat. Metro: Passeig de Gràcia. Map p 95.*

★ **Umita** RAVAL *SUSHI* Sushi by way of the creative culinary scene of Lima, Peru, Umita offers very fresh cuts of fish and creative, delicate combinations. A stool at the bar is the place to be. *c/ Pintor Fortuny 15.* ☎ *93-301-23-22. Entrees 7€–18€. AE, MC, V. Lunch & dinner daily. Metro: Catalunya. Map p 96.* ●

For classic Spanish tapas, try Taller de Tapas.

Nightlife Best Bets

Best Old-World Atmosphere
★★ L'Ascensor, c/ Bellafila, 3
(p 113)

Best Spot for Outlaw Liquor
(Absinthe)
★★★ Marsella, c/ Sant Pau, 65
(p 113)

Best Impersonation of a
French Port Bar
★★★ Pastis, c/ Santa Mónica, 4
(p 113)

Best People-Watching
Café Zurich, Plaça de Catalunya 1
(p 57)

Best Wine Bar
★★ La Vinya del Senyor, Plaça
Santa Maria, 5 (p 118)

Best Pub for Soccer & Swear-
ing in English
★ The Black Horse, c/ Allada
Vermell, 16 (p 112)

Best Classic Cocktails
★★★ Gimlet, c/ Rec, 24 (p 112)

Best Xampanyeria (Cava Bar)
★★★ El Xampanyet, c/ de la
Montcada, 22 (p 118)

Best View
★★ Mirablau, Plaça Doctor
Andreu, 2 (p 113)

Best Beach Bar on a Boat
★ Luz de Gas Port Vell, Moll de
Diposit, s/n (p 117)

Best Bar to Meet Fellow
Travelers
Travel Bar, c/ Boqueria, 27 (p 114)

Best High-Design Bar/Lounge
★★ Omm Sesion Club, c/ Rosselló,
265 (p 117)

Best Latin Dance Club
★★★ Antilla Latin Club, c/ Aragó,
141 (p 114)

Best Place for a Movie & a
Cocktail
★★ Movie Living & Food, c/ Roger
de Lluria, 50 (p 117)

Best Yesteryear Dancehall
★★★ La Paloma, c/ Tigre, 27 (p 115)

Best Drag Show
★★ Café Dietrich, c/ Consell de
Cent, 255 (p 116)

Best Open-Air Dance Club
★ La Terrazza, Av. Marquès de
Comillas, s/n (p 115)

Best Lounge for Beautiful
People & Paparazzi
★ CDLC (Carpe Diem Lounge Club)
P.g Marítim, 32 (p 117)

Previous page: Dancing after dark in Barcelona. This page: Try the absinthe at Marsella.

L'Eixample Nightlife

Aire **10**
Antilla Latin Club **11**
Bar Mut **7**
Bikini **1**
Café Dietrich **12**
Café Zurich **14**
City Hall **15**
La Terrazza **2**
Metro **13**
Mirablau **9**
Movie Living & Food **18**
New Chaps **8**
Nick Havanna **5**
Omm Sesion Club **6**
Otto Zutz **4**
Salvation **16**
Up and Down **3**
Xampú Xampany **17**

0   1/2 mile
0   1/2 km

Fontana Ⓜ

St. Martí
Parc de la Ciutadella
L'Eixample
Map Area
Ciutat Vella
Montjuïc

Balmes

Plaça Gal.la Placídia
Travessera

Riera St. Miquel

Gran de Gràcia

Torrent de l'Olla

Via Augusta

Av. Diagonal

Paris

Plaça Rei Joan Carles I

Còrsega

Diagonal Ⓜ

Rosselló

Provença

Mallorca

Balmes

Passeig de Gràcia

Rambla

GRÀCIA

Pg. Sant Joan

Bailèn

Perill

Còrsega

Casa de les Punxes

Rosselló

Casa Milà (La Pedrera)

Casa Thomas

Av. Diagonal

Provença

Verdaguer Ⓜ

Pau Claris

Roger de Llúria

Bruc

Girona

València

Aribau

Plaça Dr. Letamendi

Balmes

Catalunya

L'EIXAMPLE

Aragó

Mercat de la Concepció

Pg. Sant Joan

Aragó

Consell de Cent

Passeig de Gràcia Ⓜ

Consell de Cent

Bailèn

Girona Ⓜ

Diputació

Universitat de Barcelona

Pg. de Gràcia

Diputació

Plaça Tetuan

Gran Via Corts Catalanes

Gran Via Corts Catalanes

Tetuan Ⓜ

Universitat Ⓜ

Rda. de St. Antoni

Casa de la Caritat

Ronda Universitat

Plaça Catalunya

Casp

Pau Claris

Roger de Llúria

Bruc

Girona

Bailèn

Pg. Sant Joan

Xampú Xampany **17**

Pelai

Tallers

Urquinaona Ⓜ

Museu d'Art Contemporani de Barcelona

Fontanella

Ronda Sant Pere

EL RAVAL

Café Zurich Ⓜ Catalunya

Palau de la Música Catalana

Arc de Triomf Ⓜ

Antic Hospital de la Sta. Creu

Mercat de la Boqueria

La Rambla del Raval

Robador

La Rambla

Portaferrissa

Av. de la Catedral

Via Laietana

Sta. Maria del Pi

Catedral

Portal de l'Àngel

Mercat Sta. Caterina

Arc de Triomf

LA RIBERA

Plaça Allada i Vermell

Princesa

Montcada

Comerç

Pg. de Picasso

Riereta

St. Pau del Camp

Gran Teatre del Liceu

Generalitat

Liceu Ⓜ

Ajuntament

Jaume I Ⓜ

CIUTAT VELLA

BARRI GÒTIC

Sta. Maria del Mar

Mercat del Born

Parc de la Ciutadella

Rec

ⓘ Tourist Information
Ⓜ Metro Station

Ciutat Vella & Waterfront Nightlife

Universitat de Barcelona

L'EIXAMPLE

St. Marti

L'Eixample

Parc de la Ciutadella

Ciutat Vella

Map Area

Montjuïc

Plaça Universitari

Gran Via Corts Catalanes

Rambla Catalunya

Pg. de Gràcia

Casp

Universitat

Rda. de St. Antoni

Ronda Universitat

Plaça Castella

Pelai

Balmes

Bergara

Plaça Catalunya

Pelai

Tallers

Plaça Urquinaona

Urquinaona

Fontanella

Ronda Sant Pere

Trafalgar

Girona

Casa de la Caritat

Museu d'Art Contemporani de Barcelona

Plaça Caramelles

Elisabets

Pintor Fortuny

Xuclà

La Rambla

Santa Anna

Av. Portal de l'Angel

Comtal

Montsió

Palau de la Música Catalana

St. Pere Més Alt

LA RIBERA

St. Pere Més Baix

Carme

Betlem

Palau de la Virreïna

Portaferrissa

Via Laietana

Plaça Antoni Maura

Av. Catedral

Av. Francesc Cambó

Mercat Santa Caterina

Plaça Allada i Vermell

Antic Hospital de la Sta. Creu

Hospital

Mercat de la Boqueria

Sta. Maria del Pi

St. Felip Neri

Palau Moja

EL RAVAL

Plaça Salvador Seguí

Liceu

Boqueria

Catedral

BARRI GÒTIC

Borja

Princesa

Museu Picasso

Comerç

Gran Teatre del Liceu

Marquès de Barberà

Nou de la Rambla

La Rambla

Plaça Reial

Ferran

Cardenal Casañas

Plaça St. Jaume

Jaume I

Montcada

Rec

Pg. Born

Comerç

Arc del Teatre

Av. Drassanes

Palau Güell

Escudellers

CIUTAT VELLA

Ataülf

Ajuntament

Plaça Traginers

Via Laietana

Argenteria

Millans

Sta. Maria del Mar

Plaça del Palau

Centre d'Art Sta. Monica

Palau March

Codols

Carabassa

Avinyó

Gignàs

Ample

Correus (Post Office)

Llotja

Reials Drassanes (Museu Marítim)

Portal Sta. Madrona

Drassanes

Ample

La Mercè

Mercè

Plaça Antonio López

de Mar

Marquesa

Barceloneta

Plaça Pau Vila

Cap de Barcelona

Monument á Colom

Plaça Portal de la Pau

Passeig de Colom

(Ronda Litoral)

Moll de Dipòsit

Plaça Drassanes

Golondrinas

Moll de la Fusta

Moll d'Espanya

Palau de Mar (Museu d'Història de Catalunya)

Ginebra

La Maquinista

Moll de les Drassanes

Rambla da Mar

Port Vell

IMAX

L'Aquàrium de Barcelona

BARCELONETA

Plaça Poeta Boscà

Moll de Barcelona

Transbordador Aeri

Maremàgnum

Moll dels Pescadors

Moll de la Barceloneta

Moll de Borbó

Passeig Joan de Borbó

Sant Carles

Comte Sta. Clara

Almirall Cervera

World Trade Center

Moll de Balears

Escar

Pg. de la Escollera

Drasana

Judici

Plaça del Mar

Plaça Palmeres

Almirall Aixada

Platja St. Sebastià

(i) Tourist Information

(M) Metro Station

Almirall **3**
Apolo **4**
Baja Beach Club **27**
The Black Horse **25**
Boadas **2**
Can Paixano **18**
Casino Barcelona **29**
CDLC (Carpe Diem
  Lounge Club) **28**
Club 13 **7**
El Bosc de
  las Fades **12**
El Xampanyet **24**
The Fastnet Bar **21**
Gimlet **23**
Ginger **15**

L'Ascensor **13**
La Fianna **17**
La Paloma **1**
La Vinateria del Call **11**
La Vinya del Senyor **16**
Le Kashbah **20**
Luz de Gas Port Vell **19**
Marsella **5**
Molly's Fair City **6**
New York **8**
Pastis **9**
Pitin Bar **22**
Razzmatazz **30**
Shoko **26**
Travel Bar **10**
Va de Vi **14**

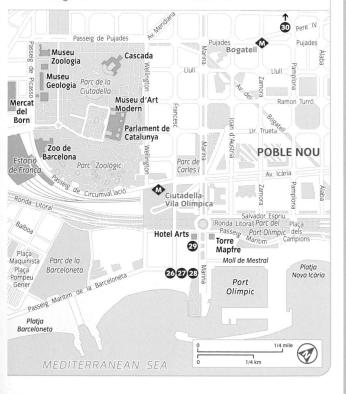

Barcelona Nightlife A to Z

Bars & Pubs

★ **Almirall** RAVAL An old-school, dimly lit place with a bohemian bent and massive Art Nouveau mirror behind the bar. *c/ Joaquín Costa, 33.* ☎ *93-412-15-35. Metro: Sant Antoni or Universitat. Map p 110.*

★ **Bar Mut** L'EIXAMPLE A smart, classic old Barcelona tapas joint and watering hole—its name is a play on the local pronunciation of vermouth—it has great snacks, all written on a chalkboard, and plentiful wines tucked behind glass. *c/ Pau Claris, 192.* ☎ *93-217-43-38. Metro: Diagonal. Map p 109.*

★ **The Black Horse** LA RIBERA With a host of British beers on tap, dart boards, and several TVs tuned to sports, this English free house with a worn pub feel is where expats come to watch soccer and put back a few pints. *c/ Allada Vermell, 16.* ☎ *93-268-33-38. Metro: Jaume I. Map p 110.*

★ **Boadas** LA RAMBLA A classic cocktail bar from the 1930s, Boadas is lined with old photos and has an intellectual, pre-revolutionary Havana vibe. A good place for a predinner drink, like a classic daiquiri. *c/ Tallers, 1.* ☎ *93-318-88-26. Metro: Catalunya. Map p 110.*

El Bosc de las Fades BARRI GOTIC A freaky plunge into a fairytale forest, complete with gnomes, fairies, mermaids, waterfalls, and trees with faces. It's fanciful and trying hard to be cinematic. *Pg. de la Banca, 7.* ☎ *93-317-26-49. Metro: Drassanes. Map p 110.*

★ **The Fastnet Bar** WATERFRONT This Irish pub with good grub has an outdoor terrace and location near the marina. Soccer and rugby fans gather around the large-screen TV. *Pg. Juan de Borbón, 22.* ☎ *93-295-30-05. Metro: Barceloneta. Map p 110.*

★★★ **Gimlet** LA RIBERA People who know their cocktails frequent this sophisticated, retro-styled bar, where excellent bartenders and cool jazz on the stereo complete the scene. Perfect for predinner drinks. *c/ Rec, 24.* ☎ *93-310-10-27. Metro: Arc de Triomf. Map p 110.*

A sign for Boadas cocktail bar.

A bartender pours a drink at Gimlet.

Picasso and Hemingway were regulars at Marsella.

hallucinogenic and still banned in some countries. They say that Picasso, Dalí, and Hemingway were regulars here. *c/ Sant Pau 65.* ☎ 93-442-72-63. *Metro: Liceu. Map p 110.*

★★ **Mirablau** TIBIDABO   The bar itself isn't anything special, really, but the view is unreal. Have a cocktail and gaze from a picture window over all of Barcelona, laid out spectacularly beneath your feet. The bar is next to the funicular near the top of Mt. Tibidabo. *Plaça Doctor Andreu, 2.* ☎ 93-418-58-79. *Tramvia Blau from Metro: Tibidabo. Map p 109.*

Molly's Fair City BARRI GOTIC   Another noisy hangout attracting mostly expats and visiting Brits and Irishmen with plenty of drinks to go around. The scene can get very animated, especially if there's a soccer match on the telly. *c/ Ferran, 7.* ☎ 93-342-40-26. *Metro: Liceu. Map p 110.*

★★★ **Pastis** LA RAMBLA/RAVAL This darkly romantic, mid-century spot, a shrine to Edith Piaf, reeks of an old seaside bar. The house special is pastis, the French anise-flavored elixir. The place isn't for everyone, but those with a sense of camp or an ascot will be in heaven here. *c/ Santa Mónica, 4.* ☎ 93-318-79-80. *Metro: Drassanes. Map p 110.*

Check out the fantastic views from Mirablau.

★★ **Ginger** BARRI GOTIC   A small but stylin' retro cocktail bar on a lovely little Gothic Quarter square. Its comfortable sofas and good selection of tapas make it a place to linger. *Palma de Sant Just, 1 (at c/ Lledó).* ☎ 93-310-53-09. *Metro: Jaume I. Map p 110.*

★ **La Fianna** LA RIBERA   This bar/restaurant's ramshackle, vaguely North African ambience appeals to late-nighters and international sorts who kick back on the cozy, cushion-topped platforms. All that's missing are hookah pipes. *c/ Banys Vells, 15.* ☎ 93-315-18-10. *Metro: Jaume I. Map p 110.*

★★ **L'Ascensor** BARRI GOTIC Named for its fantastic old-world elevator that serves as an entrance, this popular spot has been around for 3 decades and is renowned for its rum-based caipirinhas and mojitos, which might be obvious from the lineup of mint-and-sugared glasses on the bar. *c/ Bellafila, 3.* ☎ 93-318-53-47. *Metro: Jaume I. Map p 110.*

★★★ **Marsella** RAVAL   This dusty joint—around since 1820—is *the* place to try absinthe *(absenta)*, the wickedly strong anise-flavored liqueur distilled from wormwood, said to be

Pitin Bar LA RIBERA   This cool little two-story bar has been on the charming Passeig del Born since 1957. Upstairs—if you can navigate the spiral staircase—is squat and dark, perfect for just chilling out. *Pg. del Born, 34.* ☎ *93-319-50-87. Metro: Jaume I. Map p 110.*

Travel Bar BARRI GOTIC   The name says it all: This bar is a refuge for on-the-cheap travelers and backpackers to meet up, gather information, dial up the Internet, grab some cheapo grub, and, of course, pound back beers. *c/ Boqueria, 27.* ☎ *93-342-52-52. Metro: Liceu. Map p 110.*

Casino

Casino Barcelona WATERFRONT Hugely popular, this casino also contains a disco, restaurant, and all the gaming opportunities you could want. Don't forget to take your passport. *c/ Marina 19–21.* ☎ *93-225-78-78. Admission 4.50€. Metro: Citutadella/Vila Olimpica. Map p 110.*

Dance Clubs

★★★ **Antilla Latin Club** L'EIXAMPLE   A fixture among Barcelona's large Latin American and Caribbean community, this happening *salsateca* is a great place to shake it if you know what you're doing (and if you don't, check out the club's dance school, Mon and Wed–Fri 9–11:30pm, free on Tues with cover). It also gets some big-name Latino performers. *c/ Aragó, 141.* ☎ *93-451-21-51. Cover 10€. Metro: Urgell. Map p 109.*

★★ **Apolo** POBLE SEC   On Fridays and Saturdays this wildly diverse nightclub, in a venerable turn-of-the-20th-century theater/ballroom, is a dance club called Nitsa. On other nights, it plays host to movies, funk music, and rock shows; Sunday it's transformed into a very popular

gay club. *c/ Nou de la Rambla 113.* ☎ *93-318-99-17. Metro: Poble Sec. Map p 110.*

Baja Beach Club WATERFRONT A downmarket disco and meat market, with bare-chested waiters and waitresses in bikinis, this place is kind of like a danceable Hooter's on the beach. The music doesn't stray much from classic disco and cheesy '80s and '90s tunes, and the DJ booth is a speedboat on the dance floor. *Pg. Maritim, 34.* ☎ *93-225-91-00. Metro: Vila Olimpica/Ciutadella. Map p 110.*

★★ **Bikini** DIAGONAL/SANTS   This cool, sprawling bar hosts live rock music but is also a great dance club. You'll find thumping Latin tunes in one salon, alternative rock in another. *c/ Deu i Mata, 105.* ☎ *93-322-00-05. Cover 15€. Metro: Map p 109.*

★ **City Hall** L'EIXAMPLE   A popular, two-level club that draws lots of young, rambunctious clubbers and their tourist counterparts, who come to party to techno and house music. The garden out back provides a nice respite from all the

A DJ spins records late into the Barcelona night.

Head to La Paloma for dancing of all kinds.

action. *Rambla de Catalunya, 2–4.* ☎ *93-317-21-77. Cover 12€. Metro: Catalunya. Map p 109.*

★★ **Club 13** BARRI GOTIC   The action in this trendy club right in Plaça Reial is downstairs, amid glittering chandeliers, black leather chairs, and thumping electronic dance music. It was once a Capuchin convent, and it's got the old brick arches to prove it. *Plaça Reial, 13.* ☎ *93-317-23-52. Metro: Liceu. Map p 110.*

★★★ **La Paloma** RAVAL   A historic, lavish ballroom, more than a century old, this theater, with its red-velvet entry, murals, and glimmering chandeliers, is an extraordinary place to dance. In the early evening, that means fox-trot, tango, and bolero, accompanied by live orchestras. Late night Thursday to Sunday, it morphs into a much younger and hipper nightclub. Note that it was closed temporarily at press time, so call ahead. *c/ Tigre, 27.* ☎ *93-301-68-97. Cover 5€–10€. Metro: Universitat. Map p 110.*

★ **La Terrazza** MONTJUIC   This summer-only, open-air dance club is tucked inside Poble Espanyol, the faux Spanish village built for the 1929 World's Fair. La Terrazza rocks until dawn. An indoor dance option, Discotheque, is available by separate entrance and cover fee. *Poble Espanyol, Av. Marquès de Comillas, s/n.* ☎ *93-508-63-30. Metro: Espanya. Map p 109.*

★ **Le Kashbah** WATERFRONT   With a Moroccan feel near the Olympic port—in the Palau del Mar building that houses the Museu de Catalunya—this bar's dance floor heats up as the evening wears on. Nice outdoor terrace. *Plaça Pau Vila, 1.* ☎ *62-656-13-09. Metro: Barceloneta. Map p 110.*

★ **New York** BARRI GOTIC   It still looks the part of erstwhile strip club and cathouse, and the young hipsters who hang out here make very late nights of it, dancing to indie, R&B, and vintage disco. *c/ Escudellers, 5.* ☎ *93-318-87-30. Cover after 2am 10€. Metro: Drassanes. Map p 110.*

A glass of cava is sure to make your evening more bubbly.

★★★ **Otto Zutz** GRÀCIA   Probably the most famous club in Barcelona, this multi-level club still draws trendsetters, the rich, the famous, and the wannabes. With eight bars, four main dance areas, and spanning a variety of musical genres, you're bound to find something—or someone—you like. *c/ Lincoln 15.* ☎ *93-238-07-22. Cover 15€. Metro: Gràcia. Map p 109.*

★★★ **Razzmatazz** WATERFRONT This five-in-one club, a monster multi-level warehouse, offers something for everyone, as long as you're young and overflowing with energy and hormones. From techno to Goth, pop to punk and metal, a single admission to all five spaces can leave you dizzy. It's also a great live-music venue. *c/ Almogàvers 122.* ☎ *93-320-82-00. Cover (except for special concerts) 12€. Metro: Bogatell. Map p 110.*

★ **Up and Down** BARRIOS ALTOS One of Barcelona's longest-lasting clubs—heck, I danced here in the mid-80s—is still one of *the* places for a mature and elite group of regulars. That's upstairs. Youngsters head downstairs (get it? Up and Down?) to dance to louder and more current sounds. *c/ Numància 179.* ☎ *93-205-51-94. Cover 12€–18€. Metro: Maria Cristina. Map p 109.*

Gay & Lesbian Bars/Clubs

Aire L'EIXAMPLE   With few clubs catering to lesbians in Barcelona, this large, longtime favorite draws women of all ages and stripes (as well as, increasingly, straights). It has a big dance floor and a hopping bar. *c/ Valencia 236.* ☎ *93-487-83-42. Metro: Passeig de Gràcia. Map p 109.*

★★ **Café Dietrich** L'EIXAMPLE For a great drag show, you can't beat this glam cafe, one of the city's most enduring popular gay hangouts. The bartenders wear little and seem to

Even the sign is glamorous at Café Dietrich.

enjoy the attentions of their patrons. *c/ Consell de Cent 255.* ☎ *93-451-77-07. Metro: Gràcia or Universitat. Map p 109.*

★ **Metro** LA RAMBLA/RAVAL Cruisy, with two dance floors, Metro remains one of the most popular gay discos in Barcelona. The crowd ranges from pretty fashionistas to handlebar-moustache, macho types. One dance floor even spins traditional Spanish music and Spanish pop. The backroom isn't for the meek. *c/ Sepulveda 185.* ☎ *93-323-52-27. Cover 10€. Metro: Universitat. Map p 109.*

New Chaps L'EIXAMPLE   This bar is the place to find gay cowboys and bears. The downstairs darkroom is where the action is in the wee hours. *Av. Diagonal, 365.* ☎ *93-215-53-65. Metro: Diagonal. Map p 109.*

Salvation L'EIXAMPLE   A young crowd frequents this flashy dance club with two *salones,* one featuring house and DJs, the other commercial pop. *Ronda de Sant Pere, 19–21.* ☎ *93-318-06-86. Metro: Urquinaona. Map p 109.*

Lounges, Designer Cocktail Bars & Beach Hangouts

★ **CDLC (Carpe Diem Lounge Club)** WATERFRONT   This trendy place is all attitude and *gente bella* (beautiful people). If you want to see and be seen, it's appropriately swanky, and right on the edge of the beach. To chill on the luxo white beds, you'll have to pony up for a pricey bottle of whiskey. I'm partial to the outdoor terrace. Make sure you wear your best duds. *Pg. Marítim, 32.* ☎ *93-224-04-70. Metro: Vila Olímpica/Ciutadella. Map p 110.*

★ **Luz de Gas Port Vell** WATER-FRONT   A summer-only lounge bar on a boat in the marina, this sister bar of the very cool nightspot Luz de Gas is ideal in warm weather for evening cocktails. Candlelit tables and a dance floor overlook the pier. *Moll de Diposit, s/n (in front of Palau de Mar).* ☎ *93-209-77-11. Metro: Drassanes or Barceloneta. Map p 110.*

★★ **Movie Living & Food** L'EIX-AMPLE   An unusual restaurant and lounge, Movie says it's a "visual music club," and that means screens with concert videos and films, comfortable maroon sofas, and theater-style seats. It's the kind of high-tech place where a DJ doubles as a VJ. *c/ Roger de Lluria, 50.* ☎ *93-272-35-69. Metro:Passeig de Gràcia. Map p 109.*

★★ **Omm Sesion Club** L'EIXAM-PLE   Oozing with mod style, this swanky lounge in the basement of the ultra-cool Hotel Omm is a favorite of design types, models, and others with beauty and euros to spare. It's dramatically lit, with a glowing bar, and oh-so-chic, with plush club chairs and trendy house and electronica on the soundtrack. *c/ Rosselló, 265.* ☎ *93-445-40-00. Metro: Diagonal. Map p 109.*

★ **Nick Havanna** L'EIXAMPLE   Barcelona's original design bar began life in the 1980s. As other bars have caught the bug, Nick Havanna now revels in its retro glory. Its bathrooms are still conversation-worthy. *c/ Rosselló 208.* ☎ *93-217-77-32. Metro: Diagonal. Map p 109.*

Shoko WATERFRONT   A beach-side lounge bar that's also an Asian-themed restaurant, this self-conscious place draws plenty of pretty and pouty fashionable sorts who don't have a problem with the cheesy decor, an odd backdrop for the amped-up weekend *fiestas* set to house, trance, and hip-hop. *Pg. Marítim, 36.* ☎ *93-225-92-00. Metro: Vila Olímpica/Ciutadella. Map p 110.*

Wine (& *Cava*) Bars

★★ **Can Paixano** WATERFRONT   Usually jam-packed, this landmark bar with no sign out front serves the cheapest *cava* in Barcelona, as well as an interminable list of sandwiches. In the evening, the rustic standing-room-only space gets pretty crazed (and you've got to fight for a bottle of *cava,* which will only set you back about 5€). *c/ Reina Cristina 7.* ☎ *93-310-08-39. Metro: Barceloneta. Map p 110.*

Luz de Gas Port Vell is ideal for evening cocktails in summertime.

On a cava crawl? A required stop is El Xampanyet.

★★★ **El Xampanyet** LA RIBERA
A revered institution, as comfortable as an old tweed jacket, this is one place I pop into every time I'm wandering through La Ribera, for a fizzy *copa de cava* and some excellent snacks. Family-owned since the 1930s, it is as authentic as they come, with colored tiles, marble tables, an old zinc bar, and wine barrels. *c/ de la Montcada, 22.*
☎ *93-319-70-03. Closed Aug. Metro: Jaume I. Map p 111.*

★ **La Vinateria del Call** BARRI
GOTIC   A dark and romantic wine haunt, right in the midst of the ancient Jewish Quarter, this is a good, non-touristy spot to sip *vino* with locals. *c/ de Sant Domènec del Call, 9.* ☎ *93-302-60-92. Metro: Jaume I. Map p 110.*

★★ **La Vinya del Senyor**
LA RIBERA   Across from Santa María del Mar, this tiny wine bar with a gorgeous terrace draws hordes of tourists and local wine connoisseurs

for its spectacular list of Spanish wines and *cavas* and yummy selection of tapas. *Plaça Santa Maria 5.*
☎ *93-310-33-79. Metro: Barceloneta or Jaume I. Map p 110.*

★ **Va de Vi** BARRI GOTIC   This wine bar, owned by an artist and wine aficionado, inhabits a cinematic medieval house with Gothic arches. It has an extraordinary wine list, including some very coveted bottles such as L'Ermita from Priorat. *c/ Banys Vells 16.* ☎ *93-319-29-00. Metro: Jaume I. Map p 110.*

★ **Xampú Xampany** L'EIXAMPLE
Although the name may look impossible to pronounce for foreigners, this longtime *xampanyeria* (*cava* bar) is anything but intimidating. It serves up lots of excellent tapas alongside its house *cava* and wines. The tables outside are the place to be. *Gran Vía de les Corts Catalanes, 702 (corner of the Plaça de Tetuan).*
☎ *93-265-04-83. Metro: Girona. Map p 109.*

Arts & Entertainment Best Bets

Best **Concert Acoustics**
★★ L'Auditori, c/ Lepant, 150 (p 124)

Best **Jazz Club**
★★ Harlem Jazz Club, Comtessa de Sobradiel, 8 (p 126)

Best **Flamenco, Flashy Dresses & All**
★★ Tablao Flamenco Cordobés, La Rambla, 35 (p 126)

Best **Opera House**
★★★ Gran Teatre del Liceu, La Rambla, 51–59 (p 127)

Best **Summer Arts Festival**
★★ Grec, Montjuïc (p 129)

Best **Sporting Event**
★★ Fútbol Club Barcelona, Av. del Papa Joan XXIII (p 129)

Best **Theater Performances**
★★★ Teatre Mercat de Les Flors, c/ Lleida, 59 (p 130)

Best **Impression Made by a Concert Hall**
★★★ El Palau de la Música Catalana, c/ Sant Francesc de Paula 2 (p 124)

Best **All-Around Live Music Venue**
★★★ Luz de Gas, c/ Montaner 246 (p 127)

Best **Hipster Live Music Shows**
★★ Sala Razzmatazz, c/ dels Almogavers 122 (p 129)

Best **Unexpected Theater/ Music**
★ La Casa dels Músics, c/Encarnació, 25 (p 128)

Best **Hangout for Electronic Music Freaks**
Sonar, El Raval and other venues (p 129)

Best **Moviehouse for Subtitles**
★★★ Verdi, c/ Verdi, 32 (p 125)

Best **Alternative Rock Festival**
Primavera Sound, Parc del Fòrum (p 129)

Most **Unusual Venue for Live Jazz**
La Pedrera de Nit, Pg. de Gràcia, 92 (p 127)

*Previous page: A scene from a Tchaikovsky opera at Gran Teatre del Liceu.
This page: A performance at El Palau de la Mùsica Catalana.*

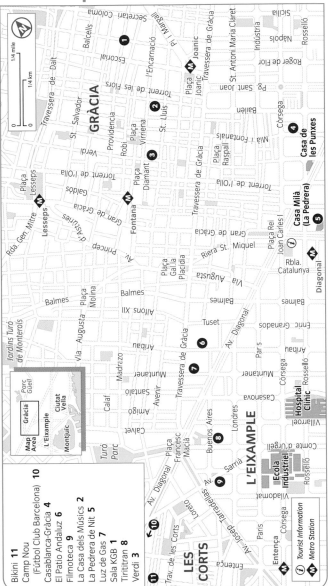

Bikini **11**
Camp Nou (Fútbol Club Barcelona) **10**
Casablanca-Gràcia **4**
El Patio Andaluz **6**
Filmoteca **9**
La Casa dels Músics **2**
La Pedrera de Nit **5**
Luz de Gas **7**
Sala KGB **1**
Tiritritran **8**
Verdi **3**

Ciutat Vella & Waterfront A & E

St. Martí
L'Eixample
Parc de la Ciutadella
Ciutat Vella
Map Area
Montjuïc

Plaça Doctor Letamendi
Aragó
Aragó

Passeig de Gràcia

Consell de Cent
Consell de Cent

L'EIXAMPLE
Girona

Diputació

Universitat de Barcelona

Gran Via Corts Catalanes
Gran Via Corts Catalanes

Plaça Universitat

Universitat

Ronda Universitat
Sepúlveda

Plaça Castella

Casa de la Caritat

Plaça Catalunya

Plaça Urquinaona

Urquinaona

Fontanella

Ronda Sant Pere

Floridablanca

Museu d'Art Contemporani de Barcelona

Elisabets

Catalunya

Santa Anna
Canuda
Comtal
Montsió

Palau de la Música Catalana

St. Pere Més Alt

LA RIBERA

St. Pere Més Baix

Pintor Fortuny

Plaça Pedro

Carme

Betlem

Palau Moja

Portaferrissa

Antic Hospital de la Sta. Creu

Mercat de la Boqueria

Av. Catedral
Plaça Antoni Maura

Av. Francesc Cambó

Mercat Santa Caterina

Plaça Allada-Vermell

EL RAVAL

St. Felip Neri

Sta. Maria del Pi

Catedral

Generalitat

BARRI GÒTIC

Plaça St. Jaume

Princesa

Bòria

Museu Picasso

Sant Pau

Gran Teatre del Liceu

Liceu

Ferran

Lleona

Jaume I

Ajuntament

St. Pau del Camp

Palau Güell

Nou de la Rambla

Arc del Teatre

CIUTAT VELLA

Plaça Traginers

Correus (Post Office)

Santa Maria del Mar

Paral.lel

Centre d'Art Sta. Monica

Palau March

La Mercè

Gignàs
Ample
Plaça Antonio López

Llotja de Mar

Plaça del Palau

Drassanes

Reials Drassanes (Museu Marítim)

Passeig de Colom

Cap de Barcelona

Barceloneta

Plaça Pau Vila

Monument à Colom

Moll de la Fusta

Moll d'Espanya

Moll de Dipòsit

Palau de Mar (Museu d'Història de Catalunya)

Plaça Drassanes
Portal de la Pau

Golondrinas

Ronda Litoral

Moll de Barcelona

Rambla da Mar

Port Vell

IMAX

Maremàgnum

L'Aquàrium de Barcelona

BARCELONETA

World Trade Center

Transbordador Aeri

Moll dels Pescadors

Moll de Balears

Moll de la Barceloneta

Plaça del Mar

Platja St. Sebastià

(i) Tourist Information
(M) Metro Station

El Palau de la Música Catalana **14**
Espai Barroc **12**
Gran Teatre del Liceu **5**
Harlem Jazz Club **10**
Icária **18**
IMAX Port Vell **11**
Jamboree **7**
Jazz Sí Club Taller de Músics **3**
L'Antic Teatre **13**

L'Auditori **15**
Los Tarantos **8**
Méliès Cinemes **2**
Renoir Floridablanca **1**
Sala Apolo **4**
Sala Razzmatazz **17**
Sidecar Factory Club **9**
Tablao Flamenco Cordobés **6**
Teatre Nacional de Catalunya **16**

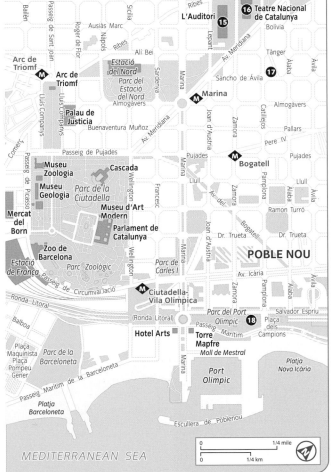

Arts & Entertainment A to Z

Classical Music & Concert Venues

★★★ El Palau de la Música Catalana LA RIBERA

This 1908 concert hall, designed by Domènech i Montaner, is a *modernista* masterpiece. Concerts are primarily classical, though the administration has sought to widen exposure to the hall by adding jazz, world, and alternative rock. For daily guided tours of the building, see p 20. A new extension called Petit Palau includes a luxury restaurant and rehearsal space. *c/ Sant Francesc de Paula 2.* ☎ *93-295-72-00. Tickets 18€–60€. www.palaumusica.org. Metro: Urquinaona. Map p 122.*

★★ L'Auditori POBLE NOU

The newest concert hall for classical music is this modern theater designed by the preeminent Spanish architect Rafael Moneo. The permanent home for the Orfeó Catala choral society and the OBC (Barcelona's Symphony Orchestra), it also plays host to renowned international musicians. Acoustics are

An orchestra plays at L'Auditori.

superb. *c/ Lepant 150.* ☎ *93-247-93-00. Tickets 15€–50€. www.auditori.org. Metro: Glòries. Map p 122.*

Film

Casablanca-Gràcia GRÀCIA

The three theaters show current and second-release mainstream and art-house films in V.O. (versión original, or original language). A sister cinema showing similar films is **Casablanca-Kaplan,** in L'Eixample. *c/ Girona, 175.* ☎ *93-459-03-26. Tickets 6€. Metro: Verdaguer. Casablanca-Kaplan: Pg. de Gràcia, 115.* ☎ *93-218-43-45. Metro: Diagonal. Map p 121.*

★★ Filmoteca L'EIXAMPLE

An art-house cinema funded by the Catalan government is a favorite of local and international *cineastes*. It shows classics and puts on festivals like "Italian Neorealism." *Cinema Aquitania, Av. Sarria 31–33.* ☎ *93-410-75-90. www.cultura.gencat.net/filmo. Tickets 2.70€. Metro: Hospital Clinic. Map p 121.*

★ Icária WATERFRONT (VILA OLÍMPICA)

This multiplex of 15 screens is in a large mall in the Port Olímpic zone. Most films are mainstream releases, although a surprising number are small independent and European movies. Online booking all the time (general admission); numbered seats on weekends only. *Salvador Espriu, 61 (Vila Olimpica).* ☎ *93-221-75-85. www.yelmocineplex.es. Tickets 6.60€. Metro: Ciutadella-Vila Olímpica. Map p 122.*

★★ IMAX Port Vell WATERFRONT

Barcelona's terrific IMAX theater shows all the latest large-format releases on three different types of projection systems (IMAX,

Flamenco dancers and a singer at El Tablao de Carmen.

OMNIMAX, 3D). *Moll de Espanya.* ☎ *93-225-11-11. Tickets 7€. Metro: Drassanes. Map p 122.*

Méliès Cinemes L'EIXAMPLE   A wide range of movies, from Spanish to foreign art, commercial, and classic films, is shown on two screens. *c/ de Villaroel, 10.* ☎ *93-451-00-51. www.cinessmelies.blogspot.com. Tickets 4€ (2.70€ Mon). Metro: Urgell. Map p 122.*

★ **Renoir Floridablanca** L'EIXAMPLE   A multitude of mainstream international releases (in their original language) show on seven screens (as many as 10 different films in a single day). A sister cinema, the **Renoir Les Corts,** has six screens with some overlap. *Floridablanca, 135.* ☎ *93-228-93-93. Tickets: 6.20€ (4.80€ Mon). www.cines renoir.com. Metro: Universitat or Sant Antoni. Renoir Les Corts: Eugenie d'Ors, 12.* ☎ *93-490-55-10. Metro: Les Corts. Map p 122.*

★★★ **Verdi** GRÀCIA   A legendary moviehouse for true film fans, and the first in Barcelona to show original-version movies, Verdi's five screens are usually devoted to the most artistic and challenging films.

A nearby annex, Verdi Park, has four additional screens. *Verdi: c/ Verdi, 32; Verdi Park, c/ Torrijos 49 (Gràcia).* ☎ *93-238-79-90. Tickets: 6.50€ (4.80€ Mon). Late shows Fri and Sat. Metro: Fontana. Map p 121.*

Flamenco

El Patio Andaluz GRÀCIA   A restaurant and flamenco stage owned by a hotel group, this congenial place puts on flamenco shows as well as *sevillanas,* which showcase traditional southern-style singing and dancing (and encourage audience participation). Shows at 8pm and 10pm; *sevillanas* at midnight. *c/ Aribau, 242.* ☎ *93-209-33-78. Metro: Gràcia. Map p 121.*

El Tablao de Carmen MONTJUÏC Within Poble Espanyol is this tourist favorite, presenting a pretty reliable flamenco show. Tues to Sun 8pm to 1am. First show 9:30pm, second 11:30pm (midnight Fri–Sat). *Poble Espanyol de Montjuïc.* ☎ *93-325-68-95. Dinner & show 55€–80€; drink & show 30€. Metro: Espanya.*

★★ **Los Tarantos** BARRI GOTIC The oldest flamenco club in

Barcelona (1963) has hosted the likes of Antonio Gades and Rosario, and respected Andalusian flamenco artists regularly make the pilgrimage here. An attractive theater space is excellent for both dance performances and music concerts. *Plaça Reial, 17.* ☎ *93-319-17-89. www. masimas.com/tarantos. Cover (includes 1 drink) 20€. Metro: Liceu. Map p 122.*

★★ Tablao Flamenco Cordobés
LA RAMBLA   Near the waterfront, this Andalusian-style club has been around since 1970. The upstairs room hosts traditional *cuadro flamenco,* performances by singers, dancers, and a guitarist. Shows, though they don't approach the passionate displays seen in the deep south, are perhaps the most authentic in Barcelona. Three shows nightly with dinner: 7, 8:30, and 10pm. *La Rambla, 35.* ☎ *93-317-57-11. www.tablaocordobes.com. Dinner & show 50€–60€; 1 drink & show 30€–35€. Metro: Drassanes. Map p 122.*

★ Tirititran L'EIXAMPLE   This *colmao flamenco*—a neighborhood restaurant-bar with live flamenco performances—near Av. La Diagonal is a good option for those uninterested in slick, costumed productions aimed primarily at tourists. Downstairs is a small stage for concerts, which are often informal. *c/ Buenos Aires, 28.* ☎ *93-410-86-77. www.tirititran.com. Metro: Urgell. Map p 121.*

Jazz & Cabaret
★ Espai Barroc LA RIBERA
This place is proudly over-the-top. Rooms in a medieval mansion, overflowing with objets d'art, busts, and Baroque-framed art, make a grand spot for a drink. But on Thursday nights, singers perform arias from opera's greatest hits. *c/ de la Montcada, 20.* ☎ *93-310-06-73. Cover varies. Metro: Jaume I. Map p 122.*

The Harlem Jazz Club.

★★ Harlem Jazz Club BARRI
GOTIC   One of Barcelona's oldest and finest jazz clubs was remodeled, but the tiny spot remains intimate and the music wide-ranging, covering bebop, blues, bossa nova, and more. *Comtessa de Sobradiel, 8.* ☎ *93-310-07-55. Admission free Mon–Thurs. 6€ Fri–Sat, 1-drink minimum. Closed Aug. Metro: Jaume I. Map p 122.*

★ Jamboree BARRI GOTIC
Tucked into Plaça Reial, this longtime standard bearer for live blues and jazz occasional draws big names (back in the day, Chet Baker and Ella Fitzgerald played here), though often the headlining acts are talented up-and-comers. Late in the evening, it gets rowdier and the space becomes a nightclub for a younger crowd, with hip-hop downstairs and world music upstairs. *Plaça Reial, 17.* ☎ *93-301-75-64. www.masimas.com/jamboree. Shows 3€–10€. Metro: Liceu. Map p 122.*

★ **Jazz Sí Club Taller de Músics** RAVAL   A free-flowing program of live music nightly is the *raison d'etre* of this intimate music school auditorium and bar. Miguel Poveda and Enrique Morente, two current stars of flamenco, have played for students, teachers, and an enthusiastic public. Every night features a different musical genre, and programs go late. *c/ Requesens, 2.* ☎ *93-329-00-20. www.tallerde musics.com. Free admission. Metro: Sant Antoni. Map p 122.*

★★ **La Pedrera de Nit** L'EIXAM-PLE   The rooftop of Gaudí's emblematic *modernista* apartment building is transformed into an extraordinary venue for cocktails and live jazz, flamenco, tango, and world music during weekend evenings in summer months. As the lights of the Eixample district flicker below, the illuminated warrior chimneys become even more surreal, an enchanted backdrop for one of the most unique live-music bars on the planet. *Pg. de Gràcia, 92 (at Provença).* ☎ *902-40-09-73 or 902-10-12-12 for advance tickets. July–Sept Fri–Sat 9–11pm. Admission (includes one drink & visit to Espai Gaudi) 10€. Metro: Diagonal or Provença. Map p 121.*

★★★ **Luz de Gas** L'EIXAMPLE For years, this glamorous turn-of-the-century music hall has reigned supreme in Barcelona for its stylish looks (chandeliers and thick red curtains) and programming of live music, which is very often Latin jazz; past artists include Charlie Haden and Danilo Pérez. Several performance areas each have their own bars. The lineup covers jazz, pop, folk, R&B, and salsa. Sala B is another space next door with a more modern, industrial look. *c/ Muntaner, 246.* ☎ *93-209-77-11. www.luzdegas.com. Cover (includes 1 drink) 20€–25€. Metro: Diagonal. Map p 121.*

Opera
★★★ **Gran Teatre del Liceu** LA RAMBLA   Barcelona's great opera house, founded in 1874, is one of the grandest theaters in the world. Though it burned in 1994, it was quickly rebuilt with donations, preserving the look and feel of the original. The Liceu has long been the

The lobby to the Gran Teatre del Liceu.

home turf of the international opera stars José Carreras and Montserrat Caballé, both from Barcelona. In addition to opera, you'll find concerts, as well as recitals and chamber music, in the smaller **El Petit Liceu.** *La Rambla, 51–59.* ☎ *93-485-99-13 or* ☎ *93-485-99-00. Tickets 20€–85€. www.liceubarcelona. com. Metro: Liceu. Map p 122.*

★ **La Casa dels Músics** GRÀCIA Claiming to be the smallest opera house in the world, this stage, in the 19th-century home of the pianist Luís de Arquer, offers a unique opportunity for music lovers. Singers in the small-scale opera productions and *bel canto* are so close that you can see them sweat. Call ahead for reservations. *c/ Encarnació, 25.* ☎ *93-284-99-20. Tickets 22€. www.lacasadelsmusics.com. Metro: Fontana. Map p 121.*

Pop & Rock

★ **Bikini** SANTS   An out-of-the-way rock club near the L'illa shopping center, this space has a great dance floor and three separate areas. It has hosted some pretty big names in pop and rock, including Thievery Corporation and Marianne Faithful. The club stays open late Wed through Sun, after shows, spinning funk and hip-hop. *c/ Déu i Mata*

105 (off Av. Diagonal), Les Corts. ☎ *93-322-08-00. Admission 12€–15€. Metro: Les Corts or Maria Cristina. Map p 121.*

★★ **Pocket Club** MONTJUÏC Part of Teatre Mercat de les Flors, this cool little club schedules infrequent performances (just two Thursdays a month), but they're the kind of shows that draw hipsters, such as Iron and Wine, Destroyer, and other indie bands. *c/ Lleida, 59 (Mercat de les Flors).* ☎ *93-285-26-26. www. pocketbcn.com. Admission 10€–25€. Metro: Espanya.*

★ **Sala Apolo** POBLE SEC   This 1940s dance hall covers the bases: on Tuesday it programs alternative cinema, Wednesday is for Latin music, Thursday it's funk night, Sunday is gay night, and on Fridays and Saturdays it becomes a dance club, Nitsa. And they fit in rock shows, too. *Nou de la Rambla 113 (Poble Sec).* ☎ *93-318-99-17. Admission varies. Metro: Poble Sec. Map p 122.*

Sala KGB GRÀCIA   Not exactly secretive, but a little out of the way, this club, a longtime hangout of young underground and garage rockers, programs independent rock, metal, and reggae bands, as well as electronic house and dance

Advance Tickets & Listings

For the latest concert, theater, and event listings, pick up a copy of the weekly *Guía del Ocio,* a guide to all entertainment in Barcelona. It's available at newsstands and written in Spanish, but it's pretty comprehensible even to non-Spanish speakers, with a small section in English at the back.

Other helpful services are **Tel-Entrada** (☎ 902-10-12-12; www. telentrada.com); **ServiCaixa** (☎ 902-33-22-11; www.servicaixa. com); and **Tick Tack Ticket** (☎ 902-15-00-25; www.ticktackticket. com [from abroad, ☎ 34/93-445-06-60]).

Barcelona Music Festivals

A summer tradition in Barcelona is **Grec** (☎ **93-301-77-75;** www. barcelonafestival.com), an annual festival of international theater, music, and dance. From the last week of June to the end of the first week in August, Grec showcases everything from blues to Brazilian bossa nova and avant-garde dance at the Teatre Grec on Montjuïc and other venues. **Primavera Sound** (www.primaverasound.com), an alternative rock festival held at the Parc del Forum in late May and early June, attracts the likes of Sonic Youth, Wilco, and Drive-By Truckers. A new 2-day festival, in both Madrid and Barcelona, is **Summercase** (www.summercase.com), also held at the Parc del Forum, in mid-July. It premiered in 2006, with New Order headlining, and the next year signed up Flaming Lips, Arcade Fire, and PJ Harvey. **Sonar** (www.sonar.es), one of the biggest electronic-music festivals in the world (held in mid-June), showcases avant-garde dance music from across Europe. But its sheer size—on multiple stages both day and night—and big-name artists like Björk and Massive Attack mean this is no marginal, niche festival. In Barcelona, it's pretty much mainstream.

music. *c/ Alegre de Dalt, 55.* ☎ *93-210-59-06. www.salakgb.net. Cover 10€. Metro: Lesseps. Map p 121.*

★ **Sala Razzmatazz** PORT OLIMPIC/POBLE NOU This sprawling, young-skewing club—with five separate music ambiences within—is also a concert venue. Its "Pop Club" hosts Spanish and international pop, alternative, hip-hop, and rock acts, such as Arctic Monkeys, LCD Soundsystem, and Tokyo Police Club. *c/ dels Almogavers 122 (at Pamplona).* ☎ *93-320-82-00. Cover varies. www.salarazzmatazz. com. Metro: Bogatell/Marina. Map p 122.*

★ **Sidecar Factory Club** BARRI GÒTIC Check out Barcelona's indigenous indie rock scene at this basement club, which occasionally scores bands with international followings, such as Portastatic. *Plaça Reial 7.* ☎ *93-302-15-86. Shows 5€–10€. Metro: Liceu. Map p 122.*

Spectator Sports

★★ Fútbol Club Barcelona

SANTS Barcelona's immensely popular football, or soccer, team—perennially one of the best in Europe—plays at Camp Nou, a 120,000-seat stadium. To see "Barça" (*bar*-sa) as the locals affectionately refer to the team, take on one of its chief rivals, such as Real Madrid, is a treat that transcends sport and approaches social anthropology. Although many games are sold out long in advance, individual tickets are frequently available. How popular is the team? The **Museu del Fútbol Club Barcelona** (Soccer Museum) is one of the most-visited museums in Spain. *Av. del Papa Joan XXIII; ticket office c/ Aristides Maillol, 12–18.* ☎ *93-496-36-00. Tickets start at 24€. www.fc barcelona.com. Museum: c/ Aristides Maillol 7–9.* ☎ *93-496-36-08. Admission 7€–11€. Metro: Maria Cristina, Palau Reial or Collblanc. Map p 121.*

Teatre Mercat de Les Flors on Montjuïc.

Theater

Institut del Teatre MONTJUÏC
A large complex of municipal theater and dance schools that contains three auditoriums. Performances range from student showcases to edgy international companies. *Plaça Margarida Xirgú, s/n.* ☎ *93-227-30-00. Tickets prices vary. www.institut delteatre.org. Metro: Espanya.*

★ **L'Antic Teatre** LA RIBERA
This small, 18th-century theater is just steps from El Palau de la Música Catalana. It programs innovative and risky performances, which are likely to be all over the cultural map: dance, theater, multimedia, circus, music, and more, from both local and touring companies. The resident company is Semolina Tomic, headed by a Croatian residing in Barcelona. Tickets are inexpensive, so it's a good place for those looking for something new. *c/ Verdaguer i Callis 12.* ☎ *93-315-23-54. Tickets 6€–10€. www.lanticteatre.com. Metro: Urquinaona. Map p 122.*

★★★ **Teatre Mercat de Les Flors** MONTJUÏC Although the structure dates to the 1929 World's Fair, this Catalan theater's first performance was *Carmen* in 1983. The theater plays host to respected companies of drama, dance, and music, and schedules occasional avant-garde art festivals. There's a restaurant overlooking the city's rooftops. *c/ Lleida 59.* ☎ *93-426-18-75. www.mercatflors.org. Ticket prices vary. Metro: Espanya.*

★★ **Teatre Nacional de Catalunya** POBLE NOU A swanky, pseudo-Roman modern theater, the work of the architect Ricardo Bofill, is home to a major Catalan company that puts on both classic and contemporary plays, including those of writers such as Tom Stoppard, Oscar Wilde, and Harold Pinter, as well as modern dance. Productions are in Catalan except in rare instances. *Plaça de les Arts 1.* ☎ *93-306-57-06. www. tnc.es. Tickets 5€–32€. Metro: Plaza de les Glòries. Map p 122.* ●

Lodging **Best Bets**

Best **Romantic Hotels**
★★★ Hotel Neri $$$ *c/ Sant Sever 5 (p 142)*

★★★ Relais d'Orsa $$$ *Mont d'Orsa, 35 (p 144)*

Best **for Would-Be Aristocrats**
★★ Hotel Palace Barcelona $$$$ *Gran Via de les Corts Catalanes, 668 (p 142)*

Best **Business Hotel**
★★★ Hotel Arts $$$$ *c/ de la Marina, 19–21 (p 139)*

Best **Backstory**
★★ Hispanos Siete Suiza $$ *c/ Sicilia 255 (p 138)*

Best **Cutting-Edge Design**
★★★ Hotel Omm $$$$ *c/ Rosselló, 265 (p 142)*

★★ Diagonal $$$ *Av. Diagonal, 205 (p 137)*

Best **In-House Museum**
★★★ Hotel Claris $$$$ *c/ Pau Claris 150 (p 140)*

Best **Service**
★★★ Prestige Paseo de Gracia $$$ *Pg. de Gràcia, 62 (p 143)*

Best **Old-City Location**
★★★ Hotel Neri $$$ *c/ Sant Sever 5 (p 142)*

Best **In-House Restaurants**
★ Hotel Condes de Barcelona $$$ *Pg. de Gràcia, 73–75 (p 140)*

★★★ Hotel Omm $$$$ *c/ Rosselló, 265 (p 142)*

Best **Gay Hotel**
★★ Hotel Axel $$$ *c/ Aribau, 33 (p 139)*

Best **Boutique Hotels**
★★★ Constanza $$ *c/ Bruc, 33 (p 137)*

Previous page: A room at the Hotel 1898.

★★★ Duquesa de Cardona $$$ *Pg. Colom, 12 (p 137)*

Best **Affordable Design**
★★ Hotel Banys Orientals $$ *c/ L'Argenteria 37 (p 139)*

Best **City Views**
★★★ Relais d'Orsa $$$ *Mont d'Orsa, 35 (p 144)*

★★★ Gran Hotel La Florida $$$$ *Carretera de Vallvidrera, 83–93 (p 138)*

Best **Sea Views**
★★★ Hotel Arts $$$$ *c/ de la Marina, 19–21 (p 139)*

Best **for Families**
★★ Hispanos Siete Suiza $$ *c/ Sicilia 255 (p 138)*

Best **Rooftop Pool**
★★ Grand Hotel Central $$$ *Via Laietana, 30 (p 138)*

Best **Step Up from a Hostel**
★★ Gat Xino $ *c/ Hospital, 155 (p 138)*

Best **Luxo Hideaway**
★★★ Relais d'Orsa $$$$ *Mont d'Orsa, 35 (p 144)*

Most **Palatial Hotel**
★★★ Gran Hotel La Florida $$$$ *Carretera de Vallvidrera, 83–93 (p 138)*

Best **Spa Pampering**
★★★ Hotel Arts $$$$ *c/ de la Marina, 19–21 (p 139)*

★★★ Gran Hotel La Florida $$$$ *Carretera de Vallvidrera, 83–93 (p 138)*

Best **Historic (Modernista) Hotel**
★★★ Hotel Casa Fuster $$$$ *Pg de Gràcia, 132 (p 140)*

Funkiest **Hipster Hotel**
★★ Casa Camper $$$ *c/ Elisabets, 11 (p 136)*

133

L'Eixample Lodging

Constanza **18**
Diagonal **10**
Duques de Bergara **14**
Fashion House B&B **19**
Gran Hotel La Florida **2**
Hispanos Siete Suiza **20**
Hostal Goya **15**
Hotel Apsis
  Atrium Palace **16**
Hotel Astoria **3**
Hotel Axel **11**
Hotel Casa Fuster **4**
Hotel Claris **8**
Hotel Condes
  de Barcelona **6**
Hotel Jazz **13**
Hotel Majestic **7**
Hotel Omm **5**
Hotel Palace Barcelona **17**
Prestige Paseo de Gracia **9**
Pulitzer **12**
Relais d'Orsa **1**

Ciutat Vella & Waterfront
Lodging

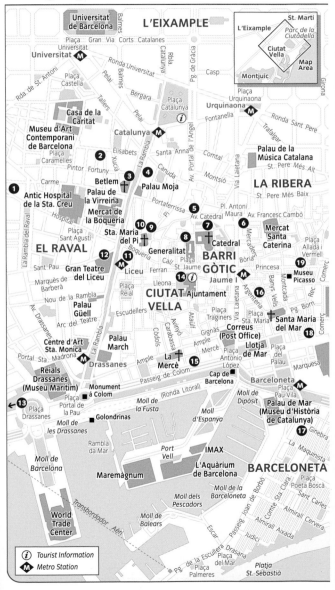

Universitat de Barcelona
L'EIXAMPLE

Plaça Gran Via Corts Catalanes
Universitat
Universitat (M)

Ronda Universitat

Rbla. Catalunya
Pg. de Gràcia
Casp

Balmes
Pelai
Bergara
Plaça Catalunya (i)

Rda. de St. Antoni
Plaça Castellà

Tallers

Casa de la Caritat

Museu d'Art Contemporani de Barcelona
Plaça Caramelles
Pintor Fortuny

Elisabets
Xuclà
La Rambla
Santa Anna
Av. Portal de l'Angel
Comtal
Montsió

Catalunya (M)

Canuda
Carme
2
Antic Hospital de la Sta. Creu
1

3 Betlem
4 Palau Moja
Palau de la Virreina
Mercat de la Boqueria
Portaferrissa
Pl. Antoni Maura

Sta. Maria del Pi **10** **9**
5
Av. Catedral
7

Hospital
Boqueria
Plaça Sant Agustí

EL RAVAL
Sant Pau
12
Gran Teatre del Liceu
Marquès de Barberà

Nou de la Rambla
Palau Güell
Arc del Teatre

Centre d'Art Sta. Monica
Portal Sta. Madrona

La Rambla del Raval

Generalitat **8**
Cardenal Casañas
Plaça Reial
11
Liceu (M)
Ferran
Lleona

6
Catedral
BARRI GÒTIC
Jaume I (M)
14 (i)

CIUTAT Ajuntament
VELLA
Plaça Traginers

Palau March
Escudellers
Còdols
Avinyó
Ataülf
Carabassa
Gignàs
Ample
Mercè
La **15** Mercè
Passeig de Colom

Plaça Antonio López

Monument à Colom
Plaça Portal de la Pau
13
Plaça Drassanes

Drassanes (M)

Reials Drassanes (Museu Marítim)

Moll de les Drassanes

Moll de Barcelona

World Trade Center

Transbordador Aeri

Rambla de Mar

Maremàgnum

Moll dels Pescadors

Moll de Balears

Palau de la Música Catalana
St. Pere Més Alt
St. Pere Més Baix
LA RIBERA

Urquinaona (M)
Fontanella
Ronda Sant Pere
Trafalgar

Via Laietana
Av. Francesc Cambó
Mercat Santa Caterina
Plaça Allada i Vermell

Allada
Montcada
Argentería
Banys Vells
Comerç
Rec

Museu Picasso **19**

Princesa
Pg. del Born
Comerç

16
Santa Maria del Mar
Plaça Sta. Maria
18

Correus (Post Office)
Llotja de Mar
Plaça del Palau
Marquesa

Moll del Dipòsit
Cap de Barcelona
Barceloneta (M)
Plaça Pau Vila

Palau de Mar (Museu d'Història de Catalunya)
17
Ginebra
La Maquinista

Moll d'Espanya
IMAX
L'Aquàrium de Barcelona
Moll de la Barceloneta

Port Vell

Pg. Joan de Borbó
Plaça Poeta Boscà
BARCELONETA

Escar
Comte Sta. Clara
Sant Carles
Almirall Cervera
Almirall Aixada

Pg. de la Escullera Drasana
Plaça del Mar
Judici

Platja St. Sebastià
Plaça Palmeres

L'Eixample
Parc de la Ciutadella
St. Marti
Ciutat Vella
Montjuïc
Map Area
Girona

(i) *Tourist Information*
(M) *Metro Station*

AC Miramar **13**
Casa Camper **2**
Ciutat Barcelona Hotel **19**
Duquesa de Cardona **15**
Gat Xino **1**
Grand Hotel Central **6**
H10 Racó Del Pi **9**
Hotel Arts **20**
Hotel Banys Orientals **16**
Hotel Barcelona Catedral **5**
Hotel Barcino **14**

Hotel Colón **7**
Hotel 1898 **3**
Hotel España **12**
Hotel Neri **8**
Jardí **10**
Marina Folch **17**
Montecarlo **4**
Park Hotel **18**
Petit Palace Opera
   Garden Ramblas **11**
Vincci Marítimo Hotel **21**

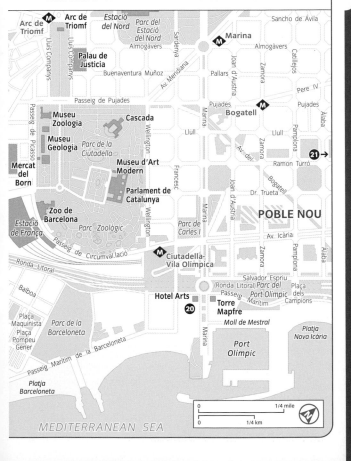

Barrios Altos Lodging

Map Area — Gràcia — Ciutat Vella

1 Gran Hotel La Florida
2 Relais d'Orsa

PARC DE COLLSEROLA

VALLVIDRERA SUPERIOR

Vallvidrera Superior

TIBIDABO

Sagrat Cor

Torre de Collserola

Tibidabo

Parc d'Atraccions

Carretera de les Aigües

2

VALLVIDRERA INFERIOR

Peu Funicular

Ctra. de les Aigües

Parc de l'Oreneta

Plaça Boràs

Ronda de Dalt

CosmoCaixa (Museu de la Ciència)

SARRIÀ-ST. GERVASI

Plaça Funicular

Barcelona **Lodging A to Z**

★ kids **AC Miramar** MONTJUÏC Tucked into the hillside, next to the Montjuïc Park gardens and with majestic views over the city and the Mediterranean, this 1920s palace was restored and converted into a hotel in 2006. A modern new addition, which is either brilliant or disastrous, depending on your taste, envelops the original mansion. The result is a chic mix of period details and modern decor. Gardens and indoor and outdoor pools make this a relaxing option. *Plaça Carlos Ibáñez, 3.* ☎ *902-29-22-95 or 93-281-16-00. www.ac-hoteles.com. 75 units. 195€–385€. AE, DC, MC, V.*

Metro: Paral.lel or Drassanes. Map p 134.

★★ **Casa Camper** RAVAL If you're a fan of funky Camper shoes, this idiosyncratic, design-trippy place, where all rooms have sitting rooms, is probably for you. The hotel's aesthetics are as playful as the company's shoe stores, though it's a little pricey for the transitional neighborhood and the young, design-obsessed crowd it courts. *c/ Elisabets, 11.* ☎ *93-295-79-00. www.camper.com/web/en/casa camper.asp. 25 units. Doubles 210€–245€. AE, DC, MC, V. Metro: Catalunya or Liceu. Map p 134.*

A room at Duqesa de Cardona.

★ **Ciutat Barcelona Hotel** LA RIBERA   A bargain hotel that offers a lot of cool design and comfort for a bargain price, this new addition to the hip neighborhood, just steps from the Picasso Museum, is a winner. Rooms are crisply contemporary and clean, and there's a nice little rooftop pool and deck. *c/ de la Princesa, 35.* ☎ *93-269-74-75. www.ciutatbarcelona.com. 78 units. Doubles 100€–120€. AE, DC, MC, V. Metro: Arc de Triomf or Jaume I. Map p 134.*

★★★ **Constanza** L'EIXAMPLE   Travelers looking for affordable Barcelona style will be pleased with this small boutique hotel. Although rooms aren't large, they are modern and comfortable, and the hotel's very well located, within walking distance of Plaça de Catalunya. A room with its own private terrace is a real bargain. *c/ Bruc, 33.* ☎ *93-270-19-10. www.hotelconstanza. com. 20 units. Doubles 120€. AE, MC, V. Metro: Urquinaona. Map p 133.*

★★ **Diagonal** L'EIXAMPLE/GRACIA   Upping the ante of cutting-edge architecture is this massive 2004 Silken hotel. Mod and flashy, it may look playful, but the hotel is dead serious about hip design. Next to Torre Agbar, some rooms have straight-shot views of La Sagrada Família. *Av. Diagonal, 205.* ☎ *93-489-53-00. www.hoteles-silken.com.*

240 units. Doubles 210€–240€. AE, DC, MC, V. Metro: Catalunya or Liceu. Map p 133.

★★★ **Duquesa de Cardona**   WATERFRONT   A sedate boutique hotel across the street from the marina, this restored 19th-century palace is elegant and intimate. It also has something unique: a large rooftop solarium terrace with a pool and great views of the port. *Pg. Colom, 12.* ☎ *866/376-7831 or 93-268-90-90. www.hduquesade cardona.com. 44 units. Doubles 185€–285€. AE, DC, MC, V. Metro: Jaume I or Drassanes. Map p 134.*

★ **Duques de Bergara** L'EIXAMPLE   An 1898 *modernista* townhouse that retains many original details, this is an elegant, traditionally styled Eixample hotel with comfortable rooms and spacious marble bathrooms. *c/ Bergara 11.* ☎ *93-301-51-51. www.hoteles-catalonia.es. 149 units. Doubles 180€–250€. AE, DC, MC, V. Metro: Catalunya. Map p 133.*

Quirky touches can be found throughout Casa Camper.

★ kids Fashion House B&B

L'EIXAMPLE One of very few bed-and-breakfasts in Barcelona, this comfortable spot, in a nicely restored 19th-century town house with a leafy communal terrace, is a good-value, homey place to stay. Each pair of bedrooms shares one bathroom. Families should check out the suite, a self-catering apartment. *c/ Bruc, 13.* ☎ *93-790-40-44. www.bcn-fashionhouse.com. 35 units. Doubles 70€–95€, including breakfast. MC, V. Metro: Urquinaona. Map p 133.*

★★ kids Gat Xino RAVAL

Just because you don't want to spend a lot of money doesn't mean you don't want some style. A major step up from hostels, this groovy place is popular with hipsters, design sorts, young families, and travelers with more style than cash. Rooms are spare, with a bright green, white, and black aesthetic, and there's a cool rooftop terrace. A sister hotel, Gat Raval (c/ Joaquín Costa, 4; ☎ 93-481-66-70), in the same 'hood, is similar in style, but cheaper and a tad plainer (not all have en-suite bathrooms). *c/ Hospital, 149-155.* ☎ *93-324-88-33. www.gataccommodation.com. 35 units. Doubles 84€–90€ including breakfast. MC, V. Metro: Liceu. Map p 134.*

★★ Grand Hotel Central LA RIBERA

In a palatial 1926 mansion owned by an old Catalan family, this new property has been beautifully converted to a contemporary luxury hotel. Rooms are warmly decorated in rich crèmes and chocolates. Use of the rooftop infinity pool, surrounded by wood decking and views of the Gothic Quarter and the sea, is a privilege. *Vía Laietana, 30.* ☎ *93-295-79-00. www.grandhotel central.com. 147 units. Doubles 185€–275 €. AE, DC, MC, V. Metro: Arc de Triomf or Jaume I. Map p 134.*

★★★ Gran Hotel La Florida MT. TIBIDABO/ENVIRONS

High above Barcelona, this palatial hotel is a magnificent refuge if pampering, luxury, and relaxation are your primary concerns. While the views across Barcelona to the sea are astounding, the hotel's not convenient if you're set on seeing and doing lots of things. Yet the hotel, originally from the 1920s, certainly earns the *gran* (great) in its name, with plush, soothing designer rooms, spa, and infinity pool. *Carretera Vallvidrera (al Tibidabo), 83–93 (7km/4.3 miles from Barcelona).* ☎ *93-259-30-00. www.hotellaflorida.com. 74 units. Doubles 320€–610€. AE, DC, MC, V. Map p 133.*

★★ kids Hispanos Siete Suiza

L'EIXAMPLE An aparthotel with the comforts of a top-flight hotel, the Suiza is perfect for families and long-term stays. Apartments in the historic house are two-bedroom, two-bath, with living room and kitchen. Incredibly, the in-house restaurant is overseen by a famed Catalan chef, Carles Gaig. But best of all, some of the hotel's profits go toward a cancer foundation established by the original owner of the house. *c/ Sicilia 255.* ☎ *93-208-20-51. www.hispanos7suiza.com. 19 units. Doubles (2-BR apt) 140€–195€, including breakfast. AE, DC, MC, V. Metro: Sagrada Família. Map p 133.*

★ Hostal Goya L'EIXAMPLE

A refreshingly smart, centrally located *hostal* and very good value, this small inn is clean and friendly. The best and quietest rooms are in the recently renovated Principal wing; others are small and dark. Most who stay here are young people in Barcelona to have a good time. *c/ Pau Claris, 74.* ☎ *93-302-25-65. www.hostalgoya.com. 19 units. Doubles 60€–80€. MC, V. Metro:*

Urquinaona or Catalunya. Map
p 133.

**★★ kids Hotel Apsis Atrium
Palace** L'EIXAMPLE   A modern
design hotel for the masses, this
congenial midsize hotel emphasizes
a high-tech angle, including Wi-Fi
and business facilities, and its
indoor swimming pool with wood
decking. Bedrooms are large and
well appointed, making this a good
value. *Gran Via de les Corts Catalanes, 656.* ☎ *93-342-80-00. www.
hotel-atriumpalace.com. 71 units.
Doubles 120€–190€. AE, DC, MC, V.
Metro: Passeig de Gràcia or
Catalunya. Map p 133.*

★★★ Hotel Arts WATERFRONT
One of only three skyscrapers in
Barcelona, this sleek, high-tech luxury hotel is on the beach and enjoys
sweeping beach views. Service is
personable and efficient, as you'd
expect from a Ritz-Carlton property,
making this a favorite of business
travelers and celebs. The outdoor
pool, swanky new spa overlooking
the marina, and restaurant by star
chef Sergi Arola only add to the
allure. *c/ de la Marina, 19–21.*
☎ *800/241-3333 or 93-221-10-00.*

*The Hotel Arts offers spectacular water
views.*

*www.ritzcarlton.com/hotels/
barcelona. 482 units. Doubles
350€–800€. AE, DC, MC, V. Metro:
Ciutadella–Vila Olímpica. Map p 134.*

★ kids Hotel Astoria L'EIXAMPLE
A renovated 1950s hotel with enduring style, this winning member of
the Derby chain (which owns the
Claris) is elegant but relaxed. One
of the best hotels in Barcelona, its
warmly decorated accommodations
and new rooftop pool and sauna
make it a very good value. At the
upper end of L'Eixample, you'll have
to walk a few blocks to restaurants
and attractions near Pg. de Gràcia.
c/ París, 203. ☎ *93-209-83-11. www.
derbyhotels.es. 115 units. Doubles
140€–195€. AE, DC, MC, V. Metro:
Diagonal. Map p 133.*

★★ Hotel Axel L'EIXAMPLE   Fill-
ing a niche in Barcelona is this midsize hotel serving an international
gay population. It's confident
enough to call the surrounding
neighborhood the "Gayxample" and
decorate rooms with erotic art (but
it's also "heterofriendly"). Rooms are
stylish, with top-quality bedding,
and the hip cocktail bar, rooftop
pool, and sundeck are prized. *c/
Aribau, 33.* ☎ *93-323-93-93. www.
hotelaxel.com. 66 units. Doubles
137€–226€. AE, DC, MC, V. Metro:
Universitat. Map p 133.*

★★ Hotel Banys Orientals LA
RIBERA   A pioneer leading the way
for stylish but inexpensive boutique
hotels, this cool place is immensely
popular, as much for its bargain
rates and hip style as its terrific location near El Born. Rooms are small
but chic, though noise-sensitive
guests should seek one at the back;
the area is full of late-night revelers.
c/ L'Argenteria, 37. ☎ *93-268-84-60.
www.hotelbanysorientals.com. 43
units. Doubles 100€. AE, DC, MC, V.
Metro: Jaume I. Map p 134.*

The Banys Orientals.

★ **kids Hotel Barcelona Catedral** BARRI GOTIC   One of Barcelona's newest hotels is in the oldest part of town, right across from the Cathedral. It's stylishly modern but affordably priced. Unexpected bonuses are the pool, terrace, and wireless Internet access, as well as cooking lessons, wine tastings, and guided tours around the old city. *c/ Capellans, 4.* ☎ *93-304-22-55. 80 units. Doubles 120€–160€. AE, DC, MC, V. Metro: Jaume 1. Map p 134.*

★ **Hotel Barcino** BARRI GOTIC   In a central Ciutat Vella location, just paces from Plaça Jaume I and the halls of government, this well-maintained, mid-size hotel is pleasant. It's an especially good choice if you score a room with a private terrace and views over the rooftops and the cathedral. *Plaça Jaume I, 6.* ☎ *93-302-20-12. www.hotelbarcino.com. 53 units. Doubles 225€. AE, DC, MC, V. Metro: Jaume I or Catalunya. Map p 134.*

★★★ **Hotel Casa Fuster** GRÀCIA   Converted into a luxury hotel in 2004, Casa Fuster, which occupies one of the city's more significant *modernista* buildings, has made a splash. No expenses were spared, giving it a feel of period indulgence with every modern amenity, including pool, restaurant, bar, lounges, and business center. *Pg de Gràcia,* 132. ☎ *902-20-23-45 or 93-255-30-00. www.hotelcasafuster.com. 105 units. Doubles 380€–475€. AE, DC, MC, V. Metro: Diagonal. Map p 133.*

★★★ **Hotel Claris** L'EIXAMPLE   Long one of my favorite hotels in Barcelona, where modern design commingles with a landmark 19th-century palace facade and a for-guests-only museum of Egyptian art. Rooms, many of which are split-level and even two-story, are a mix of cool chic and warm sophistication. On the top-floor terrace is a small pool and lovely views of the surrounding Eixample neighborhood. *c/ Pau Claris 150.* ☎ *90-099-00-11 or 93-487-62-62. www.derby hotels.com. 120 units. Doubles 300€–395€. AE, DC, MC, V. Metro: Passeig de Gràcia. Map p 133.*

Hotel Colón BARRI GOTIC   With an enviable location opposite the cathedral, this mainstay is conservatively decorated and even old-fashioned. But some sixth-floor rooms have small terraces and dramatic views. Of course, rooms at the back of the building are quieter. *Av. de la Catedral, 7.* ☎ *800/845-0636 or 93-301-14-04. www.hotelcolon.es. 145 units. Doubles 250€. AE, DC, MC, V. Metro: Jaume I. Map p 134.*

★ **Hotel Condes de Barcelona** L'EIXAMPLE   With a prestigious corner location on Passeig de Gràcia, this late 19th-century mansion is elegant and sophisticated, though an annex across the street doesn't have quite the same style. The recent arrival of one of the Basque Country's most celebrated chefs, Martín Berasategui, and his restaurant, Lasarte, have given the hotel a new verve. *Pg de Gràcia, 73–75.* ☎ *93-488-22-00. www.condesde barcelona.com. 183 units. Doubles 175€–350€. AE, DC, MC, V. Metro: Passeig de Gràcia. Map p 133.*

★★ **Hotel 1898** LA RAMBLA
This large hotel, opened in 2002, occupies a late-19th-century building that was once the Philippine Tobacco Co. headquarters. It has been strikingly converted, with bold artwork, stripes, and colors; most spectacular is the underground pool beneath brick arches. *La Rambla, 109 (entrance on Pintor Fortuny).* ☎ *93-552-95-52. www.nnhotels.es. 169 units. Doubles 165€–370€. AE, DC, MC, V. Metro: Catalunya or Liceu. Map p 134.*

Hotel España RAVAL   Off the lower part of La Rambla, this classic old hotel is known primarily for its foyer and dining room, the work of the preeminent *modernista* architect Domènech i Montaner. Guest rooms are comparatively bland, but clean; the neighborhood, though, continues to be transitional and may give some guests pause, especially at night. *c/ Sant Pau 11.*

☎ *93-318-17-58. www.hotelespanya. com. 60 units. Doubles 100€ including breakfast. AE, DC, MC, V. Metro: Liceu or Drassanes. Map p 134.*

★ **Hotel Jazz** L'EIXAMPLE
Around the corner from La Rambla, Hotel Jazz aims, by name and middle-of-the-road contemporary design, for a wide international clientele (many of whom appear to be young people on group junkets). The impressive lobby has plenty of glass and bleached wood floors; soundproofed rooms are attractive if a bit generic. But the star of the show is the rooftop pool and wood-deck terrace. *c/ Pelai, 3.* ☎ *93-552-96-96, 0870-120-1521 (U.K.), or 207/ 580-2663 (U.S.). www.nnhotels.es. 180 units. Doubles 140€–195€. AE, DC, MC, V. Metro: Catalunya or Universitat. Map p 133.*

★ **Hotel Majestic** L'EIXAMPLE
With a great location on Passeig de Gràcia, the Majestic is one of the city's most visible hotels, and though it has large rooms, decorated in bright colors and patterns, it's also popular with tour groups and can seem a bit impersonal. It has one of the most acclaimed, but obscenely expensive, hotel restaurants, Drolma. *Pg de Gràcia, 68.* ☎ *93-488-17-17. www.hotel majestic.es. 303 units. Doubles 200€–375€. AE, DC, MC, V. Metro: Passeig de Gràcia. Map p 133.*

The underground pool at the Hotel 1898.

The Hotel Neri is well-located on the delightful Plaça Felip Neri.

★★★ **Hotel Neri** BARRI GOTIC   A

sumptuous Gothic palace discretely tucked away on charming Plaça Felip Neri, this small, upscale hotel is romance incarnate, all velvet drapes and soft-lit rooms. Rooms are luxurious, with fine linens, and the restaurant and cafe on the square are unexpected bonuses. A true find in the Old City, it's the kind of place you won't want to leave. *c/ Sant Sever 5.* ☎ *93-304-06-55. www.hotelneri.com. 22 units. Doubles 180€–225€. AE, DC, MC, V. Metro: Jaume I. Map p 134.*

★★★ **Hotel Omm** L'EIXAMPLE

The hotel with the most buzz in Barcelona is this sleek temple of hip, Zen-like design and an even cooler clientele. Its restaurant, Moo (p 104), is one of the city's best. Design freaks will be in heaven; the place

was created for them. The rooftop lap pool and deck have views of La Pedrera. *c/ Rosselló, 265.* ☎ *93-445-40-00. www.hotelomm.es. 59 units. Doubles 320€–375€. AE, DC, MC, V. Metro: Diagonal. Map p 133.*

★★ **Hotel Palace Barcelona**

L'EIXAMPLE   Though this 1919 Art-Deco hotel has changed names, many still refer to it as the Ritz, and the grace and old-money elegance remain. It's white-glove treatment all the way here; public rooms are grand and aristocratic, guest rooms are large and formal. The restaurant Caelis, with a new chef, is getting a lot of attention. *Gran Via de les Corts Catalanes, 668.* ☎ *93-318-52-00. www.hotelpalacebarcelona. com. 122 units. Doubles 400€–585€. AE, DC, MC, V. Metro: Passeig de Gràcia. Map p 133.*

★ **H10 Racó Del Pi** BARRI GOTIC

A member of a small, Barcelona-based hotel chain, this attractive, small hotel is intimate and perfectly located, in a historic building on one of the most atmospheric streets in the Gothic Quarter. Rooms aren't huge, but they do feature a clean, stylish aesthetic. *Plaça del Pi, 7.* ☎ *93-342-61-90.*

The hip lobby of Hotel Omm.

www.hotelracodelpi.com. 37 units.
Doubles 195€. AE, DC, MC, V. Metro:
Jaume I or Liceu. Map p 134.

Jardí BARRI GOTIC   Simple and
easygoing, this small hotel has an
extraordinary location, overlooking
two of the prettiest plazas in the
heart of Ciutat Vella. Rooms are
somewhat austere, with bright lighting, but five have private terraces.
Plaça Sant Josep Oriol, 1. ☎ 93-301-
59-00. hoteljardi@retemail.es. 40
units. Doubles 80€–100€. MC, V.
Metro: Liceu. Map p 134.

kids Marina Folch WATERFRONT
If you're looking for beachside
accommodations without busting
your budget, this small and friendly
guesthouse in Barceloneta is a good
bet. Rooms—some of which have
balconies and port views—are no-
nonsense but clean and comfortable, worth every euro. c/ Mar 16.
☎ 93-310-37-09. 10 units. Doubles
50€–65€. AE, DC, MC, V. Metro:
Barceloneta. Map p 134.

★ Montecarlo LA RAMBLA   This
opulent 19th-century building has
been a hotel since 1945. It con-
serves period details, including
carved wood doors, a baronial
fireplace, and crystal chandeliers.
Midsize guest rooms are smartly
decorated in a traditional style.
La Rambla 124. ☎ 93-412-04-04.
www.montecarlobcn.com. 55 units.
Doubles 160€–340€. AE, DC, MC, V.
Metro: Catalunya. Map p 134.

Park Hotel LA RIBERA   This
reserved hotel at the edge of El
Born is an interesting example of
mid-century architecture, notable
for its spiral staircase and lobby's
mosaic-tiled bar. Rooms are small
and very understated. Av. Marquès
de l'Argentera 11. ☎ 93-319-60-00.
www.parkhotelbarcelona.com. 91
units. Doubles 110€–190€. AE, DC,
MC, V. Metro: Barceloneta or Jaume I.
Map p 134.

The luxurious lobby at the Hotel Palace
Barcelona.

**★ Petit Palace Opera Garden
Ramblas** LA RAMBLA   One of
Barcelona's newest hotels is this
member of a successful, value-
priced Spanish chain. It's near, but
not on, La Rambla, and just seconds
from La Boquería food market.
Rooms have laptop computers
with free Wi-Fi connections. c/ La
Boqueria 10. ☎ 93-302-00-92. www.
hthoteles.com. 69 units. Doubles
95€–200€. Metro: Liceu. Map p 134.

**★★★ Prestige Paseo de Gra-
cia** L'EIXAMPLE   This exquisite
boutique hotel has a prestigious
address but inside is all Zen cool.
Rooms are minimalist—some even
have their own quiet bamboo garden terraces. Services and amenities are impeccable, from the hip
"Zeroom" lounge to the "Ask Me"
friendly service staff. Pg de Gràcia,
62. ☎ 93-272-41-80. www.prestige
paseodegracia.com. 45 units. Doubles 210€–270€. AE, DC, MC, V.
Metro: Diagonal or Passeig de Gràcia. Map p 133.

★★ Pulitzer L'EIXAMPLE   Sleek
and trendy, but affordable for a
hotel of its design and amenities,

The staff is top-notch at the Prestige Paseo de Gracia.

this relative newcomer to the scene is understandably popular. With a stylish cocktail bar and alluring candle-lit rooftop terrace, the hotel is bound to win a design prize or two. *c/ Bergara, 8.* ☎ *93-481-67-67. www.hotelpulitzer.es. 91 units. Doubles 150€–225€. AE, DC, MC, V. Metro: Catalunya. Map p 133.*

★★★ **Relais d'Orsa** MT. TIBID-ABO/ENVIRONS   This tiny, gorgeous inn, occupying a restored 1900 seigniorial palace, overlooks the whole of Barcelona. Romantic and seemingly ripped from the pages of design magazines, the hotel is a place where guests happily sacrifice convenience for luxury and tranquility. The two front rooms have small terraces and unparalleled views. *Mont d'Orsa, 35.* ☎ *93-406-94-11. 6 units. Doubles 220€. AE, DC, MC, V. Metro: FGC train, Vallvidrera. Map p 133.*

★ **Vincci Maritimo Hotel** WATERFRONT (POBLE NOU)   In a newly developing waterfront district near Mar Bella beach, this forward-looking hotel pushes the envelope of sleek design, with miles of glass, warm wood, and brushed steel. Perfect if you're mostly interested in hanging out at less-populated beaches. *c/ Llull 340.* ☎ *902-45-45-85 or 93-356-26-00. www.vincci hoteles.com. 144 units. Doubles 140€–190€. AE, DC, MC, V. Metro: Poble Nou. Map p 134.* ●

Montserrat

1. Aeri de Montserrat
2. La Moreneta
3. Escolanía
4. Museu de Montserrat
5. Funiculars

A **very popular half-day trip,** this spectacularly jagged peak (the "saw-tooth mountain"), 50km (31 miles) northwest of Barcelona, is home to a Benedictine monastery and La Moreneta (the Black Madonna), the patron saint of Catalonia. A sacred place of pilgrimage, Montserrat is overrun on the holy days April 27 and September 8.

1 ★★ Aeri de Montserrat.
The most scenic way to Montserrat is by cable car. The FGC train leaves from Barcelona and connects to it both ways. *Cable car tickets 8€ roundtrip; 5€ one-way.*

2 ★ La Moreneta. The Bene-dictine monastery, tucked into the 1,219m (4,000-ft.) ridges of Montserrat, holds a shrine to the famous Black Madonna icon, which according to legend was discovered

Previous page: Montserrat Monastery.

The Montserrat monastery nestled into the mountain.

in the 12th century (and said to have been carved by St. Luke in 50 A.D.).

❸ ★★ Escolanía. One of the oldest boys' choirs in Europe (dating to the 14th century) performs Monday to Friday at 1pm and Monday to Thursday at 6:45pm. On Sundays and holidays, you can hear them during noon mass and again at 6:45pm.

❹ Museu de Montserrat. The museum next door to the Basilica contains minor paintings by such artists as Caravaggio, Degas, Monet, and El Greco, as well as an early Picasso and Dalí. *Plaça de Santa María, s/n.* ☎ *93-877-77-77. Admission 6.50€. Mon–Fri 10am–6:45pm.*

❺ ★ Funiculars. A funicular climbs to the peak of **Sant Joan,** where there's a small hermitage and panoramic views, but the only way up to the **Sant Jeroni** hermitage and summit beyond that is by foot (about a 45-minute walk). A separate funicular goes to **Santa Cova,**

The cable car to Montserrat.

a 17th-century chapel built in the shape of a cross, where La Moreneta was allegedly discovered. *Combined funicular ticket 7.30€ round-trip; included in Tot Montserrat and TransMontserrat tickets.*

Practical Matters: Montserrat

The **Tot Montserrat** ticket (35€) includes trains, entry into the Montserrat museum, funiculars, and lunch at the Montserrat restaurant; the **TransMontserrat** ticket (21€), is for the train and funiculars only. Trains depart from Barcelona's Plaça d'Espanya station (☎ 93-205-15-15; www.fgc.net; Metro: Espanya). By car, take the A-2 out of Barcelona toward Tarragona and Martorell, or the Barcelona–Terrassa highway via the Túneles de Vallvidrera. The **Tourist Information Office** is on Plaça de la Creu, s/n; ☎ 93-877-77-77.

Sitges

1. Museu Cau Ferrat
2. Museu Maricel del Mar
3. Cafe-Bar Roy
4. Beaches
   - Aiguadolç
   - Sant Sebastià
   - La Fragata
   - La Ribera
5. Sitges nightlife:
   carrer St. Bonaventura

(i) Information
✉ Post Office

An excellent day or overnight trip is to the beach town of Sitges, 35km (22 miles) southwest of Barcelona along the Costa Daurada (Golden Coast). Long a cultural and intellectual center, Sitges was a favorite of the painters Santiago Rusiñol and Salvador Dalí, as well as the poet Federico García Lorca. This is no quiet beach town, though; it's one of Spain's most prominent gay resorts.

1 ★★ **Museu Cau Ferrat.** The former home of Rusiñol is packed to the rafters with *modernista*-period paintings, artworks by El Greco, Ramón Casas, Ignacio Zuloaga, and others; ceramics and wrought iron; and a collection of the artist's personal effects. The house served as a bohemian refuge from the end of the 19th century until Rusiñol's death in 1931. The edifice of the home is worth the visit alone. *c/ del Fonollar, s/n.* ☎ *93-894-03-64.*

Admission 3€. Tues–Sun 10am–2pm and 5–9pm.

2 ★ **Museu Maricel del Mar.** This early 20th-century mansion, the one-time residence of the painter Ramon Casas and the American Charles Deering, houses a collection of Gothic and Romantic artworks, as well as modern Catalan sculpture, ceramics, and drawings. *c / del Fonollar, s/n.* ☎ *93-894-03-64. Admission 3€. Daily 10am–1pm and 4–6pm.*

The hall at Cau Ferrat.

3 **Cafe-Bar Roy.** A good stop for a coffee or a glass of *cava* and snacks, this classic, old-fashioned coffee house has marble tables, hand-painted tiles and Art Nouveau touches (and, shockingly, free Wi-Fi). *c/ de les Parellades, 9. ☎ 938-11-00-52. $.*

4 ★★ **Beaches.** Sitges's biggest draw is its 17 beaches. Those in the town center and along the eastern end are the most laid-back. The most popular are **Aiguadolç** and **Balmins. Sant Sebastià** and **La Fragata** are known as family beaches, something that would probably not be said for those to the west. A young crowd heads to **La Ribera,** and farthest west are the beaches, such as **Platges del Mort,** that are the haunts of the least inhibited beachgoers, including nudists and large groups of gays.

5 ★ **Nightlife.** In the town center, **Carrer Sant Bonaventura,** a 5-minute walk from the beach, teems with gay party spots. **Mediterráneo,** c/ Sant Bonaventura, 6 (no phone), is the largest gay disco. One of Spain's most flamboyant parties is **Carnaval** in Sitges, celebrated the week before Lent.

Practical Matters: Sitges

Trains (40 minutes; ☎ 902-24-02-02; www.renfe.es) make frequent departures from Barcelona's Sants station. By car, take C-246 or toll highway A-7 (40 km/25 miles south of Barcelona; allow 45 minutes to an hour). The **Tourist Information Office** (☎ 93-894-42-51; www.sitgestour.com) is at c/ Sinia Morera, 1. A combined ticket to all Sitges museums is available for 6.40€, 3.50€ students.

Lodging: Hotel Romàntic de Sitges, c/ de Sant Isidre 33 (☎ 93-894-83-75; www.hotelromantic.com; doubles 85€–95€), is composed of three art-filled 19th-century town houses and is a short walk from the beach; **El Xalet,** Isla de Cuba, 33–35 (☎ 93-811-00-70), is a fairly priced *modernista* house with original furnishings in the center of town and within walking distance of the beach.

Dining: Good restaurants on Paseo de la Ribera include **El Velero de Sitges,** at No. 38 (☎ 93-894-20-51), and **Mare Nostrum**, at No. 60 (☎ 93-894-33-93).

Girona

0 100 yds
0 100 m

ⓘ Information
✉ Post Office

Pont de Sant Feliu
St. Feliu
Plaça Sant Feliu
Catedral
Museu d'Art
Jardins dels Alemanys
Plaça Catedral
Plaça Llendoners
Museu d'Història
Força
EL CALL ❶
Plaça de Sant Domènec
Sant Domènec
Pont d'en Gomèz
Ballesteries
Jardins Maristes
Sant Martí Sacosta
Berenguer Carnicer
Passeig
Real de Font Clara
Canalejas
Plaça de la Independencia
Pont de Sant Agustí
B. Carreras P.
BARRI VELL
Portal Nou
Argenteria
Fontana d'Or
Plaça Mercaders
Llebre
Torre dels Socors
Santa Clara
Pont de Ferro
Ciutadans
Llibertat
Plaça del Vi
Andorra France
Girona CATALUNYA
BARCELONA
MEDITERRANEAN SEA
Sèquia Obra
Riu Onyar
ⓘ
Aragón
Pont de Pedra
❽

❶ El Call
❷ Banys Àrabs
❸ Catedral
❹ Roman walls
❺ Museu d'Art
❻ Monestir de St. Pere de Galligants (city archaeology museum)
❼ Cases de l'Onyar/ Pont de Ferro
❽ Museu del Cinema

An hour north of Barcelona is Girona, one of Spain's most historic cities. Its pristine old quarter is among the most beautiful in Spain. Built on an old Roman settlement and steeped in the layered histories of the Romans, Moors, and Jews, the town center is a compact jumble of narrow stone streets, dark alleyways, and the medieval arches of El Call—the ancient Jewish neighborhood. Bustling by day, the cobblestone streets of the old quarter turn quiet as night falls. Though one of Spain's wealthiest cities, Girona has a reputation as a provincial and emphatically Catalan city.

❶ ★★★ **El Call.** Girona was home to a prosperous Jewish community for more than 6 centuries, until its members were expelled in 1492. The Jewish district ("El Call" in Catalan) is a tangle of narrow, dark, atmospheric streets tucked within the Old Quarter and said to be the best-preserved ghetto in Western Europe. Carrer de la Força is the principal street, where buildings date from the 13th to 15th centuries. The **Museu d'Historia dels Jueus** is a well-designed history center that documents the Jewish population of Girona; the last known synagogue in the city, built in the 15th century, is part of the center. *c/ de la Força, 8.* ☎ *972-21-67-61. www.ajuntament.gi/call. Admission*

A street in Girona's El Call neighborhood.

to museum: 2€ adults, 1.50€ students and seniors. May–Oct Mon–Sat 10am–8pm, Sun 10am–3pm, Nov–Apr Mon–Sat 10am–6pm and Sun 10am–3pm.

❷ ★ Banys Àrabs. The 12th-century Arab baths are one of the few reminders of Girona's Moorish community. Restored in the 1920s, the Romanesque baths are among the best preserved in Spain. *c/ Ferran el Católic, s/n.* ☎ *972-21-32-62. www.banysarabs.org. Admission 1.60€ adults, .80€ seniors and students. Apr–Sept Mon–Sat 10am–7pm and Sun 10am–2pm, Oct–Mar daily 10am–2pm.*

Banys Àrabs.

❸ ★ Catedral. Steep Baroque stairs climb to Girona's imposing cathedral overlooking the city. The cloister and tower are the only surviving elements of the original, early-11th-century Romanesque building. The single nave is the widest Gothic nave in the world (and the second-widest of any style, after St. Peter's in the Vatican). In the treasury is a magnificent collection of religious art. Perhaps the most important piece is the 11th– or 12th–century *Tapestry of the Creation,* an embroidered depiction of humans and animals in the Garden of Eden. *Plaça de la Catedral.* ☎ *972-21-44-26. Admission (cloister and museum) 3.50€. Oct–Feb Tues–Sat 10am–2pm and 4–6pm, Mar–June Tues–Sat 10am–2pm and 4–7pm, July–Sept Tues–Sat 10am–8pm.*

❹ ★ Roman Walls. For great views of the old town, walk along a 5km (3.1-mile) portion of the original Roman wall, which dates to the first century A.D. Afterward, don't miss the pretty, serene gardens tucked behind the cathedral and just below the city wall: Jardines de la Francesa (French Woman's Gardens) and Jardines de los Alemanes (German Gardens).

❺ ★★ Museu d'Art. Girona's Art Museum, in a former Episcopal

The Tapestry of the Creation *in the Girona cathedral.*

palace, covers almost 1,000 years of history and art. It features excellent Catalan Romanesque and Gothic paintings, as well as a significant collection of contemporary art. Among the highlights is a 15th-century altarpiece, Sant Miquel de Cruïlles, one of the finest works of Catalan Gothic art anywhere. The museum also boasts its altarstone of Sant Pere de Roda, from the 10th and 11th centuries; this work in wood and stone, depicting figures and legends, was once embossed in silver. *Pujada de la Catedral, 12.* ☎ *972-20-38-34. www.museuart. com. Admission 2€ adults, 1.50€ students and seniors, free for children under 16. Mar–Sept Tues–Sat 10am–7pm, Oct–Feb Tues–Sat 10am–6pm and Sun 10am–2pm.*

⑥ **Monestir de Sant Pere de Galligants.** This 12th-century, Catalan Gothic Benedictine monastery houses the city archaeology museum, with several items culled from the Roman ruins at nearby Empúries. *Plaça de Santa Llúcia, s/n.* ☎ *972-20-26-32. Admission 2€. Tues–Sat 10:30am–1:30pm and 4–7pm, Sun 10am–2pm.*

⑦ **Lola Cafe.** On the most atmospheric street in the old Jewish Quarter, this hip, dark cafe frequently features live music on weekend nights. *c/ de la Força, 7.* ☎ *972-22-88-24. $.*

⑧ ★ **Cases de l'Onyar.** The picturesque, multi-colored houses (*cases*) along the Onyar River shimmer in the water's reflection, with drying laundry fluttering in the

Houses on the Onyar River.

breeze. Many of the houses date to the Middle Ages, when they were outside the original walls of the Old City. Leading to the modern city is the **Pont de Ferro,** an iron bridge built by the Eiffel Company in 1877, 12 years before the Eiffel Tower.

➒ ★ Museu del Cinema.
Spain's only cinema museum is the extensive private collection of one man, Tomàs Mallol. The museum houses his collection of some 25,000

cinema artifacts, including photo-graphs, posters, engravings, and drawings, as well as the original cam-era of the Luimière brothers. There are numerous interactive exhibits and a library with film-related publica-tions. *c/ Sèquia, 1.* ☎ *972-41-27-77. www.museudelcinema.org. Admission 4€ adults, 2€ students and seniors. May–Sept Tues–Sun 10am–8pm, Oct–Apr Tues–Fri 10am–6pm, Sat 10am–8pm and Sun 11am–3pm.*

Practical Matters: Girona

By car from Barcelona, take the ronda (beltway) in the direction of France and then the A-7 to Girona; the trip is 97km (60 miles). Fre-quent (90-minute) trains leave from Barcelona's Estació Sants and arrive at Girona's Plaça Espanya (☎ 902-24-02-02; www.renfe.es). The main **Oficina de Turisme** is on the pedestrian-only main drag, Rambla de la Llibertat, 1 (☎ 972-22-65-75).

   Lodging: Bellmirall is a small, charming guest house in the heart of the Old Quarter, in a restored 14th-century stone mansion (c/ Bellmirall,3; ☎ 972-20-40-09; www.grn.es/bellmirall; doubles 60€–70€; no credit cards; closed Jan–Feb). **Hotel Citutat de Girona** (c/ Nord 2; ☎ 972-48-30-38; www.hotel-ciutatdegirona.com; dou-bles 116€–143€) is a modern and hip midsize hotel at the edge of the Old Quarter.

   Dining: Blanc ($$), connected to the Hotel Ciutat de Girona, is a stylish and excellent-value restaurant that serves Catalan and Mediterranean specialties (c/ Nord, 2; ☎ 972-41-56-37). El **Celler de Can Roca** ($$$$) is one of the top upscale restaurants in Catalonia, if not in all of Spain—by itself it may be worth a trip to Girona (Car-retera de Taialá, 40 [direction of Les Planes, northeast of the Old Quarter]; ☎ 972-22-21-57).

L'Empordà & Costa Brava

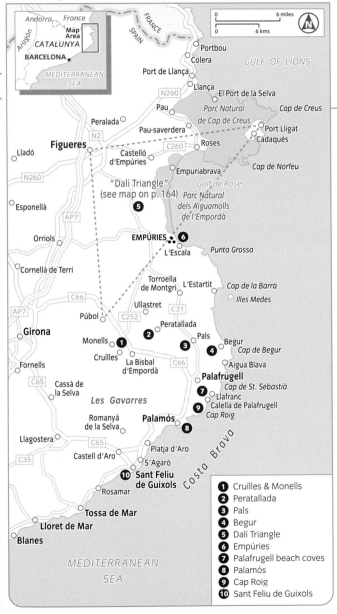

Andorra France
Aragon CATALUNYA
Map Area
BARCELONA
MEDITERRANEAN SEA

0   6 miles
0   6 kms

FRANCE
SPAIN

Portbou
Colera
Port de Llança
Llança
El Port de la Selva
Pau
Peralada
Pau-saverdera
Figueres
Castelló d'Empúries
Roses
Empuriabrava

GULF OF LIONS

Parc Natural de Cap de Creus
Cap de Creus
Port Lligat
Cadaqués
Cap de Norfeu

Golf de Roses

Lladó
Esponellà
Orriols
Cornellà de Terri

"Dalí Triangle" (see map on p. 164)
❺

Parc Natural dels Aiguamolls de l'Empordà

EMPÚRIES ❻
L'Escala

Punta Grossa

Torroella de Montgrí
L'Estartit
Cap de la Barra
Illes Medes

Ullastret
Púbol
Peratallada
Pals
Begur
Cap de Begur
Aigua Blava

Girona
Monells ❶
Cruïlles
La Bisbal d'Empordà
❷
❸
❹

Fornells
Cassà de la Selva

Les Gavarres

Romanyà de la Selva
Palamós

Palafrugell
❼ Cap de St. Sebastià
Llafranc
Calella de Palafrugell
❾
Cap Roig
❽

Llagostera
Castell d'Aro
Platja d'Aro
S'Agaró
❿ Sant Feliu de Guixols
Rosamar

Tossa de Mar
Lloret de Mar
Blanes

Costa Brava

MEDITERRANEAN SEA

❶ Cruïlles & Monells
❷ Peratallada
❸ Pals
❹ Begur
❺ Dalí Triangle
❻ Empúries
❼ Palafrugell beach coves
❽ Palamós
❾ Cap Roig
❿ Sant Feliu de Guixols

L'Empordà, the plains and rolling green hills surrounding Girona, is Spain's Tuscany. Inland from the coast are small and mostly unassuming medieval villages with ancient stone houses, many of which have been converted into weekend and summer homes by affluent Barcelonans. The Costa Brava, the "untamed coast," is a stretch of rocky coves and sandy beaches, with deep cobalt blue Mediterranean waters and whitewashed fishing villages. The natural beauty of the coastline's southern end, nearest Barcelona, has been greatly marred by sand-and-sun mass-market tourism.

❶ ★ Cruïlles & Monells. These two quiet villages are attractive enclaves of medieval stonework. Monells's main claim to fame is a magnificent porticoed main square, while at the center of Cruïlles, once enclosed by walls, is a Romanesque 11th-century monastery.

❷ ★★ Peratallada. Less slick than Pals (see below), this picturesque town grew up around an unusual castle. You'll also find a 14th-century palace, a porticoed main square, and houses rich with Gothic details, several of which house inns and antique shops.

❸ ★★ Pals. Almost too pretty and perfect, this medieval town rising above the plains is hugely popular with tourists. Pals's alleyways and stone walls look as though they might be part of a movie set.

❹ ★ Begur. This attractive hilltop town is topped by the ruins of a 13th-century castle, with commanding 360-degree views of the whole of L'Empordà and the Costa Brava, all the way up the coast to Cadaqués. Many houses below are colonial in style, built by returning locals who set out for Cuba in the early 19th century. On the outskirts of Begur are excellent beaches, including Aiguablava, Sa Riera, and Sa Tuna.

❺ ★★★ Dalí Triangle. The Empordà region is marked by the trail of Spain's famous oddball, the surrealist painter Salvador Dalí, who hailed from northern Catalonia and lived much of his life on the Costa Brava. Three points, including a museum and two curious homes, form the Dalí Triangle. Together they are a must-see for anyone with an appreciation for Dalí and the absurd.

Pals, a picturesque town.

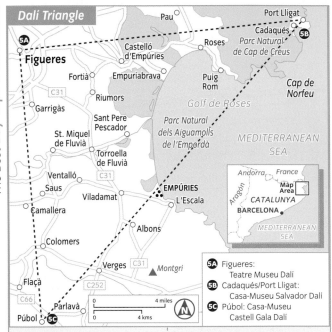

Dalí Triangle

Pau
Port Lligat
Cadaqués **5B**
Figueres **5A**
Castelló d'Empúries
Roses
Parc Natural de Cap de Creus
Fortià
Empuriabrava
Puig Rom
Cap de Norfeu
Riumors
Golf de Roses
Garrigàs
C31
Sant Pere Pescador
MEDITERRANEAN SEA
St. Miquel de Fluvià
Parc Natural dels Aiguamolls de l'Empordà
Torroella de Fluvià
C31
Ventalló
Andorra France
Saus
Viladamat
EMPÚRIES
Map Area
CATALUNYA
Aragón
Camallera
L'Escala
BARCELONA
MEDITERRANEAN SEA
Colomers
Albons
Verges C31
Montgri
Flaçà
C252
C66
Parlavà
0   4 miles
0   4 kms
Púbol **5C**

5A Figueres:
Teatre Museu Dalí
5B Cadaqués/Port Lligat:
Casa-Museu Salvador Dalí
5C Púbol: Casa-Museu
Castell Gala Dalí

5A ★★★ Figueres: Teatre Museu Dalí. Dalí's Museum-Theater, which he designed as his legacy in his birthplace of Figueres, is part theater, part amusement park—fittingly idiosyncratic and witty. The red building is topped by giant white eggs and decorated with glazed ceramic loaves of bread; inside are a salon with furniture re-creating Mae West's face and a long black Cadillac with sprinklers inside. Dalí is buried in a crypt here. *Plaça de Gala-Salvador Dalí, 5.* ☎ *972-67-75-00. www.salvador-dali.org.*

5B ★★ Cadaqués/Port Lligat: Casa-Museu Salvador Dalí. Next to the seaside village of Cadaqués, Dalí built his first home with Gala, his eccentric Russian-born

wife. They cobbled together several fishers' residences and decorated them in Daliesque fashion: with stuffed swans, a lip sofa, and Dalí-designed chimneys. ☎ *972-25-10-15. www.salvador-dali.org.*

5C ★ Púbol: Casa-Museu Castell Gala Dalí. Dalí bought a medieval castle in an isolated L'Empordà village for his beloved princess in the late 1960s, but Gala allowed Dalí to visit only when she invited him. Even into her late 60s, she entertained a coterie of much younger men here. There are odd Daliesque touches throughout, though the castle is less nutty than the other two points in the Triangle. ☎ *972-48-86-55. www. salvador-dali.org.*

The bizarre meets the absurd at the Dalí Museum in Figueres.

6 ★★ **Empúries.** The extensive ruins of a Greco-Roman city, one of the most fascinating archaeological finds in Spain, are on view at the **Museu d'Empúries.** Three different civilizations settled on the coast here between the 7th and 3rd centuries B.C. Empúries is the only place in Spain with incarnations as a Greek village, an Iberian settlement, and a Roman town. ☎ *972-77-02-08. www.mac.es. Admission 2.50€ adults, 2€ seniors and students 16–18, children under 16 free.*

June–Sept daily 10am–8pm, Oct–May daily 10am–6pm.

7 ★★ **Palafrugell Beach coves.** Several of the most beautiful coves and sandy beach spots along the Costa Brava are near Palafrugell. Calella de Palafrugell, Llafranc, and Tamariu are gentle, protected spots with good swimming and walking paths through pine-forested hills.

8 **Palamós.** The tensions of a Costa Brava town caught between tradition and modern development

Calella de Palafrugell.

focused on tourism are apparent in this old fishing village.

9 ★ Cap Roig. On a clifftop peninsula is a magnificent estate that once belonged to a Russian army general and is now home to beautiful Mediterranean botanical gardens (Jardí Botànic) with extraordinary views of the coast. In summer months, the **Festival Jardins de Cap Roig** features live jazz, rock, flamenco, world music, theater, and opera (including big names like Bob Dylan). ☎ *972-61-45-82. www.caproig.cat. The gardens are open daily, April–Sept 9am–8pm and Oct–Mar 9am–6pm. On concert days (July–Aug), they close at 2pm. Free admission.*

10 Sant Feliu de Guixols. The beginning of the "good" Costa Brava after miles of overdevelopment, this easygoing town has a 10th-century church and chapel, Sant Martí, high on a hill overlooking the coastline. ●

Practical Matters: L'Empordà & Costa Brava

Car is by far the best way to travel around the region. Figueres is 150km (93 miles) north of Barcelona on A-7 and 50km (31 miles) north of Girona. To get to Cadaqués, take C-260 from Figueres and then a long, twisting, maddening road (GI-614). Púbol is 40km (25 miles) south of Figueres along highway C-252 or 16km (10 miles) east of Girona along C-255. From Girona, **trains** go to the Costa Brava towns of Llança, Blanes, and Colera, as well as Figueres.

Lodging & Dining: El Far Hotel Restaurant is a cliff-top property formed by a 17th-century hermitage and a 15th-century lighthouse. The views of the bay and Mediterranean are astounding (Platja de Llafranc, near Palafrugell; ☎ 972-30-16-39; www.elfar.net; doubles 175€–300€). In L'Empordà, near the coast, is **Castell de'Empordà,** a 700-year-old castle converted to a luxurious small hotel. It's 3km (2 miles) from La Bisbal (☎ 972-64-62-54; www. castelldemporda.com; doubles 95€–235€; closed: Nov–Mar). **La Plaça de Madremanya,** in a small Catalan village halfway between Girona and the coast, is a gorgeous country hotel, with one of the region's finest restaurants (c/ Sant Esteve 17, Madremanya; ☎ 972-49-04-87; www.laplacamadremanya.com; doubles 99€–155€).

The **Savvy Traveler**

Before You Go

Government Tourist Offices

In the U.S.: 666 Fifth Ave., Fifth Floor, New York, NY 10103 (☎ 212/265-8822); 8383 Wilshire Blvd., Suite 956, Beverly Hills, CA 90211 (☎ 323/658-7188); 845 N. Michigan Ave., Suite 915E, Chicago, IL 60611 (☎ 312/642-1992); and 1221 Brickell Ave., Suite 1850, Miami, FL 33131 (☎ 305/358-1992). **In Canada:** 102 Bloor St. W., Suite 3402, Toronto, Ontario M5S 1M9, Canada (☎ 416/961-3131). **In the U.K.:** 22–23 Manchester Sq., London W1M 5AP (☎ 020/7486-8077).

The Best Times to Go

March to May and **September to late October** are the best times to visit Barcelona, with fewer crowds than in summer. Weather-wise, however, almost any time of year is the right time to go. Barcelona is not nearly as dreadfully hot in summer as Madrid and the south. In **August,** much of the city shuts down as its citizens head for the beaches. August is the major vacation month in Europe, and traffic from England, France, the Netherlands, and Germany to Spain becomes a stampede. **November** to **February** can be pleasantly temperate, crowds are nonexistent, and prices drop for hotels and airfares. But some coastal resorts, especially on the Costa Brava, shut down during this slow season. The **Christmas** season in Barcelona, beginning in early **December** and extending through the first week of **January,** is especially festive.

Barcelona is officially Spain's most popular destination, and tourism is now year-round; it is also a major international trade fair and conference destination throughout the

year, so mid- to high-range hotels should be booked well in advance.

Festivals & Special Events

SPRING. One of the high points is **Semana Santa (Holy Week).** On Palm Sunday, palm leaves are blessed in La Sagrada Família, while in the city cathedral's cloister, the curious *L'ou com balla*—a hollowed-out egg shell—is placed on top of a fountain to bob around and "dance." **La Diada de St. Jordi,** on April 23, is the colorful celebration of Saint George (St. Jordi in Catalan), the patron saint of Catalonia; the tradition is for men to give a single red rose to the significant women in their lives (mother, girlfriend, sister, etc.), and for women to give a book in return (though many forward-thinking men now also give women books). Rose-sellers are everywhere, and bookshops set up open-air stalls along Passeig de Gràcia. May 1 is **May Day,** or Labor Day, and the streets are full of marching trade-union members. During **Corpus Christi,** which falls in either May or June, the streets of Sitges are carpeted in flowers.

SUMMER. During the **Verbena de Sant Juan** (June 23), Catalonia celebrates the Twelfth Night with fireworks ablaze in streets and squares, bonfires lit along the beach, and liters of *cava* consumed. It's traditional to have the first dip of the year in the sea at dawn (officially the first day of summer). **El Grec,** at the beginning of July, is a culture festival that brings marquee names in all genres of music and theater to perform in various open-air venues. **Festa Major de Gràcia** (early–mid-August) is a week-long *festa* held in the Gràcia neighborhood, which is elaborately decorated; by day, long tables are set up for communal lunches and board games, and at night, thousands invade the narrow streets for outdoor concerts and revelry.

FALL. La Diada de Catalunya (September 11), the National Day of Catalonia, is the most politically and historically significant holiday in the region, celebrating the region's autonomy and the date the city was besieged by Spanish and French troops in 1714 during the War of Succession. Demonstrations calling for independence are everywhere, and the *senyera,* the flag of Catalonia, is hung from balconies. **La Mercè** (September 24) honors Our Lady of Mercy, the city's patron saint (who according to legend rid Barcelona of a plague of locusts). Free concerts are held in squares, and folkloric figures such as the *gigants* (giants) and *cap grosses* (fat heads) take to the streets. People come out to perform the *sardana* (traditional Catalan dance) and to watch the forming of *castellers* (human towers). Firework displays light up the night, and the hair-raising *correfoc,* a parade of firework-brandishing "devils" and dragons, is the grand finale. One of the best times to be in Barcelona, especially for children.

WINTER. All Saints' Day (November 1), a public holiday, is reverently celebrated: relatives and friends lay flowers on the graves (or *nichos*—in Spain, people are often buried one on top of another in tiny compartments) of the dead. The night before, some of the bars in the city hold Halloween parties. The weeks leading to **Nadal,** or Christmas, are marked by *Fira de Santa Llucia,* a huge open-air market near the cathedral selling handicrafts, Christmas decorations, trees, and figurines (including *caganers;* see p 62) for their *pessebres* (nativity dioramas). A life-size nativity is constructed in Plaça Sant Jaume. **Día de los Reyes** (Three Kings Day), January 6, remains the traditional Catholic celebration of Christmas gift-giving (even though Santa Claus has made inroads and many families now exchange gifts on Dec. 25). The evening prior public celebrations take place in cities and towns across Spain; in Barcelona, three costumed Magi arrive by boat at the port to dispense candy to children. **Carnaval** (just prior to Lent) in Barcelona is low-key, with dressing up only by groups of children or stall owners in the local markets. Not so in Sitges, the seaside town south of Barcelona, where locals, especially the gay community, go all out with hedonistic costumes, parades, and other forms of revelry.

The Weather

Barcelona is blessed with a Mediterranean climate, and spring and fall are unfailingly pleasant, with sunny skies and moderate temperatures. Even in the winter, days are crisp but not exceedingly cold and often sunny. Snow is rare and never lasts more than a day or two. Most rainfall occurs in April. July and August are hot and humid, even at night, as the temperature often only drops minimally. The surrounding sea is warm enough to swim in from the end of June to early October. Inland, the temperatures drop slightly, as does the humidity. North on the Costa Brava, a strong wind known as the *tramontana* often blows.

Cellphones *(Móviles)*

World phones—or GSM (Global System for Mobiles)—work in Spain (and most of the world). If your cellphone is on a GSM system, and you have a world-capable multiband phone, you can make and receive calls from Spain. Just call your wireless operator and ask for "international roaming" to be activated. You can also rent a GSM phone. The French-owned store **FNAC** (main

Useful Websites

- **www.okspain.org:** Tourist Office of Spain official U.S. site; it has detailed "Before You Go" information (including U.S. air departures).
- **www.tourspain.es:** Turespaña's Web site, with helpful primers on leisure travel, adventure travel, or business travel, as well as a feature of Spanish news from around the world.
- **www.spaininfo.com:** Loads of practical tips on driving, destinations, bringing in pets, and even learning Spanish.
- **www.renfe.es:** The official site of Spanish rail, for routes, schedules, and booking.
- **www.barcelonaturisme.com:** The city's official tourism site, with excellent information in English as well as Catalan and Spanish.
- **www.barcelona.com:** For one-stop tour, hotel, and activity booking.
- **www.cbrava.es:** Information about Costa Brava, the city of Girona, and other parts of Catalonia, including L'Empordà.

branch at Plaça Catalunya, 4; metro: Catalunya; ☎ 93-344-18-00; www.fnac.es) provides a pay-as-you-go mobile phone package, which actually works out to be cheaper than renting if you're staying just a few weeks or less. North Americans can rent a GSM phone before leaving home from **InTouch USA** (☎ 800/872-7626; www.intouchglobal.com) or **RoadPost** (☎ 888/290-1606 or 905/272-5665; www.roadpost.com).

Car Rentals

Driving in Barcelona isn't advised, especially with the preponderance of inexpensive taxis and metro services. A car is pretty much indispensable, however, for exploring L'Empordà and Costa Brava. North America's biggest car-rental companies, including Avis, Budget, and Hertz, maintain offices in Barcelona and Catalonia, including at El Prat airport and the Girona rail station. **Avis** (☎ 800/331-1212; www.avis.com), **Hertz** (☎ 800/654-3131; www.hertz.com), and **Budget** (☎ 800/472-3325; www.budget.com) have offices at Sants railway station and other spots in Barcelona. Two other agencies of note include **Kemwel Holiday Auto** (☎ 877/820-0668; www.kemwel.com) and **Auto Europe** (☎ 800/223-5555; www.autoeurope.com).

Getting **There**

By Plane

From Barcelona's **El Prat** airport (13km/8m from the city center), there are several ways to get into town. One is the **Aerobús** (3.60€), which leaves from just outside all three terminals every 15 minutes from 6am to midnight and stops at

Plaça Espanya, Gran Vía de les Corts Catalanes, Plaça Universitat, and Plaça de Catalunya (taking about 40 minutes to reach the last stop). Another is by half-hourly **rail service** (2.75€) that departs between 6:15am and 11:15pm from El Prat to Estació Sants (25 minutes), which has connections with the Metro. The third is by **taxi** (about 25€) from ranks outside all terminals.

Travelers arriving from within the European Union on budget airlines such as Ryanair may land at **Girona** airport (103km/64miles northeast of Barcelona) or **Reus** (110 km/68 miles west of the city). **Barcelona Bus** (☎ 93-232-04-59) travels to Barcelona from the airport in Girona (12€; 70 min.) and Reus (11€; 90 min.). The train from either city is cheaper, but you'd have to catch a bus to either town's rail station. A taxi to Barcelona from Girona or Reus will cost as much as 120€ or more.

By Car
Highway **A-7** leads to Barcelona from France and northern Catalonia (Costa Brava and Girona). The **A-2** leads to Barcelona from Madrid, Zaragoza, and Bilbao. From Valencia or the Costa del Sol, take the **E-15** north. Close to the city, look for one of two signs into downtown Barcelona: *Centre Ciutat* takes you downtown into the Eixample district, while *Ronda Litoral* is a beltway that takes you quickly to the port area.

By Train
Most national (RENFE; www.renfe. es) and international trains arrive at **Estació Sants,** Plaça dels Països Catalans, s/n (☎ 93-495-62-15; Metro: Sants).

Getting **Around**

By Metro
The **Metro** (☎ **010** or 93-298-70-00; www.tmb.net) is Barcelona's excellent, modern, and clean subway. Its five lines are by far the fastest and easiest way to navigate the city. Red diamond symbols mark stations. Single-ticket fares (*senzill,* or *sencillo*) are 1.20€, although you can get a T1 pass (good for 10 trips) for 6.65€. You can also get free rides on all public transport with purchase of the Barcelona Card discount pass (www.barcelonacard. com). The Metro runs Mon to Thurs 5am to 11pm; Fri and Sat 5am to 2am; and Sun 6am to midnight.

The Metro shares some terminals with **FGC Trains** (☎ 93-205-15-15), run by the provincial government (they cost the same as the Metro, and you can use the same Metro multitrip tickets) and connecting the city center to upper neighborhoods, including Sarrià, Vallvidrera, Tibidabo, and Gràcia. The only problem you may encounter is when you need to switch between an FGC train and a regular Metro train: You have to exit the first and reenter the second, paying separately for each line.

By Taxi
Black-and-yellow taxis are plentiful and reasonably priced; few journeys cost more than 7€. You can either hail a cab in the street (the green light on the roof means it's available) or grab one where they're lined up (usually outside hotels). Fares begin at 1.30€ (1.40€ at night). Reliable taxi companies include **Servi Taxi** (☎ 93-330-03-00) and **Barna Taxi** (☎ 93-357-77-55).

By Bus

Buses are plentiful, but much less convenient than the Metro. Most bus routes stop at the Plaça de Catalunya. Routes are clearly marked on each stop, as are timetables—but most buses stop running well before the Metro closes. The **Nitbus** (☎ 010 or 93-223-51-51; change made; no passes), which runs from 11pm to 4am and is often the only alternative to the dearth of taxis in the wee hours, is bright yellow and clearly marked with an N; most leave from Plaça Catalunya. Travel Cards and other TMB passes are not valid on Nitbuses. Tickets (1.20€) are bought directly from the driver.

By Car

Trying to negotiate Barcelona's unfamiliar, traffic-clogged streets can be nerve-racking, and parking is an expensive nightmare. However, a car is useful if you plan to head out on daytrips to Sitges, Montserrat, or the Penedès wine country, or to travel to the Costa Brava or L'Empordà. See p 162 for a list of rental car companies.

On Foot

Strolling in Barcelona is a pastime and art, and the compact city is ideal for walking, especially along La Rambla, Passeig de Gràcia, and in the labyrinthine Barri Gòtic.

Fast **Facts**

APARTMENT RENTALS Among the options are **La Casa de les Lletres** (☎ 93-226-37-30; www.cru2001.com); **www.visit-bcn.com**, which offers everything from Barri Gòtic town houses to loft-style apartments; and **www.friendlyrentals.com**, offering stylish properties at a surprisingly good value.

ATMS/CASHPOINTS Maestro, Cirrus, and Visa cards are readily accepted at all ATMs. Exchange currency either at banks or *casas de cambio* (exchange houses). You can also find currency exchange offices at the Sants rail station and El Prat airport. Spanish banks include La Caixa, Caixa de Catalunya, BBV, and Central Hispano. Branches of these are located near Plaça Catalunya. Most banks offer 24-hour ATMs. Currency-exchange houses include BCN World and BCN Change & Transfer.

BUSINESS HOURS Banks are open Monday through Friday from 8:30am to 2pm. Most offices are open Monday through Friday from 9am to 6 or 7pm. (In July, 8am–3pm.) In August, businesses are on skeleton staff if not closed altogether. At restaurants, lunch is usually from 1:30 or 2 to 4pm and dinner from 9 to 11:30pm or midnight. Major stores are open Monday through Saturday from 9:30 or 10am to 8pm; staff at smaller establishments, however, often still close for siesta in the mid-afternoon, doing business from 9:30am to 2pm and 4:30pm to 8 or 8:30pm.

CONSULATES & EMBASSIES **U.S. Consulate,** Pg. Reina Elisenda, 23, in Sarrià (☎ 93-280-22-27); **Canadian Consulate,** c/ Elisenda Pinós 10 (☎ 93-204-27-00); **U.K. Consulate,** Av. Diagonal, 477 (☎ 93-419-90-44); **Australian Consulate,** Gran Vía Carles III, 98 (☎ 93-490-90-13); **New Zealand Consulate,** Travessera de Gràcia, 64 (☎ 93-209-03-99).

DOCTORS Dial ☎ 061 to find a doctor.

ELECTRICITY Most hotels operate on 220 volts AC (50 cycles). Some older places have 110 or 125 volts AC.

EMERGENCIES For an ambulance or medical emergencies, dial ☎ 061; for fire ☎ 080. For other emergencies, call ☎ 112.

GAY & LESBIAN TRAVELERS In 1978, Spain legalized homosexuality among consenting adults, and in 1995, Spain banned discrimination based on sexual orientation. Marriage between same-sex couples became legal in 2005. Catalonia has helped paved the way in rights for gay couples, pre-empting national laws by granting same-sex couples the same official status and conjugal rights as heterosexual ones. Barcelona is one of the major centers of gay life in Spain, and Sitges, one of Europe's most popular resorts for gay travelers, is just south of Barcelona. The website www.gayinspain.com has very complete and destination-specific listings for gay travelers.

HOLIDAYS Holidays observed include January 1 (New Year's Day), January 6 (Feast of the Epiphany), March/April (Good Friday and Easter Monday), May 1 (May Day), May/June (Whit Monday), June 24 (Feast of St. John), August 15 (Feast of the Assumption), September 11 (National Day of Catalonia), September 24 (Feast of Our Lady of Mercy), October 12 (Spain's National Day), November 1 (All Saints' Day), December 8 (Feast of the Immaculate Conception), December 25 (Christmas) and December 26 (Feast of St. Stephen).

INSURANCE Check your existing insurance policies before you buy travel insurance to cover trip cancellation, lost luggage, medical expenses, or car rental insurance. For more information, contact one of the following recommended insurers: **Access America** (☎ 866/807-3982; www.accessamerica.com); **Travel Guard International** (☎ 800/826-4919; www.travelguard.com); **Travel Insured International** (☎ 800/243-3174; www.travelinsured.com); and **Travelex Insurance Services** (☎ 888/457-4602; www.travelex-insurance.com). For travel overseas, most U.S. health plans (including Medicare and Medicaid) do not provide coverage, and the ones that do often require payment for services upfront. If you require additional medical insurance, try **MEDEX Assistance** (☎ 410/453-6300; www.medexassist.com) or **Travel Assistance International** (☎ 800/821-2828; www.travelassistance.com; for general information on services, call the company's Worldwide Assistance Services, Inc., at ☎ 800/777-8710).

INTERNET Internet access is plentiful, both in cybercafes (*cafés Internet*) and frequently in hotels, several of which now offer Wi-Fi. The **Internet Gallery Cafe** is down the street from the Picasso Museum, Barra de Ferro 3 (☎ 93-268-15-07). To find cybercafes in Barcelona, check **www.cybercaptive.com** and **www.cybercafe.com**.

LOST PROPERTY Call credit card companies the minute you discover your wallet has been lost or stolen and file a report at the nearest police precinct. Your credit card company or insurer may require a police report number or record. **Visa's** U.S. emergency number is ☎ 800/847-2911, or 90-099-11-24 in Spain. **American Express** cardholders and traveler's check holders should call ☎ 800/221-7282 in the U.S., or 90-237-56-37 in Spain. **MasterCard** holders should call ☎ 800/307-7309 in the U.S., or 90-097-12-31 in Spain.

MAIL & POSTAGE Spanish post offices are called *correos* (koh-*ray*-os), identified by yellow-and-white signs with a crown and the words *Correos y Telégrafos*. Main offices are generally open from 9am to 8pm Mon through Fri and Sat 9am to 7pm. The Central Post Office is at Plaça de Antoni López, s/n, at the end of Vía Laietana (☎ 902-19-71-97). Other branches are at Aragó, 282; and Ronda Universitat; 23.

MONEY The single European currency in Spain is the **euro**. At press time, the exchange rate was approximately 1 € = $1.33 (or .68£). For up-to-the minute exchange rates between the euro and the dollar, check the currency converter website **www.xe.com/ucc**.

PASSPORTS No visas are required for U.S. or Canadian visitors to Spain providing your stay does not exceed 90 days. Australian visitors do need a visa. If your passport is lost or stolen, contact your country's embassy or consulate immediately. (See "Consulates & Embassies," p 164.) Make a copy of your passport's critical pages and keep it separate from your passport.

PHARMACIES Pharmacies *(farmàcies)* operate during normal business hours and one in every district remains open all night and on holidays. The location and phone number of this *farmàcia de guàrdia* is posted on the door of all the other pharmacies. A very central pharmacy open 24/7 is **Farmàcia Álvarez,** Pg. de Gràcia, 26 (☎ 93-302-11-24). You can also call ☎ 010 or ☎ 93-481-00-60 to contact all-night pharmacies.

POLICE The national police emergency number is ☎ 091. For local police, call ☎ 092.

SAFETY Violent crime in Barcelona is a rarity, but criminals frequent tourist areas and major attractions such as museums, restaurants, hotels, beach resorts, trains, train stations, airports, subways, and ATMs. Exercise care around major tourist sights, especially La Rambla (in particular, the section closest to the waterfront); Barri Gòtic; Raval neighborhood; and La Sagrada Família. You shouldn't walk alone at night in either the Gothic Quarter or the Raval district. **Turisme Atenció** (Tourist Attention Service), La Rambla, 43 (☎ 93-256-24-30), has English-speaking attendants who can aid crime victims in reporting losses and obtaining new documents. The office is open 24/7.

SMOKING A new law banning smoking in public places, including on public transportation and in offices, hospitals, and some bars and restaurants, was enacted in early 2006. Nonsmoking sections in restaurants remain relatively rare, but expect this to change as Spaniards adapt to the new reality. If you feel strongly about avoiding second-hand smoke, ask establishments if they have a *no fumadores* (nonsmoking) section.

TAXES The value-added (VAT) tax (known in Spain as *IVA*) ranges from 7% to 33%, depending on the commodity being sold. Food, wine, and basic necessities are taxed at 7%; most goods and services (including car rentals) at 13%; luxury items (jewelry, all tobacco, imported liquors) at 33%; and hotels at 7%. Non EU residents are entitled to a reimbursement of the 16% IVA tax on most purchases worth more than 90€ made at shops offering "Tax Free" or "Global Refund" shopping. Forms, obtained from the store where you made your purchase, must be stamped at Customs upon departure. For more information see **www.globalrefund.com**.

TELEPHONES For national telephone information, dial ☎ 1003. For international telephone information, call ☎ 025. You can make international calls from booths identified with the word *Internacional*.

To make an international call, dial ☎ 00, wait for the tone, and dial the country code, area code, and number. If you're making a local call, dial the two-digit city code first (**93** in Barcelona) and then the seven-digit number. To make a long-distance call within Spain, the procedure is exactly the same because you must dial the city prefix no matter where you're calling.

TIPPING   More expensive restaurants add a 7% tax to the bill and cheaper ones incorporate it into their prices. This is *not* a service charge, and a tip of 5% to 10% is expected in these establishments. For coffees and snacks most people just leave a few coins or round up to the nearest euro. Taxis do not expect tips. Tip hotel porters and doormen 1€ and maids about the same amount per day.

TOILETS   In Catalonia they're called *aseos, servicios,* or *lavabos,* and are labeled *caballeros* for men and *damas* or *señoras* for women.

TOURIST INFORMATION   **Turisme de Barcelona,** Plaça de Catalunya, 17 (underground) (☎ 93-285-38-34), is open daily 9am to 9pm. **Informació Turística de Catalunya** has information on Barcelona and the entire region; it's located in Palau Robert, Pg. de Gràcia, 107 (☎ 93-238-40-03). Tourism information offices are also at Sants train station and the airport. Call ☎ 010 for general visitor information.

TRAVELERS WITH DISABILITIES   Many buildings in Barcelona have stairs, making it difficult for visitors with disabilities to get around, though conditions are slowly improving. Newer hotels are more sensitive to the needs of persons with disabilities, and more expensive restaurants are generally wheelchair-accessible. However, because most places have very limited, if any, facilities for people with disabilities, you might consider taking an organized tour specifically designed to accommodate such travelers. **Flying Wheels Travel** (☎ 507-451-5005; www.flying wheelstravel.com) offers escorted tours to Spain ("Spanish Symphony"), and **Access-Able Travel Source** (☎ 303-232-2979; www.access-able. com) has access information for people traveling to Barcelona. TMB (the public transportation system for both bus and Metro) has a help line for disabled travelers (☎ 93-486-07-52), and ECOM is a federation of private disabled organizations (☎ 93-451-55-50).

Barcelona: **A Brief History**

550 B.C. Greeks settle at Empúries in northern Catalonia.

212 B.C. The Romans, using Empúries as an entry point, subjugate Spain.

206 B.C. Romans defeat Carthaginians.

1ST C. A.D. Christians spread throughout Catalonia.

15 Barcino founded by Romans.

70 First Jewish settlements in Barcino.

415 Barcelona occupied by the Visigoths; capital until 554.

719 Moorish invasion of Iberian Peninsula reaches Barcelona.

878 Guifré el Pilós (Wilfred the Hairy) defeats Moors and founds dynasty of Counts of Barcelona (5-century-long autonomous rule).

1064 The *Usatges,* the first Catalan Bill of Rights, is drafted.

1137 A royal marriage unites Catalonia and neighboring region of Aragón.

1213–35 Jaume I consolidates empire, conquers Mallorca, Ibiza, and Valencia.

1249 Barcelona forms the *Consell de Cent* (Council of 100) municipal government.

1283 Corts (Parliament) to govern Catalonia created.

1347–59 The Black Plague halves the city's population. The *Generalitat* (autonomous government) is founded.

1469 Fernando II, monarch of Catalonia-Aragón, marries Isabel, queen of Castile, uniting all of Spain.

1492 Columbus discovers America. The "Catholic Monarchs" expel all remaining Jews and Muslims.

1494 Catalonia falls under Castilian rule.

1522 Under the rule of Charles V, Catalans refused permission to trade in the New World.

1640–50 Catalan revolt known as the *Guerra dels Segadors* (Harvesters' War); Catalonia declares itself a republic, allied with France.

1701–13 Spanish War of Succession.

1759 Barcelona falls to Franco-Spanish army; the Catalan language is banned.

1808–14 French occupy Catalonia in Peninsular War with England.

1832 The Industrial Revolution begins in Barcelona with the first steam-driven factory.

1854–1865 Old City walls torn down; work begins on the "new city," expansion called *L'Eixample.*

1873 First Spanish Republic established.

1888 First Universal Exposition in Barcelona held at *Parc de la Ciutadella.*

1892–93 Collectives demand Catalan autonomy. Anarchist throws bombs in the Teatre Liceu Opera House.

1909 *Setmana Tràgica* (Tragic Week); anarchists go on anticlerical rampage in Barcelona.

1924 Dictatorship established by General Primo de Rivera; Catalan language banned.

1929 Second International Exhibition held, on Montjuïc.

1931 Francesc Macià negotiates autonomy for Catalonia during the Second Republic and declares himself president.

1936–1939 Spanish Civil War; ends with anarchist-occupied Barcelona taken by Franco's army.

1960s Package tourism boom takes off on Catalonia's Costa Brava.

1975 Franco dies; Juan Carlos becomes king.

1978 King Juan Carlos grants Catalonia autonomous rule; Catalan language restored.

1981 Coup attempt by right-wing officers fails; democracy prevails.

1982 Socialists gain power after 43 years of right-wing rule.

1986 Spain joins the European Community (now the European Union).

1992 Barcelona hosts 25th Summer Olympic Games.

1998 Generalitat introduces "linguistic normalization" laws to strengthen Catalan as the region's primary language.

2004 Spanish Prime Minister José Luis Zapatero officially requests that Catalan, along with Basque and Galician, be recognized as working languages of the E.U.

2006 A new *Estatut* (Statute) granting Catalonia additional autonomous powers is passed by the Spanish Socialist government.

Barcelona's **Architecture**

Roman (2nd c. b.c.–4th c. a.d.)

The early conquerors of Spain were extraordinary engineers. Relics of the Roman colony of Barcino can be seen in the surviving columns of the **Temple d'Augustus,** originally part of the Roman forum, and gates and sections of the 3rd- and 4th-century walls that encircled the city. The finest Roman ruins are beneath **Plaça del Rei,** in the **Museu d'Història de la Ciutat.**

Medieval (Romanesque, 9th–12th c.; & Gothic, 12th–16th c.)

Beautiful in its simplicity and austerity, Romanesque architecture featured wide aisles, round arches, and heavy walls (mostly in churches). The finest example in Barcelona is **Sant Pau del Camp** (9th–12th centuries).

Catalan Gothic emerged in Catalonia in the 12th century, with harsher lines and more austere ornamentation than traditional Gothic architecture. Employed in both civic and religious buildings, it featured pointed arches, soaring buttresses and spires, airy naves, and massive columns. The purest example anywhere is **Santa Maria del Mar,** the basilica in La Ribera. Other examples include the **Church of Santa Maria del Pi** and the **Saló del Tinell** (on the stunning Plaça del Rei). Though the entire Barri Gòtic is named for the style, the neighborhood reflects an evolution and mix of styles, of which the **Cathedral** is the best example.

Modernisme (late 19th–early 20th c.)

It's not "modernism," or what is usually defined as 20th-century functionality, but Catalan Art Nouveau, a derivative of the European movement in the arts of the late 19th century. In Barcelona, *modernista* architecture was spearheaded by **Antoni Gaudí** (**La Sagrada Familia, La Pedrera**), but many other celebrated *modernista* architects, including **Domènech i Montaner** and **Puig i Cadafalch,** transformed the city with

Catedral de Barcelona

La Pedrera

elegant mansions and concert halls perfectly suited to the enlightened prosperity of the Catalan bourgeoisie. Though there are excellent examples outside of Barcelona, in Girona, Valencia, Sitges, Reus, and even the Basque Country, the Catalan capital boasts the highest concentration of *modernista* architecture in the world. The mid-19th century L'Eixample district, the new city expansion by **Ildefons Cerdà,** is the style's finest showcase (it's not called the ***Quadrat d'Or,*** or Golden Square, for nothing).

Modern & Contemporary (1929–present)

The stark pavilion built by **Mies Van der Rohe** for the 1929 International Exposition in Barcelona is a landmark of modern architecture. Barcelona took advantage of the 1992 Olympic Games to reorient the city to the sea and create new urban beaches, new residential neighborhoods, a port and marina, ring roads, and introduce daring public sculptures, promenades, and squares weaving through the Old City. In 1999 the Royal Institute of British Architects presented Barcelona's City Council with their Gold Medal, the first time a city (rather than an architect) had received the accolade. Spanish (Rafael Moneo and Santiago Calatrava) and international (Arata Isozaki and Norman Foster) architects have also made their mark on the city, as have a number of young, daring Catalans. The French architect Jean Nouvel's audacious **Torre Agbar** is the newest symbol of a city embracing the future with bravado.

Mies Van der Rohe pavilion

Useful Phrases

Useful Words & Phrases

ENGLISH	SPANISH/CATALAN	PRONUNCIATION
Good day	Buenos días/Bon dia	*bweh*-nohs dee-ahs/bohn *dee*-ah
How are you?	¿Cómo está?/Com està?	*koh*-moh es-*tah*/com ehs-*tah*
Very well	Muy bien/Molt bé	mwee byehn/mohl beh
Thank you	Gracias/Gràcies	*grah*-thee-ahs/*grah*-see-uhs
You're welcome	De nada/De res	*deh nah*-dah/duh ress
Goodbye	Adiós/Adéu	ah-*dyos*/ah-*deh*-yoo
Please	Por favor/Si us plau	por fah-*vohr*/see yoos plow
Yes	Sí/Sí	see
No	No/No	noh
Excuse me	Perdóneme/Perdoni'm	pehr-*doh*-neh-meh/per-*don*-eem
Where is . . . ?	¿Dónde está . . . ?/ On és . . . ?	*dohn*-deh es-*tah*/ohn ehs
To the right	A la derecha/A la dreta	ah lah deh-*reh*-chah/ah lah *dreh*-tah
To the left	A la izquierda/ A l'esquerra	ah lah ees-*kyehr*-dah/ahl ehs-keh-*ra*
I would like . . .	Quisiera/Voldría	kee-*syeh*-rah/ vohl-*dree*-ah
I want . . .	Quiero/Vull	*kyeh*-roh/*boo*-wee
Do you have . . . ?	¿Tiene usted?/Té?	tyeh-neh oo-*sted*/teh
How much is it?	¿Cuánto cuesta?/ Quant és?	*kwahn*-toh *kwehs*-tah/kwahnt ehs?
When?	¿Cuándo?/Quan?	*kwahn*-doh/kwahn
What?	¿Qué?/Com?	Keh/Cohm
There is (Is there . . . ?)	(¿)Hay (. . . ?)/ Hi ha? *or* Hi han?	aye/ee ah/ee ahn
What is there?	¿Qué hay?/Que hi ha?	keh aye/keh ee ah
Yesterday	Ayer/Ahir	ah-*yehr*/ah-*yeer*
Today	Hoy/Avui	oy/ah-*wee*
Tomorrow	Mañana/Demá	mah-*nyah*-nah/ deh-*mah*
Good	Bueno/Bon	*bweh*-noh/bohn
Bad	Malo/Mal	*mah*-loh/mahl
Better (Best)	(Lo) Mejor/Millor	(loh) meh-*hohr*/ mee-*yohr*
More	Más/Mes	mahs/mehss
Less	Menos/Menys	*meh*-nohs/*meh*-nyus
Do you speak English?	¿Habla inglés?/ Parla anglès?	ah-blah een-*glehs*/ *pahr*-lah ahn-*glehs*

I speak a little Spanish/Catalan	Hablo un poco de español/Parlo una mica de Catalá	*ah*-bloh oon *poh*-koh deh es-pah-*nyol*/*pahr*-loh oo-nah *mee*-kah *deh* kah-tah-*lah*
I don't understand	No entiendo/No comprenc	noh ehn-*tyehn*-doh/noh cohm-*prehnk*
What time is it?	¿Qué hora es?/Quina hora és?	keh *oh*-rah ehss/*kee*-nah *oh*-rah ehss
The check, please	La cuenta, por favor/El compte, si us plau	lah *kwehn*-tah pohr fah-*vohr*/ehl *cohmp*-tah see yoos plow
the station	la estación/la estació	lah es-tah-*syohn*/la esta-*cyo*
a hotel	un hotel/l'hotel	oon oh-*tehl*/ehl ho-*tehl*
the market	el mercado/el mercat	ehl mehr-*kah*-doh/ehl mehr-*kaht*
a restaurant	un restaurante/un restaurant	oon rehs-tow-*rahn*-teh/oon rehs-tow-*rahn*
the toilet	el baño/el lavabo	ehl *bah*-nyoh/ehl lah-*vah*-boh
a doctor	un médico/un metge	oon *meh*-dee-koh/oon meht-*jah*
the road to . . .	el camino a/al cami per	ehl kah-*mee*-noh ah/ahl kah-*mee* pehr
to eat	comer/menjar	ko-*mehr*/mehn-*jahr*
a room	una habitación/un habitació	*oo*-nah ah-bee-tah-*syohn*/oon ah-bee-tah-*syohn*
a book	un libro/un llibre	oon *lee*-broh/oon *yee*-breh
a dictionary	un diccionario/un diccionari	oon deek-syoh-*nah*-ryoh/oon deek-syoh-*nah* ree

Numbers

NUMBER	SPANISH	CATALAN
1	uno (*oo*-noh)	*un (oon)*
2	dos (dohs)	*dos (dohs)*
3	tres (trehs)	*tres (trehs)*
4	cuatro(*kwah*-troh)	*quatre (kwah-trah)*
5	cinco (*theen*-koh)	*cinc (sink)*
6	seis (says)	*sis (sees)*
7	siete (*syeh*-teh)	*set (seht)*
8	ocho (*oh*-choh)	*vuit (vweet)*
9	nueve (*nweh*-beh)	*nou (noo)*
10	diez (dyehht)	*deu (deh-yoo)*
11	once (*ohn*-theh)	*onze (ohn-zah)*
12	doce (*doh*-theh)	*dotze (doh-tzah))*

NUMBER	SPANISH	CATALAN
13	trece (*treh*-theh)	*tretze (treh-tzah)*
14	catorce (kah-*tohr*-theh)	*catorza (kah-tohr-zah)*
15	quince (*keen*-seh)	*quinza (keen-zah)*
16	dieciséis (dyeh-thee-*says*)	*setze (seh-tzah)*
17	diecisiete (dyeh-thee-*syeh*-teh)	*disset (dee-seht)*
18	dieciocho (dyeh-thee-*oh*-choh)	*divuit (dee-vweet)*
19	diecinueve (dyeh-thee-*nweh*-beh)	*dinou (dee-noo)*
20	veinte (*bayn*-teh)	*vint (vehnt)*
30	treinta (*trayn*-tah)	*trenta (trehn-tah)*
40	cuarenta (kwah-*rehn*-tah)	*quaranta (kwah-rahn-tah)*
50	cincuenta (theen-*kwehn*-tah)	*cinquanta (theen-kwahn-tah)*
60	sesenta (seh-*sehn*-tah)	*seixanta (see-shahn-tah)*
70	setenta (seh-*tehn*-tah)	*setanta (seh-tahn-tah)*
80	ochenta (oh-*chehn*-tah)	*vuitanta (vwee-tahn-tah)*
90	noventa (noh-*behn*-tah)	*noranta (noh-rahn-tah)*
100	cien (*thyehn*)	*cent (sent)*

Recommended **Spanish Wines**

I recommend seeking out the following wines while touring Spain.

Reds (Tintos)
Rioja Viña Ardanza, Allende, Imperial, CVNE, Marqués de Riscal, La Rioja Alta, San Vicente, Castillo de Ygay, López Heredia, Muga, Remírez Ganuza, Roda, Artadi

Riber del Duero Reds Condado de Haza, Pago de los Capellanes, Emilio Moro, Pesquera, Hacienda Monasterio, Aalto, Atauta, Alíon, Mauro, Leda, Vega Sicilia

Toro Quinta Quietud, San Román, Dos Victorias, Pintia, Numanthia

Priorat Cims de Porrera, Clos Martinet, Clos Mogador, Mas Doix, Vall Llach, L'Ermita

Jumilla Casa Castillo, Finca Sandoval

Monsant Celler de Capçanes, Joan d'Anguera

Others Dominio de Valdepusa/ Marqués de Griñón (Toledo), Castillo de Perelada (Penedès), Chivite (Navarra), Dominio de Tares (Bierzo), Torres (Penedès)

Whites (Blancos)
Ablariño (from Galicia) Lagar de Cervera, Laxa, Martin Codax, Terras Gaudia, Pazo de Señorans

Rioja Muga, Marqués de Riscal, López-Heredia

Rueda Dos Victorias José Pariente, MartinSancho, Belondrade y Lurton

Other
Cava (sparkling wine from Catalonia) Agusti Torelló, Avinyó, Gramona, Juvé y Camps, Segura Viudas

Sherry San León (manzanilla), Tío Pepe (fino), Alvear (Pedro Ximénez)

Recommended Vintages for Rioja & Ribera del Duero Wines

YEAR	RIOJA	RIBERA DEL DUERO
1990	Good	Excellent
1991	Average	Average
1992	Good	Good
1993	Average	Fair
1994	Outstanding	Excellent
1995	Outstanding	Outstanding
1996	Excellent	Outstanding
1997	Good	Good
1998	Excellent	Excellent
1999	Excellent	Excellent
2000	Excellent	Excellent
2001	Outstanding	Outstanding
2002	Average	Average
2003	Good	Good
2004	Outstanding	Outstanding
2005	Excellent	Very good

Toll-Free Numbers & Websites

AER LINGUS
☎ 800/474-7424 in the U.S.
☎ 01/886-8844 in Ireland
www.aerlingus.com

AIR CANADA
☎ 888/247-2262
www.aircanada.ca

AIR FRANCE
☎ 800/237-2747 in the U.S.
☎ 0820-820-820 in France
www.airfrance.com

AIR NEW ZEALAND
☎ 800/262-1234 or -2468 in the U.S.
☎ 800/663-5494 in Canada
☎ 0800/737-000 in New Zealand
www.airnewzealand.com

ALITALIA
☎ 800/223-5730 in the U.S.
☎ 8488-65641 in Italy
www.alitalia.it

AMERICAN AIRLINES
☎ 800/433-7300
www.aa.com

AUSTRIAN AIRLINES
☎ 800/843-0002 in the U.S.
☎ 43/(0)5-1789 in Austria
www.aua.com

BMI
No U.S. number
☎ 0870/6070-222 in Britain
www.flybmi.com

BRITISH AIRWAYS
☎ 800/247-9297 in the U.S.
☎ 0870/850-9-850 in Britain
www.british-airways.com

CONTINENTAL AIRLINES
☎ 800/525-0280
www.continental.com

DELTA AIR LINES
☎ 800/221-1212
www.delta.com

EASYJET
No U.S. number
www.easyjet.com

IBERIA
☎ 800/772-4642 in the U.S.
☎ 902/400-500 in Spain
www.iberia.com

ICELANDAIR
☎ 800/223-5500 in the U.S.
☎ 354/50-50-100 in Iceland
www.icelandair.is

KLM
☎ 800/374-7747 in the U.S.
☎ 020/4-747-747 in the Netherlands
www.klm.nl

LUFTHANSA
☎ 800/645-3880 in the U.S.
☎ 49/(0)-180-5-838426 in Germany
www.lufthansa.com

NORTHWEST AIRLINES
☎ 800/225-2525
www.nwa.com

QANTAS
☎ 800/227-4500 in the U.S.
☎ 612/131313 in Australia
www.qantas.com

SCANDINAVIAN AIRLINES
☎ 800/221-2350 in the U.S.
☎ 0070/727-727 in Sweden
☎ 70/10-20-00 in Denmark
☎ 358/(0)20-386-000 in Finland
☎ 815/200-400 in Norway
www.scandinavian.net

SWISS INTERNATIONAL AIRLINES
☎ 877/359-7947 in the U.S.
☎ 0848/85-2000 in Switzerland
www.swiss.com

UNITED AIRLINES
☎ 800/241-6522
www.united.com

US AIRWAYS
☎ 800/428-4322
www.usairways.com

VIRGIN ATLANTIC AIRWAYS
☎ 800/862-8621 in continental U.S.
☎ 0870/380-2007 in Britain
www.virgin-atlantic.com

Index

See also Accommodations and Restaurant indexes, below.

A

Access-Able Travel Source, 167
Access America, 165
Accommodations, 131–144.
    See also Lodging Index
        Barri Gòtic, 140, 142, 143
        Barrios Altos, 136
        Ciutat Vella and Waterfront, 134–135
        Girona, 153
        Gràcia, 137, 140, 143
        La Rambla, 141, 143
        L'Eixample, 133, 137–143
        L'Empordà and Costa Brava, 158
        Raval, 136, 138, 141
        Sitges, 149
        Tibidabo, 138, 144
        Waterfront, 137, 139, 143, 144
Aeri de Montserrat, 146
Aer Lingus, 175
Aerobús, 162
Agatha Ruiz de la Prada, 78–79
Aiguadolç (Sitges), 149
Air Canada, 175
Aire, 116
Air France, 175
Airlines, 163
    toll-free numbers and websites, 175
Air New Zealand, 175
Air travel, 162
Alitalia, 175
All Saints' Day, 161
Almirall, 112
Alsina, Antoni, 85
Ambit, 38
American Airlines, 175
American Express, 165
Antic Mercat del Born, 66
Antilla Latin Club, 108, 114
Antiques, 76, 77, 155
Antonio Miró, 45, 72, 78
Apartment rentals, 164
Apolo, 114
Aquàrium de Barcelona, 16
Architecture, 169–170. See
    also individual architects
    modernista, 24–29, 169
    L'Eixample, 69, 91

Architecture fans, tour for, 40–45
Armand Basi, 45
Arnau, Eusebi, 27
Art galleries, 37–39, 76
ArticketBCN Discounts, 11
Art-lovers' tour, 36–39
Art museums
    ArticketBCN Discounts, 11
    Fundació Antoni Tàpies, 37
    Fundació Joan Miró, 37
    Museu Barbier-Mueller d'Art Precolombí, 32, 33
    Museu Cau Ferrat (Sitges), 148
    Museu d'Art (Girona), 151
    Museu d'Art Contemporani de Barcelona (MACBA), 38, 44
    Museu de Montserrat, 147
    Museu Frederic Marès, 34
    Museu Maricel del Mar (Sitges), 148
    Museu Nacional d'Art de Catalunya (MNAC), 19
    Museu Picasso, 13, 38–39
    Teatre Museu Dalí (Figueres), 156
Arts and entertainment, 119–130
    Barri Gòtic, 125, 126, 129
    best, 120
    Ciutat Vella and Waterfront, 122–123
    classical music and concert venues, 124
    current listings, 128
    flamenco, 125–126
    Gràcia, 124, 125, 128
    jazz and cabaret, 126–127
    La Rambla, 126, 127
    La Ribera, 124, 126, 130
    L'Eixample, 121, 124–127
    Montjuïc, 125, 128–130
    movies, 124–125
    music festivals, 129
    opera, 127–128
    theater, 130
    tickets, 128
Artur Ramón Espai Contemporani, 39

ATMs (automated teller machines), 164
Australian Consulate, 164
Austrian Airlines, 175
Auto Europe, 162
Avis, 162

B

Baja Beach Club, 114
Balmins (Sitges), 149
Banys Arabs (Girona), 151
Barça, 54
Barcelona Bici, 92
Barcelona Bus, 163
Barceloneta, 89
Barcino, 15
Bar del Pi, 17
Bar Lobo, 38
Bar Mut, 112
Barna Taxi, 163
Barri Gòtic, 4
    accommodations, 140, 142, 143
    arts and entertainment, 125, 126, 129
    neighborhood walk, 60–63
    nightlife, 113–115, 118
    restaurants, 98, 100, 101, 103–106
    shopping, 76–77, 79–82
Barrios Altos, 116
    accommodations, 136
    restaurants, 98
Bars
    best, 108
    Cor Caliu, 70
    Cuines Santa Caterina, 43
    El Xampanyet, 39
    gay and lesbian, 116
    Mirablau, 22
    wine (and cava), 117–118
Bars and pubs, 112–114
    lounges, designer cocktail bars and beach hangouts, 117
BCN Original Shops, 81
Beaches, 17, 89, 91
    Palafrugell Beach coves, 157
    Sitges, 149
Beardsley, 81
Begur, 155
Berenguer de Montagut, Santa María del Mar, 31
Biciclot, 92
Biking, 5, 91–92
Bikini, 114, 128
The Black Horse, 108, 112

Block of Discord (Manzana de la Discórdia), 10, 26, 27
Blue Tram (Tramvia Blau), 6
BMI, 175
Boadas, 112
Boat tours and cruises, 52, 89
Bofill, Ricardo, 45
Bogatell, 89, 91
Bookstores, 76
Botanic Gardens (Jardí Botànic), 85
British Airways, 175
Budget, 162
Buffet y Ambigú, 72, 76
Bulevar dels Antiquaris, 76
Business hours, 164
Bus travel, 164

C

Cable car (Transbordador Aèri), 43, 84
Cacaolat, 48
Cacao Sampaka, 48, 80
Cadaqués, 156
Caelum, 35, 72, 80
Cafe-Bar Roy (Sitges), 149
Café de la Opera, 12, 59
Café Dietrich, 108, 116
Cafes
  Bar del Pi, 17
  Caelum, 35
  Cafe-Bar Roy (Sitges), 149
  Café de la Opera, 12, 59
  Café Zurich, 57
  Els Quatre Gats, 28
  La Font de Gat, 20, 85
  Lola Cafe (Girona), 152
  Mesón del Café, 15, 61
  Tèxtilcafé, 33
Café Zurich, 57, 108
CaixaForum, 42
Calatrava, Santiago, 45
Camper, 82
Camper Foodball, 44
Camp Nou, 54
Canada
  Consulate, 164
  government tourist offices in, 160
Can Paixano, 117–118
Cap de Barcelona (Lichtenstein), 16, 38
Capella del Marcús, 67
Cap Roig, 158
Carnaval, 161
  Sitges, 149
Car rentals, 162
Carrer Consell de Cent, 37
Carrer de Comerç, 66

Carrer de l'Argenteria, 65
Carrer del Bisbe, 62
Carrer de les Mosques, 32, 67
Carrer del Rec, 66
Carrer dels Banys Nous (carrer dels antiquaris), 63
Carrer dels Sombrerers, 67
Carrer de Montcada, 31–33, 67
Carrer Sant Bonaventura (Sitges), 149
Car travel, 163
  L'Empordà and Costa Brava, 158
Casa Amatller, 10, 27
Casa Batlló, 10, 27
Casablanca-Gràcia, 124
Casablanca-Kaplan, 124
Casa Calvet, 29, 69
Casa de la Caritat, 44
Casa de la Ciutat, 35
Casa de les Punxes (Casa Terrades), 70
Casa del Llibre, 76
Casa Lleó Morera, 10, 27
Casa Milà (La Pedrera), 4, 9, 26, 27
  jazz on the rooftop, 120
Casa-Museu Castell Gala Dalí (Púbol), 156–157
Casa-Museu Salvador Dalí (Cadaqués), 156
Casas, 82
Casas, Ramón, 27
Casa Thomas, 70
Cascada fountain, 87
Cases de l'Onyar (Girona), 152
Cases dels Canonges, 62
Cashpoints, 164
Casino Barcelona, 114
Castell de Montjuïc, 84
Catedral, Girona, 151
Catedral de Barcelona, 12, 33, 61
Cava bars, 117–118
Cavas, 6
CCCB (Centre de Cultura Contemporània de Barcelona), 44
CDLC (Carpe Diem Lounge Club), 108, 117
Cellphones (móviles), 161–162
Centre d'Art Santa Mònica, 59
Centre de Cultura Contemporània de Barcelona (CCCB), 44
Ceramics and pottery, 76–77
Cerdà, Ildefons, 170

Cereria Subira, 82
Cheetah Girls, 53
Chillida, Eduardo, 38, 61
Chocolate
  Escribà, 57
  Granja Viader, 48
  Museu de la Xocolata, 49
Christmas (Nadal), 161
Churches and cathedrals
  Catedral de Barcelona, 12, 33, 61
  Església dels Sants Just i Pastor, 62
  La Sagrada Família, 5, 9, 25
  Santa María del Mar, 6, 13, 31, 65
  Santa María del Pi, 63
  Sant Pau del Camp, 35
  Sant Pere de les Puel.les, 67
CicloBus Barcelona, 92
Cinemas, 124–125
City Hall (club), 114–115
Ciutat Vella, 30–35
  art galleries, 39
  arts and entertainment, 122–123
  restaurants, 96–97
  shopping, 74, 77
Classic Bikes Barcelona, 92
Climate, 161
Club 13, 115
Colmado Quílez, 48, 80
Columbus, Christopher, Monument à Colom, 16, 59
Conjunt Monumental de la Plaça del Rei, 15, 33
Consulates, 164
Continental Airlines, 175
Cor Caliu, 70
Corpus Christi, 160
Cosmetics, 77
CosmoCaixa (Museu de la Ciència), 54
Costa Brava, 154–158
Credit cards, lost or stolen, 165
Cruïlles, 155
Cuines Santa Caterina, 43
Currency, 166
Custo-Barcelona, 79

D

Dalí, Salvador
  Casa-Museu Castell Gala Dalí (Púbol), 156–157
  Teatre Museu Dalí (Figueres), 156
Dalí Triangle, 155, 156

Dance clubs, 114–116
best, 108
Day trips and excursions, 145–158
Girona, 150–153
L'Empordà and Costa Brava, 154–158
Montserrat, 146–147
Sitges, 148–149
Delta Air Lines, 175
Demasié, 80
Department stores/shopping centers, 77–78
Design and architecture fans, tour for, 40–45
Designer home goods and furnishings, 78
Día de los Reyes, 161
Diagonal, 77
Dining, 5. See also Restaurant Index
Barri Gòtic, 98, 100, 101, 103–106
Barrios Altos, 98
best bets, 94
Ciutat Vella and Waterfront, 96–97
Girona, 153
hours, 98
L'Eixample, 95
L'Empordà and Costa Brava, 158
Sitges, 149
Vila Olimpica, 99
Disabilities, travelers with, 167
Discos Castelló, 82
Doctors, 164
Dom, 78
Domènech i Montaner
Casa Lleó Morera, 10, 27
Casa Thomas, 70
Castle of Three Dragons, 87
El Palau de la Música Catalana, 5, 20, 28, 67, 120, 124
Fundació Tàpies, 27
Hospital de Santa Creu i Sant Pau, 25–26
Drassanes Reials, 59

E

E & A Gispert, 49, 67, 72, 80
Easyjet, 175
El Born. See also La Ribera
shopping, 76, 77, 79–81
El Bosc de las Fades, 112
El caganer, 62
El Call (Jewish district)
Barcelona, 61, 63
Girona, 150

El Corte Inglés, 72, 77
Electricity, 165
El Grec, 160
El Palau de la Música Catalana, 5, 20, 28, 67, 120, 124
El Patio Andaluz, 125
El Poble Espanyol, 19
El Prat airport, 162
El Quim de la Boqueria, 47
El Raval
accommodations, 136, 138, 141
nightlife, 112, 113, 115, 116
shopping, 79, 82
Els Quatre Gats, 28
El Tablao de Carmen, 125
El Triangle, 78
El Xampanyet, 39, 108, 118
Embassies, 164
Emergencies, 165
Empúries, 157
Entertainment and arts, 119–130
Barri Gòtic, 125, 126, 129
best, 120
Ciutat Vella and Waterfront, 122–123
classical music and concert venues, 124
current listings, 128
flamenco, 125–126
Gràcia, 124, 125, 128
jazz and cabaret, 126–127
La Rambla, 126, 127
La Ribera, 124, 126, 130
L'Eixample, 121, 124–127
Montjuïc, 125, 128–130
movies, 124–125
music festivals, 129
opera, 127–128
theater, 130
tickets, 128
Escribà, 47, 57
Església dels Sants Just i Pastor, 62
Esolanía (Montserrat), 146–147
Espai Barroc, 120, 126
Estació Sants, 163
Estadi Olímpic, 20
Etxart & Panno, 79
Euro, 166
Excursions and day trips, 145–158
Girona, 150–153
L'Empordà and Costa Brava, 154–158

Montserrat, 146–147
Sitges, 148–149

F

Falqués, Pere, 27
Families with children
best hotel for, 132
tour for, 50–54
Farmàcia Alvarez, 166
Farmacia Genové, 58
Fashion and accessories, 6, 78–80
La Ribera, 67
The Fastnet Bar, 112
Favorita, 70
FC Barcelona/Camp Nou, 54
Festa Major de Gràcia, 160–161
Festival Grec, 85
Festival Jardins de Cap Roig, 158
Festivals and special events, 160–161
FGC Trains, 163
Film, 124–125
Filmoteca, 124
Fish sculpture, 43
Flamenco, 125–126
Flying Wheels Travel, 167
FNAC, 82, 161–162
Font, Josep, 45, 72, 79
Font de Gat, 85
Font Màgica, 54, 85
Fontserrè, Josep, 87
Food stores and markets, 47, 80
Cacao Sampaka, 80
Caelum, 80
Colmado Quílez, 48, 80
Demasié, 80
E & A Gispert, 49, 80
gourmet tour, 46–49
Mercat de la Boqueria, 4–5, 11, 47, 58
Mercat de Santa Caterina, 44, 67
Montiel, 67
Origen 99, 9%, 49, 72, 80
Queviures J. Murrià, 70
Tot Formatge, 80
Forvm Ferlandina, 81
Fossar de les Moreres, 65
Fundació Antoni Tàpies, 37
Fundació Joan Miró, 20, 37
Fundació Tàpies, 27
Funiculars, Montserrat, 147
Fútbol Club Barcelona, 120, 129

G
Galería Carles Tache, 38
Galería Eude, 38
Galería Lluciá Homs, 38
Galería Maeght, 39
Galería René Metras, 38
Galleries, 37–39, 76
Ganiveteria Roca, 82
García Lorca, Federico, 57
Gargallo, Pau, 28
Gaudí, Antoni
    Casa Batlló, 10, 27
    Casa Calvet, 29, 69
    Casa Milà (La Pedrera),
        4, 9, 26, 27
        jazz on the rooftop,
        120
    La Sagrada Família, 5, 9,
        25
    Palau Güell, 28–29
    Parc Güell, 21, 25
Gay and lesbian travelers,
    165
    bars and clubs, 116
    best hotel for, 132
    Sitges, 149
Gehry, Frank, Fish sculpture,
    38, 43
Gifts, 81
Giménez & Zuazo, 79
Gimlet, 108, 112
Ginger, 113
Girona, 150–153, 163
Gourmet food shops, 80.
    See also Food stores and
    markets
Gourmet tour, 46–49
Gràcia
    accommodations, 137,
        140, 143
    arts and entertainment,
        124, 125, 128
Granja Viader, 48
Gran Teatre del Liceu, 58,
    120, 127
Grec, 120, 129
GSM (Global System for
    Mobiles), 161–162
Guía del Ocio, 128
Guifré el Pilós, 35

H
Harlem Jazz Club, 120, 126
Hemingway, Ernest, 59, 113
Herbolisteria del Rei, 72, 82
Heritage, 76
Hertz, 162
Highways, 163
History of Barcelona, 167–168
Hivernacle, 87
Holidays, 165

Holy Week (Semana Santa),
    160
Homage to Picasso (Home-
    natge a Picasso), 38, 66
Home goods and furnish-
    ings, 78
Hospital de Santa Creu i Sant
    Pau, 25–26
Hotel Oriente, 59
Hotels. See Lodging
Hugo, Victor, 57

I
Iberia, 175
Icária, 124
Icelandair, 175
Ici Et Là, 78
IMAX Port Vell, 54, 124–125
Informació Turística de
    Catalunya, 167
Institut del Teatre, 130
Insurance, 165
Internet access, 165
Internet Gallery Cafe, 165
InTouch USA, 162
Isozaki, Arata, 42–43
Itaca, 77
Ivo & Co., 81

J
Jamboree, 126
Jardí Botànic (Botanic Gar-
    dens), 85
Jardins del Claustre, 85
Jazz and cabaret, 4, 126–127
Jazz Sí Club Taller de Músics,
    127
Jewelry, 81
Jewish district (El Call)
    Barcelona, 61, 63
    Girona, 150
Jocomomola de Sybilla, 79
Jordi Barnadas, 37–38
Josep Font, 45, 72, 79
Jujol, Josep María, 25

K
Kemwel Holiday Auto, 162
KLM, 175
Kukuxumusu, 72, 81

L
La Bombeta, 89
La Boqueria, 4–5, 11, 47, 58
La Casa de les Lletres, 164
La Casa dels Músics, 120, 128
La Catedral, 12, 33, 61
La Diada de Catalunya, 161
La Diada de St. Jordi, 160
La Fianna, 113

La Font de Gat, 20
La Fragata (Sitges), 149
La Galería de Santa María
    Novella, 77
LAIE, 76
Lake (Parc de la Ciutadella), 87
La Mercè, 6, 161
La Moreneta (Montserrat),
    146
L'Antic Teatre, 130
La Paloma, 108, 115
La Pedrera (Casa Milà), 4, 9,
    26, 27
    jazz on the rooftop, 120
La Pedrera de Nit, 127
La Plaça de Madremanya, 158
L'Aquàrium de Barcelona, 16
La Rambla (Les Rambles), 4,
    11, 52
    accommodations, 141,
        143
    arts and entertainment,
        126, 127
    neighborhood walk,
        56–59
    nightlife, 112, 113, 116
    shopping, 76, 78
La Rambla de Catalunya, 77
L'Arca de l'Avia, 72, 76
La Ribera (Barcelona), 6
    accommodations,
        137–139, 143
    arts and entertainment,
        124, 126, 130
    neighborhood walk,
        64–67
    nightlife, 112–114
    restaurants, 98,
        100–103, 105
    shopping, 77–81
La Ribera (Sitges), 149
La Sagrada Família, 5, 9, 25
L'Ascensor, 108, 113
Las Golondrinas, 52, 89
La Terrazza, 108, 115
L'Auditori, 45, 120, 124
La Vinya del Senyor, 13, 108,
    118
L'Eixample
    accommodations, 133,
        137–143
    arts and entertainment,
        121, 124–127
    biking, 92
    neighborhood walk,
        68–70
    nightlife, 112, 114,
        116–118
    restaurants, 95, 100, 101
    shopping, 44–45, 73,
        76–81

Le Kashbah, 115
L'Empordà, 154–158
Les Rambles. *See* La Rambla
L'Estel Matinal, 37
L'Hivernacle/L'Umbracle, 87
Liceu, 58, 128
Lichtenstein, Roy, 16, 38, 89
Lodging, 131–144. *See also*
    Lodging Index
        Barri Gòtic, 140, 142,
            143
        Barrios Altos, 136
        Ciutat Vella and Water-
            front, 134–135
        Girona, 153
        Gràcia, 137, 140, 143
        La Rambla, 141, 143
        L'Eixample, 133,
            137–143
        L'Empordà and Costa
            Brava, 158
        Raval, 136, 138, 141
        Sitges, 149
        Tibidabo, 138, 144
        Waterfront, 137, 139,
            143, 144
Loewe, 81
Lola Cafe (Girona), 152
Los Tarantos, 125–126
Lost property, 165
Lufthansa, 175
Lupo Barcelona, 72, 81–82
Luz de Gas, 120, 127
Luz de Gas Port Vell, 108, 117

M

MACBA (Museu d'Art Con-
    temporani de Barcelona),
    38, 44
Magic Fountain (Font Màg-
    ica), 54, 85
Mail and postage, 165–166
Manzana de la Discórdia
    (Block of Discord), 10, 26,
    27
Mar Bella, 89, 91
Maremàgnum, 72, 78
Marès, Frederic, 87
Mariscal, Xavier, 16, 17, 38
Marsella, 108, 113
MasterCard, 165
May Day, 160
MEDEX Assistance, 165
Medieval Barcelona. *See*
    Ciutat Vella
Mediterráneo (Sitges), 149
Meier, Richard, Museu d'Art
    Contemporani de
    Barcelona (MACBA), 38,
    44
Méliès Cinemes, 125

Mercat de La Boquería, 4–5,
    11, 47, 58
Mercat de Santa Caterina,
    44, 48, 67
Mercat de Sant Josep (La
    Boquería), 4–5, 11, 47, 58
Mesón del Café, 15, 61
Metro, 116, 163
Mies van der Rohe, Ludwig,
    170
        Pavelló, 42
Mirablau, 22, 108, 113
Mirador de l'Alcalde, 84–85
Mirador del Rei Martí, 33
Miró, Antonio, 45, 72, 78
Miró, Joan
        Barcelona Airport
            mosaic mural, 38
        Fundació Joan Miró, 20,
            37
        La Rambla mosaic, 58
        Pla de l'Os, 38
        Woman and Bird, 38
MNAC (Museu Nacional
    d'Art de Catalunya), 19
Modernista architecture,
    24–29, 169
        L'Eixample, 69, 91
Moll de la Fusta, 16, 89
Molly's Fair City, 113
Monells, 155
Moneo, Rafael, 45
Monestir de Sant Pere de
    Galligants (Girona), 152
Money, 166
Montiel, 67
Montjuïc, 84–85
        accommodations, 136
        arts and entertainment,
            125, 128–130
Montserrat, 6, 146–147
Mont Tibidabo, 21–22
        accommodations, 138,
            144
        biking, 91–92
        Tramvía Blau (Blue
            Tram) to, 6
Monument à Colom, 16, 59
Moors, 35
Moovida, 45
Movie Living & Food, 108,
    117
Movies, 124–125
Museu Barbier-Mueller d'Art
    Precolombí, 32, 33
Museu Cau Ferrat (Sitges),
    148
Museu d'Art (Girona), 151
Museu d'Art Contemporani
    de Barcelona (MACBA),
    38, 44

Museu de la Ciència (Cosmo-
    Caiixa), 54
Museu de la Xocolata, 49
Museu del Cinema (Girona),
    153
Museu del Fútbol Club
    Barcelona, 129
Museu de Montserrat, 147
Museu d'Empúries, 157
Museu d'Història de la
    Ciutat, 15
Museu d'Historia dels Jueus
    (Girona), 150–151
Museu d' Textil i d' Indumen-
    tària, 33
Museu Frederic Marès, 34
Museu Maricel del Mar
    (Sitges), 148
Museu Marítim, 15, 59
Museums
        Museu del Cinema
            (Girona), 153
        Museu del Fútbol Club
            Barcelona, 129
        Museu d'Història de la
            Ciutat, 15
        Museu d'Historia dels
            Jueus (Girona),
            150–151
        Museu d' Textil i d' Indu-
            mentària, 33
        Museu Marítim, 15, 59
Museu Nacional d'Art de
    Catalunya (MNAC), 19
Museu Picasso, 13, 38–39
Museus de Zoologia i Geolo-
    gia, 86–87
Museu Tèxtil i d'Indumen-
    tària, 32
Music festivals, 129
        Festival Jardins de Cap
            Roig, 158
Music stores, 82

N

Nadal (Christmas), 161
Natalie Capell Atelier de
    Moda, 72, 79
Neighborhood walks, 55–70
        Barri Gòtic, 60–63
        La Rambla, 56–59
        La Ribera, 64–67
        L'Eixample, 68–70
New Chaps, 116
New York, 115
New Zealand, Consulate,
    164
Nick Havanna, 117
Nightlife, 107–118
        bars and pubs, 112–114
        best bets, 108

casino, 114
dance clubs, 114–116
gay and lesbian bars
and clubs, 116
Sitges, 149
Nitbus, 164
Northwest Airlines, 175
Nouvel, Jean, 45, 170
Nova Icària, 89, 91

O

Olympic Games (1992),
42–43, 89
Omm Sesion Club, 108, 117
Opera, 127–128
Origen 99, 9%, 49, 72, 80
Otto Zutz, 116
Outdoor activities, 83–92
La Ribera (waterfront),
88–91
Montjuïc, 84–85
Parc de la Ciutadella,
86–87

P

Palafrugell Beach coves,
157
Palamós, 157
Palau Aguilar, 32
Palau Dalmases, 32
Palau de Baró de Quadras,
70
Palau de la Generalitat, 62
Palau de la Música Catalana,
5, 28, 67, 120, 124
Palau de la Virreina, 58
Palau dels Cervelló, 32
Palau dels Marquesos de
Lliò, 32
Palau d'Esports Sant Jordi,
42–43
Palau Güell, 28–29, 59
Palau Moxó, 63
Palau Nadal, 32
Pals, 155
Parc d'Atraccions Tibidabo,
22, 54
Parc de la Ciutadella,
86–87
Parc Güell, 21, 25, 53
Parc Zoològic, 52, 87
Parks
Parc de la Ciutadella,
86–87
Parc Güell, 21, 25, 53
Parleament de Catalunya, 87
Passatge de Permanyer, 69
Passeig Colom, 16
Passeig de Gràcia, 26, 77
Passeig del Born, 65–66
Passeig dels Til.lers, 87
Passeig de Picasso, 66

Passports, 166
Pastis, 108, 113
Pati de les Aigües, 69
Pavelló Mies van der
Rohe, 42
Peratallada, 155
Pharmacies, 166
Picasso, Pablo, 28
Museu Picasso, 13,
38–39
Piñón, Helio, 44
Pitin Bar, 114
Plaça de Catalunya, shop-
ping, 78, 81, 82
Plaça de les Olles, 65
Plaça del Pi, 63
Plaça del Rei, 61
Conjunt Monumental de
la, 15, 33
Plaça de Ramon Berenguer
el Gran, 61
Plaça de Sant Felip Neri, 63
Plaça de Sant Jaume, 34–35,
62
Plaça de Sant Josep Oriol, 63
Plaça de Sant Just, 62
Plaça Nova, 61
Plaça Ramon Berenguer, 33
Plaça Reial, 11, 59
Placeta del Pi, 63
Pla de l'Os, 38
Platamundi, 81
Platges (beaches), 89, 91
Platges del Mort (Sitges),
149
Poble Nou, arts and enter-
tainment, 124, 129, 130
Pocket Club, 128
Police, 166
Pont Bac de Roda, 45
Pont de Ferro (Girona), 152
Portal de Bisbe, 61
Portal de l'Angel, 33
Port Lligat, 156
Port Olímpic, 17, 89
Post offices, 165–166
Prim, General, statue
of, 87
Primavera Sound, 120, 129
Puig i Cadafalch, Josep
CaixaForum, 42
Casa Amatller, 10, 27
Casa de les Punxes
(Casa Terrades), 70
Els Quatre Gats, 28
La Font de Gat, 20
Palau de Baró de
Quadras, 70

Q

Qantas, 175
Queviures J. Murrià, 48, 70

R

Rafa Teja Atelier, 79
Rambla de Canaletes, 57
Rambla de les Flors, 57
Rambla dels Caputxins, 59
Rambla dels Estudis (Rambla
dels Ocells), 57
Rambla de Santa Mónica, 59
Raval
accommodations, 136,
138, 141
nightlife, 112, 113, 115,
116
shopping, 79, 82
Razzmatazz, 108, 116
Regia, 77
Renoir Floridablanca, 125
Renoir Les Corts, 125
Restaurants, 5. See also
Restaurant Index
Barri Gòtic, 98, 100,
101, 103–106
Barrios Altos, 98
best bets, 94
Ciutat Vella and Water-
front, 96–97
Girona, 153
hours, 98
L'Eixample, 95
L'Empordà and Costa
Brava, 158
Sitges, 149
Vila Olimpica, 99
Reus, 163
RoadPost, 162
Romans, 31
Temple d'Augustus, 34
Roman walls
Barcelona, 33, 61
Girona, 151
Ruta del Modernisme de
Barcelona, 28

S

Safety, 166
Sala Apolo, 128
Sala Dalmau, 37
Sala d'Art Artur Ramón, 76
Sala KGB, 128
Sala Parés, 39
Sala Razzmatazz, 120, 129
Saló de Cent, 35
Salvation, 116
Santa Cova, 147
Santa María del Mar, 6, 13,
31, 65
Santa María del Pi, 63
Sant Feliu de Guixols, 158
Sant Jeroni, 147
Sant Joan, 147
Sant Pau del Camp, 35
Sant Pere de les Puel.les, 67

Sant Sebastià (Sitges), 149
Scandinavian Airlines, 175
Scenic, 92
Seasons, 160
Semana Santa (Holy Week), 160
Senda, 38
ServiCaixa, 128
Servi Taxi, 163
1748 Artesana i Coses, 76
Shoes, 82
Shoko, 117
Shopping, 71–82
    antiques and art, 76
    Barri Gòtic, 76–77, 79–82
    best, 72
    bookstores, 76
    ceramics and pottery, 76–77
    Ciutat Vella, 74, 77
    department stores/shopping centers, 77–78
    designer home goods and furnishings, 78
    El Born, 76, 77, 79–81
    El Raval, 79, 82
    fashion and accessories, 6, 67, 78–80
    gifts, 81
    gourmet food shops, 80
    jewelry, 81
    La Rambla, 76, 78
    La Ribera, 74–75, 78
    leather goods, 81–82
    L'Eixample, 44–45, 73, 76–81
    music stores, 82
    Old City, 17
    Plaça de Catalunya, 78, 81, 82
    shoes, 82
    Waterfront, 75, 78
Sidecar Factory Club, 129
Sinagoga Medieval de Barcelona, 63
Sitges, 148–149
Smoking, 166
Sombrerería Obach, 82
Sonar, 129
Special events and festivals, 160–161
Spectator sports, 129
Subway, 163
Summercase, 129
Swiss International Airlines, 175

T
Tablao Flamenco Cordobés, 120, 126
Tapaç 24, 10

Tàpies, Antoni
    Fundació Antoni Tàpies, 27, 37
    Homage to Picasso (Homenatge a Picasso), 38, 66
    Tapis de la Fundació, 37
Taxes, 166
Taxis, 163
Teatre Grec, 85
Teatre Mercat de Les Flors, 120, 130
Teatre Museu Dalí (Figueres), 156
Teatre Nacional de Catalunya, 45, 130
Tel-Entrada, 128
Telephones, 166–167
Temple d'Augustus, 34
Tèxtilcafé, 33
Theater, 130
Tibidabo Mountain, 21–22
    accommodations, 138, 144
    biking, 91–92
    Tramvia Blau (Blue Tram) to, 6
Tick Tack Ticket, 128
Tipping, 167
Tirititran, 126
Toilets, 167
Topos V, 38, 61
Torre Agbar, 45, 170
Tot Formatge, 49, 80
Tot Montserrat ticket, 147
Tourist information, 160, 167
    Girona, 153
    Montserrat, 147
    Sitges, 149
Tours
    art-lovers', 36–39
    boat, 52, 89
    for design and architecture fans, 40–45
    for families with children, 50–54
    gourmet, 46–49
    one-day, 9–13
    two-day, 14–17
    three-day, 18–22
Train travel, 163
    L'Empordà and Costa Brava, 158
    Sitges, 149
Trama, 39
Tramvia Blau (Blue Tram), 6
Transbordador Aèri (cable car), 43, 84
TransMontserrat ticket, 147
Transportation, 163–164
Travel Assistance International, 165

Travel Bar, 108, 114
Travelex Insurance Services, 165
Travel Guard International, 165
Travel Insured International, 165
Turisme Atenció, 166
Tusquets, Oscar, 28

U
Umbracle, 87
Un Cotxe Menys/Bike Tours Barcelona, 92
United Airlines, 175
United Kingdom
    Consulate, 164
    government tourist offices in, 160
United States
    Consulate, 164
    government tourist offices in, 160
Up and Down, 108, 116
US Airways, 175

V
Va de Vi, 118
Vaho Works, 72, 81
Verbena de Sant Juan, 160
Verdi, 120, 125
Verd Poma, 79
Viaplana, Albert, 44
Vila Olímpica restaurants, 99
Vila Viniteca, 49, 72, 80
Vinçon, 27, 72, 78
Virgin Atlantic Airways, 175
Visa, 165
Visitor information, 160, 167
    Girona, 153
    Montserrat, 147
    Sitges, 149
Vocabulary, 171–173

W
Walking, 164
Waterfront, 52
    accommodations, 137, 139, 143, 144
    arts and entertainment, 122–125
    nightlife, 112, 114–117
    outdoor activities, 88–91
    restaurants, 98–101, 104–106
    shopping, 74–75, 78
Weather, 161
Websites, 162
Wheelchair accessibility, 167

Wine (and cava) bars, 117–118
Wines
recommended, 173–174
Vila Viniteca, 49, 80
Woman and Bird, 38

X

Xampanyerias, 6
Xampú Xampany, 118

Z

Zara, 79–80
Zoo, Barcelona, 52, 87

Accommodations

AC Miramar, 136
Bellmirall (Girona), 153
Casa Camper, 132, 136
Castell de'Empordà, 158
Ciutat Barcelona Hotel, 137
Constanza, 132, 137
Diagonal, 132, 137
Duquesa de Cardona, 132, 137
Duques de Bergara, 137
El Xalet (Sitges), 149
Fashion House B&B, 138
Gat Xino, 132, 138
Grand Hotel Central, 132, 138
Gran Hotel La Florida, 132, 138
Hispanos Siete Suiza, 132, 138
Hostal Goya, 138
Hotel 1898, 141
Hotel Apsis Atrium Palace, 139
Hotel Arts, 132, 139
Hotel Astoria, 139
Hotel Axel, 132, 139

Hotel Banys Orientals, 132, 139
Hotel Barcelona Catedral, 140
Hotel Barcino, 140
Hotel Casa Fuster, 132, 140
Hotel Citutat de Girona, 153
Hotel Claris, 132, 140
Hotel Colón, 140
Hotel Condes de Barcelona, 132, 140–141
Hotel España, 141
Hotel Jazz, 141
Hotel Majestic, 141
Hotel Neri, 132, 142
Hotel Omm, 132, 142
Hotel Palace Barcelona, 132, 142
Hotel Romàntic de Sitges, 149
H10 Racó Del Pi, 142–143
Jardí, 143
Marina Folch, 143
Montecarlo, 143
Park Hotel, 143
Petit Palace Opera Garden Ramblas, 143
Prestige Paseo de Gracia, 132, 143
Pulitzer, 143–144
Relais d'Orsa, 132, 144
Vincci Marítimo Hotel, 144

Restaurants

Abac, 94, 98
Agua, 53, 94, 98
Agut d'Avignon, 94, 98
Arola, 99
Bestial, 99–100
Blanc (Girona), 153
Botafumeiro, 94, 100
Café de L'Academia, 94, 100
Cal Pep, 94, 100
Can Costa, 100

Can Culleretes, 100
Can Majó, 94, 100
Casa Calvet, 94, 100
Cinc Sentits, 94, 101
Comerç 24, 94, 101
Cor Caliu, 70
Cuines Santa Caterina, 43
El Celler de Can Roca (Girona), 153
El Far Hotel Restaurant (near Palafrugell), 158
El Japonés, 101
El Quim de la Boqueria, 47
Els Pescadors, 94, 101
Els Quatre Gats, 28, 101
El Velero de Sitges, 149
Espai Sucre, 94, 102
Flash-Flash Tortillería, 102
Font de Gat, 85
Gente de Pasta, 102
Hisop, 94, 102
Hofmann, 94, 102–103
Inopia, 94, 103
La Bombeta, 89
La Dentellière, 94, 103
La Font de Gat, 20
La Paradeta, 94, 103
Lasarte, 94, 103
La Vinateria del Call, 63, 118
Les Quinze Nits, 104
Lonja de Tapas, 104
Los Caracoles, 104
Mare Nostrum (Sitges), 149
Montiel, 67
Moo, 94, 104
Moovida, 45
Organic, 104–105
Senyor Parellada, 94, 105
7 Portes, 94, 105
Sikkim, 105
Talaia Mar, 106
Taller de Tapas, 106
Tapaç 24, 106
Umita, 106

Photo **Credits**

Raga/AGE Fotostock; p 25 bottom: © Quim Roser i Puig Photography; p 26 top: © Neil Schlecht; p 26 bottom: © San Rostro/AGE Fotostock; p 28 top: © Quim Roser i Puig Photography; p 29 top: © JTB Photo Communications, Inc. / Alamy; p 31 bottom: © Matz Sjöberg/AGE Fotostock; p 33 top: © Imagebroker / Alamy; p 34 top: © Jordi Sans/AGE Fotostock; p 34 bottom: © Neil Setchfield/Lonely Planet Images; p 37 top: © Javier Larrea/AGE Fotostock; p 38 top: © Quim Roser i Puig Photography; p 38 bottom: © Matz Sjöberg/AGE Fotostock; p 39 top: © Krzysztof Dydynski/Lonely Planet Images; p 39 bottom: © Quim Roser i Puig Photography; p 42 bottom: © Jordi Cami/AGE Fotostock; p 43 top: © Jon Arnold/Danita Delimont; p 43 bottom: © Sergio Pitamitz/AGE Fotostock; p 44 top: © Neil Schlecht; p 45 bottom: © Guido Krawczyk/AGE Fotostock; p 47 top: © Quim Roser i Puig Photography; p 48 top: © Quim Roser i Puig Photography; p 48 bottom: © Rough Guides/Alamy; p 49 top: © Rough Guides/Alamy; p 49 bottom: © Oliver Strewe/Lonely Planet Images; p 52 bottom: © Tom & Therisa Stack/Tom Stack & Associates / drr.net; p 53 top: © R. Matina/AGE Fotostock; p 54 top: © Andres Kudacki/Corbis; p 55: © Michael Melford/Getty Images; p 57 top: © Kevin Foy/Alamy; p 57 bottom: © Quim Roser i Puig Photography; p 58 top: © Color Point Photo/Index Stock Imagery; p 58 bottom: © Neil Setchfield/Lonely Planet Images; p 59 top: © Peter Holmes/AGE Fotostock; p 59 bottom: © Jon Hicks/eStock Photo; p 61 top: © Jordi Sans/AGE Fotostock; p 61 bottom: © Age Fotostock/SuperStock; p 62 top: © Neil Schlecht; p 62 bottom: © Neil Schlecht; p 63 top: © Quim Roser i Puig Photography; p 63 bottom: © Toni Vilches / Alamy; p 65 bottom: © Age Fotostock/SuperStock; p 66 top: © Rene Mattes/AGE Fotostock; p 66 bottom: © Frederic Comi/AGE Fotostock; p 67 top: © Quim Roser i Puig Photography; p 67 bottom: © Quim Roser i Puig Photography; p 69 top: © Bora / Alamy; p 69 bottom: © Quim Roser i Puig Photography; p 70 top: © PhotoBliss / Alamy; p 70 bottom: © Toño Labra/AGE Fotostock; p 71 © Quim Roser i Puig Photography; p 72 bottom: © Quim Roser i Puig Photography; p 76 top: © Quim Roser i Puig Photography; p 77 top: © Quim Roser i Puig Photography; p 78 top: © Oscar García Bayerri/AGE Fotostock; p 78 bottom: © Quim Roser i Puig Photography; p 79 top: © Quim Roser i Puig Photography; p 80 bottom: © Neil Schlecht; p 81 top: © Quim Roser i Puig Photography; p 82 top: © Dino Fracchia / drr.net; p 82 bottom: © Quim Roser i Puig Photography; p 83: © Art Kowalsky/Alamy; p 85 top: © Oscar García Bayerri/AGE Fotostock; p 85 bottom: © Xavier Subias/AGE Fotostock; p 87 top: © Quim Roser i Puig Photography; p 87 bottom: © John Elk III/Lonely Planet Images; p 89 bottom: © Josep Curto/AGE Fotostock; p 91 top: © travelstock44/Alamy; p 92 top: © Quim Roser i Puig Photography; p 93: © Neil Schlecht; p 99 top: © Richard Bryant/Arcaid / Alamy; p 99 bottom: © Oso Media / Alamy; p 100 top: © Quim Roser i Puig Photography; p 101 bottom: © Quim Roser i Puig Photography; p 102 bottom: © Rough Guides/Alamy; p 103 top: © Quim Roser i Puig Photography; p 103 bottom: © Quim Roser i Puig Photography; p 104 top: © Quim Roser i Puig Photography; p 105 top: © Quim Roser i Puig Photography; p 105 bottom: © Quim Roser i Puig Photography; p 106 bottom: © Quim Roser i Puig Photography; p 107: © Karolina Krasuska/Everynight Images/Alamy; p 108 bottom: © Quim Roser i Puig Photography; p 112 top: © Quim Roser i Puig Photography; p 112 bottom: © Quim Roser i Puig Photography; p 113 top: © Quim Roser i Puig Photography; p 113 bottom: © Rough Guides / Alamy; p 114 bottom: © Andrew Butterton/Alamy; p 115 top: © Quim Roser i Puig Photography; p 115 bottom: © John Ferro Sims / Alamy; p 116 bottom: © Quim Roser i Puig Photography; p 117 top: © Quim Roser i Puig Photography; p 118 top: © Quim Roser i Puig Photography; p 119: © Quim Roser i Puig Photography; p 120 bottom: © Quim Roser i Puig Photography; p 124 bottom: © Quim Roser i Puig Photography; p 125 top: © Quim Roser i Puig Photography; p 126 top: © Quim Roser i Puig Photography; p 127 bottom: © Quim Roser i Puig Photography; p 130 top: © Xavier Florensa/AGE Fotostock; p 131: © Quim Roser i Puig Photography; p 137 top: © Quim Roser i Puig Photography; p 137 bottom: © Quim Roser i Puig Photography; p 139 bottom: © Neil Schlecht; p 140 top: © Quim Roser i Puig Photography; p 141 bottom: © Quim Roser i Puig Photography; p 142 top: © Quim Roser i Puig Photography; p 142 bottom: © Quim Roser i Puig Photography; p 143 top: © Quim Roser i Puig Photography; p 144 top: © Quim Roser i Puig Photography; p 145: © Brian Lawrence/SuperStock; p 146 bottom: © Dirk Hedemann/Alamy; p 147 top: © Dirk Hedemann/Alamy; p 149 top: © Jordi Cami/AGE Fotostock; p 151 top: © Jordi Cami/AGE Fotostock; p 151 bottom: © Tolo Balaguer/AGE Fotostock; p 152 top: © Victor Kotler/AGE Fotostock; p 152 bottom: © Toño Labra/AGE Fotostock; p 155 bottom: © Peter Adams Photography/Alamy; p 157 top: © Jerónimo Alba/AGE Fotostock, Inc.; p 157 bottom: © Xavier Subias/AGE Fotostock; p 159: © Justin Kase/Alamy